CHEERLEADER! CHEERLEADER!

An American Icon

Natalie Guice Adams

Pamela J. Bettis

CPL

palgrave
macmillan

To
John and Bonnie Guice
and
John and Louise Bettis,
Loving Parents Who Have Never
Stopped Cheering for Us.

First published 2003 by
PALGRAVE MACMILLAN™
175 Fifth Avenue, New York, N.Y. 10010 and
Houndmills, Basingstoke, Hampshire, England RG21 6XS.
Companies and representatives throughout the world.

PALGRAVE MACMILLAN is the global academic imprint of the Palgrave
Macmillan division of St. Martin's Press, LLC and of Palgrave Macmillan
Ltd. Macmillan® is a registered trademark in the United States, United
Kingdom and other countries. Palgrave is a registered trademark in the
European Union and other countries.

ISBN 1-4039-6184-0 hardback

Library of Congress Cataloging-in-Publication Data
Adams, Natalie Guice, 1962–
    Cheerleader! : an American icon / Natalie Guice Adams, Pamela Bettis.
       p.   cm.
    Includes bibliographical references and index.
    ISBN 1-4039-6184-0 (cloth)
    1. Cheerleading—United States.   I. Bettis, Pamela, 1955–   II. Title.

LB3635.A33   2004
791.6'4—dc—21

                                                           2003048738

A catalogue record for this book is available from the British Library.

Design by Letra Libre.

First edition: November 2003
10   9   8   7   6   5   4   3
Printed in the United States of America.

CONTENTS

ACKNOWLEDGEMENTS

I t sounds cliché to say that this book would not have been possible had it not been for the hard work and support of many people. But, in our case, this really is true. Over the past four years, we have had incredible support from our family, friends, new and former cheerleading acquaintances, and our academic colleagues and students. To try to name everyone is a danger because inevitably we will omit someone, but here is our attempt to say in a small way, "thanks so much" to all of you. First, to the girls, cheerleading coach, principals, and teachers of Wichita Middle School, we thank you for allowing us into your world. It was in conversations with you that we began to recognize the power of cheerleading in this culture, and your words and insights formed the initial foundation of this work. Further, hanging out with the WMS girls during lunch gave us access to all sorts of culinary delights: pickles dipped in Kool-Aid being our favorite. We would also like to acknowledge the support of Oklahoma State University and the University of Alabama. Portions of this book were written through the financial help of these institutions, particularly the three Oklahoma State University College of Education Faculty Development and Research Committee grants and the University of Alabama Faculty Development Research Grant. We also want to thank Drs. Deb Jordan and Diane Montgomery, from Oklahoma State University, for their help in our initial study of girls and leadership. To the many graduate assistants over the last four years who have contributed in so many ways: Ann Wasilewski, Stacey Elssasser, Laura Jewett, Anne Kanga, Samantha Briggs, Gerald Wood, Judy German—your help was immeasurable. To Natalie's colleague, Dr. Harold Bishop, who provided a wealth of factual information about African American cheerleaders prior to desegregation, thank you for your vote of confidence. To an old friend, Sandi Eley, whose connections in the cheerleading world are vast, we appreciate your perkiness (obviously she was a cheerleader) and willingness to do so much "behind the scenes" to make this book a reality. To our newfound friends, Kim Irwin, Steve Burke, Mary Jones, Debbie Purifoy, Barby Ingle, Shelley Femwright, and Georgie Kerby, your expertise about cheerleading and willingness to share your insider views of the cheerleading world helped us immeasurably. All of the people at UCA/Varsity deserve a special note of appreciation for allowing us free rein to wander around, ask questions, and get an in-depth look at the business of cheerleading. To our many family members and friends who read portions of this book and provided thoughtful feedback: Diane Storr (who also played cheerleading detective), Lynda Comeaux, Emily Gruss Gillis (who is writing her own book and thought about all of our dilemmas), Becky Chastain, Bill Armaline, and Dave Bergin; and to those who listened to our endless cheerleading yammering but who offered encouragement nevertheless: Edward Jones, Elizabeth Lohrman, Kathy Farber, Lisa Cary, Yunsil Lee, Jeannie Christainsen, Jim Christiansen, Jamie Nekich, "Peepsie" Gregson, Nirmala Erevelles, John Petrovic, and Stephen Tomlinson. To Collin Harer of Videoland, Jonathan Billing of Archer Photography in Moscow, Idaho, and Edward Guy, thanks for the technical help. To Amanda Johnson, who first approached us about the book and continued to be so helpful as our editor throughout this process, thanks for believing in the project and doing so many things that went beyond your call of duty as editor. Thanks also to Matthew Ashford, who was always available to help in any way we needed and did it cheerfully (he must have been a former cheerleader!). To our college students at three different institutions who have read through various chapters of this book, provided valuable feedback, created some interesting titles, and shared their own cheerleading stories—thanks for indulging your professor. To our husbands, Jim Adams and Jim Gregson, what can we say?—other than we promise we will wear that cute little cheerleading uniform for you one night. Your encouragement, your patient listening, your solicited and unsolicited advice, your willingness to do more than your share as a co-nurturer of our children, are all appreciated more than these words can ever express. To our children, Hunter, Chris, Rebecca, and Hank, we hope our dedication to this book will serve to inspire you to pursue your own dreams. We love you for understanding that missed soccer games, missed cello practices, missed school events were one of the hazards of writing the book. We will make it up to you (particularly if the book sells well). And to our parents, to whom we dedicate the book, thanks for your unwavering belief in our ability, not simply while writing this book, but throughout our lives. Both of us are who we are and where we are today because of you. Last, but certainly not least, to the hundreds of cheerleaders and former cheerleaders who allowed us to ask them what cheerleading meant to them, we thank you for what you have taught us about passion, joy, and having fun.

PREFACE

Ola Ola A
Roll now, roll now, to the beat
I don't know
Just what it is
But Cheerleaders are funky
We dance like monkeys
Cheerleaders are humble
Cause we flip flop and tumble
Cheerleaders are spastic
Cause we stretch like elastic
Cheerleaders are crazy
Always wearing our daisies
Cheerleaders got spirit
So come on let's hear it!

(Universal Cheerleading Association
camp boogie song, summer 2002)

Four years ago, through a series of chance happenings, we fell into a research project studying cheerleading at a middle school in the Midwest. Many years ago, Natalie had been a junior high and high school cheerleader in Winnsboro, Louisiana, and Pam had tried out for the Churchland Truckers ninth-grade squad in Portsmouth, Virginia, and was not selected. Since that time, both of us had become public school teachers, married, returned to graduate school in the early 1990s, earned Ph.D.s in education, and had children. Certainly, neither of us had given any serious thought to cheerleading in a very long time. But as we began studying cheerleading at this one particular middle school, we found ourselves fascinated by the passion so many people, young and old alike, hold for cheerleading. It was hard not to be a cheerleading convert as we listened to Ms. Stone, a 48-year-old cheerleader coach in the school district we were studying, say with such sincerity: "I'm a real loyal person. So being a cheerleader sponsor for this school is a real honor because I'm an Eagle [the team mascot]. I came through this system. My parents worked for this system. I've got roots here, so my school spirit comes from my heart." We also became intrigued with the significance of the cheerleader in American popular culture. Once we started paying attention, we found cheerleaders popping up everywhere—in music videos, movies, sit-com's, newspapers, advertisements, and even in interviews with First Ladies. Often after a glass of wine, we found ourselves practicing herkeys (a cheerleader jump) on Pam's back deck, making up cheers, trying on the various cheerleader T-shirts that people began giving us, and laughing outrageously as we tried to imagine George W. Bush and Trent Lott (former cheerleaders themselves) in cheerleading skirts.

As we began to present our cheerleading research to our academic colleagues, we did not necessarily receive a cheery reception. Our feminist colleagues quickly dismissed our work, since it was obvious to them that cheerleading, like the Miss America pageant, was a pre-feminist relic that positioned girls and women as not-so-bright sex objects and that for some reason had lingered on even in the post-Title IX era. For the most part, academics were not willing to see any merit, first of all, in even studying cheerleading. Typically, in informal conversations, there would be silence after we announced the topic of our research; only when we wrapped the topic in academic jargon (i.e., "the multiple gendered subjectivities of cheerleading") did the silence break, and the conversation began. Sometimes, our topic provoked a playfulness not usually found in higher education. At one conference, when we informed a North Carolina colleague that we were presenting our study of cheerleading, he told us that he would only attend our presentation if we wore cheerleading skirts. We responded that varicose veins were not complimentary of short cheerleading skirts; he laughed and commented that, at his age, he wouldn't be able to see our flaws, but that this wasn't his point. The idea of us wearing kicky cheerleading skirts, the image of cheerleading itself, was still very provocative for him. This playful exchange along with the more reserved responses from our more serious colleagues provided us with the beginning clues of the power of cheerleading.

Even academics, we found, had lots of stories to tell about cheerleading, once they got past thinking about it in academic terms. When we presented some of our research to a small group of colleagues we knew fairly well, the group members spent a good part of a two-hour meeting telling personal cheerleader stories, many of which were fueled by anger and pain. One woman told the group, "I hated cheerleaders in high school and have really never gotten over that." One of the men, who did not have children, told the group with forceful certainty, "If I ever have a daughter, one thing I can assure you, she will NOT be a cheerleader." Others told stories about returning to their class reunions and finding that the petite cheerleaders were the ones who had become overweight and had not achieved much after high school. When we talked about our writing project at dinner parties peopled by an assortment of academics, men confided long-ago crushes on head cheerleaders, and scrapbooks were pulled out of storage with pictures of former cheerleaders from the 1970s and 1980s. Clearly, although disdained as a topic of research for many academics, cheerleading still evoked powerful reflections on one's youth and one's position in the typical school hierarchy.

However, we never intended to write a book about it, since few academics seemed to take our cheerleading work very seriously. But prompted by an insightful and very hip Palgrave Macmillan representative, Amanda Johnson, who we met at an academic conference, and encouraged by all types of cheerleaders from all over the country, we decided to write a book about cheerleading that would appeal to both academics and to a more general audience. It was a struggle at times to find a voice that would speak to both audiences, but, for the most part, writing this book was, well, fun. We have read, watched, listened, and even lived cheerleading for the last four years. Natalie retrieved her old high school cheerleading uniform, tried it on, broke the zipper, and then forced her children to watch her perform an old cheer. Pam bought a cheerleading uniform with poms for Halloween, wore it to teach her Qualitative Research class, and cheered smart commentary. We have even begun communicating with each other by leaving phone messages in cheer form. It has been the kind of fun that girls at the UCA cheer camp on the University of Idaho campus had when they cheered and sang the camp boogie song presented at the beginning of this preface: "Cheerleaders are funky. We dance like monkeys." They couldn't help but laugh out loud. We hope this book at times makes you laugh out loud while at the same time reflect on why an activity that brings pleasure to so many has been neglected as a worthy topic of study for so long.

CHEERLEADING

What's There to Cheer About?

We are Cheerleaders
Couldn't be Prouder
If you Can't Hear Us
We'll Shout a Little Louder.

Every Friday night in small towns, suburbs, and cities across the United States, a motley group of individuals gather in stadiums, gymnasiums, and coliseums to root for their hometown football, basketball, wrestling, or volleyball team. Center stage is the players themselves, but just to the left, on the sidelines, is another permanent fixture of this great American spectacle—the cheerleaders. Like jazz and baseball, cheerleading is a cultural icon native to the United States. However, cheerleading has not acquired the status that jazz and baseball hold in our culture. No Cheerleading Hall of Fame has been built, and, to date, Ken Burns, director of two extraordinary documentaries on jazz and baseball, has yet to film a documentary on cheerleading. Unlike jazz performers or baseball players, cheerleaders are typically presented in a negative light or at least not taken very seriously. Often when people think about cheerleading, these images come to mind: the cleavage-revealing Dallas Cowboys Cheerleaders in hotpants; the Texas cheerleading mom in handcuffs, after her plan to have the mother of her daughter's cheerleading rival killed is uncovered; the silly and shallow Spartan Cheerleaders on *Saturday Night Live* in search of the perfect cheer; and high school cheerleaders in short skirts and earmuffs motivating football teams on chilly Friday nights across this country. Writing about cheerleaders in *Sports Illustrated,* journalist Rick Reilly paints this picture: "Cheerleaders have no more impact on the game than the night janitorial staff. They don't even face the game. They face the crowd, lost in their bizarre Muffy World."[1] Even less sympathetic to cheerleading, Marty Beckerman, author of *Death to All Cheerleaders,* describes cheerleaders as "a urine stain on the toilet seat of America."[2] However, the 3.8 million people who participate in cheerleading in the United States would vehemently disagree with Reilly's and Beckerman's characterizations of cheerleading.[3]

Although a staple of American life and culture, cheerleading is an ambiguous cultural icon, having very different meanings for different people. For example, Terry Ventura (married to the former Minnesota governor Jesse Ventura) related in an interview that she was "not exactly cheerleading material."[4] What was she implying in that statement? Was she too smart to be a cheerleader? Too dumb? Too ugly? Too poor? Too wild? Too innocent? Too uncoordinated? This ambivalence regarding cheerleading is not new. In 1911, when all cheer leaders[5] or yell leaders were males, the president of Harvard University attacked "organized cheering" as a deplorable avenue for college men to express emotion, and contended that this new college tradition offered nothing of value to respectable educated men.[6] This attack did not keep the activity from growing, and by the 1920s, cheer-leaders on college campuses were highly respected: "the position of cheer-leader nowadays is fraught with great responsibility and rated as a high honor, so much so that in many colleges competitions and examinations are held to select the cheer-leaders."[7]

Almost one hundred years later, we are still unclear about what the cheerleader represents in American culture. However, an important difference from the past is that today, cheerleading is seen as an almost exclusively female activity. Many would argue that cheerleaders are nothing more than half-naked girls jumping senselessly up and down for the sole purpose of worshipping male athletes. Others would claim that cheerleading is a sport and deserves the respect paid to other forms of athletics. Some would contend that cheerleading opens the door for professional advancement. After all, the list of famous cheerleaders is rather impressive: Presidents Franklin Roosevelt, Dwight Eisenhower, Ronald Reagan, George Bush Sr., and George W. Bush, Senator Trent Lott, and entertainers Raquel Welch, Meryl Streep, Jimmie Stewart, Kirk Douglas, Katie Couric, Halle Berry, Renee Zellweger, Sandra Bullock, Samuel L. Jackson, Reba McEntire, and Madonna, to name a few. Mary Ellen Hanson, author of an in-depth historical account of cheerleading in the United States, argues that the cheerleader symbolizes all of the above: "youthful prestige, wholesome attractiveness, peer leadership, and popularity [as well as] mindless enthusiasm, shallow boosterism, objectified sexuality, and promiscuous availability."[8]

The movie, music video, advertising, and television industries certainly recognize how cheerleaders can be used to convey particular meanings about social and cultural life in America. However, once again, the cultural ambiguities of the contemporary cheerleader are present. So, for example, when Toby Keith in the music video "How Do You Like Me Now?" sings about a high school girl who shuns the advances of a now famous musician, the cheerleader is used to represent the popular all-American girl whom all high school boys want to date. When Lester Burnham in the Academy Award - winning film *American Beauty* has a midlife crisis and begins fantasizing about sex with someone other than his wife, his sexual dreams center around his daughter's friend, Angela, a young, seemingly innocent yet sexy cheerleader. Making fun of the inanity of shallow boosterism in American culture, *Saturday Night Live* provides the audience with the Spartan cheerleaders, whose sole aim in life is to find the perfect cheer. The movies *Sugar and Spice,* which features cheerleaders who rob a bank, and *But I'm a Cheerleader,* about a cheerleader sent to a homosexual rehabilitation camp, work only if the audience brings to the viewing the preconceived notion that cheerleaders represent wholesomeness rather than criminal intent or lesbianism. The supposed humor of these movies is built around the understanding that the audience will find it amusing to juxtapose such seemingly contradictory images of cheerleading.

If only because of the sheer numbers of people involved, cheerleading deserves the same kind of serious study that jazz and baseball have received. But more important, a study of cheerleading offers a glimpse into broader areas of American social and cultural life. Although it has been often characterized as a superfluous activity, cheerleading holds a myriad of meanings about many facets of American culture. It is a ubiquitous image and metaphor in American society. As Pamela Grundy points out in her fascinating history of North Carolina sports: " . . . in the multifaceted society of twentieth-century America, the most successful cultural institutions have been those that can support multiple meanings, be put to many ends."[9] Cheerleading is one such cultural institution. What then can we learn by studying the multiple meanings of this American cultural icon?

First, a careful examination of cheerleading can tell us much about patriotism, nationalism, and an American identity. Greg Webb, vice president of the Universal Cheerleading Association (UCA), explains: "cheerleading for the large part really is small town patriotism; it's nationalism at the very local level."[10] Across the United States, small towns build an identity around their high school sports, and you can see the importance of that identity when you drive through such a town and read the sign at the town limits saying, "Welcome to Shady Bluff, Home of the AA 1996 State Football Runner Ups."[11] That identity focuses on the talent of the local athletic teams, but it also includes the local cheerleaders, who are present for most male athletic events, particularly football and basketball. Just as male football players are symbols of ideal boy/manhood, cheerleaders, not surprisingly as perceived brides of the football heroes, are the symbols of ideal girl/womanhood. Furthermore, the role of the cheerleader as the eternally optimistic all-American girl, who leads the fans to cheer for team members even when they have obviously been beaten, represents the essence of traditional American patriotism.

Second, a study of cheerleading reveals how gender roles in the United States have changed over the last 135 years. Few people, for example, realize that cheerleading began as an exclusively male activity and represented desirable masculinity. In fact, as late as 1939 women were barred from being chosen for the All-American Cheerleading squad that was selected by sportswriters.[12] At the collegiate level, women first entered cheerleading squads (albeit in small numbers) during the 1920s, when early movies, advertisements, and beauty pageants began the mass commercialization, use, and some might say exploitation of feminine beauty. Further, sororities became major players in campus life during this time period, and cheerleading squads reflected this in their composition. Women becoming cheerleaders also closely parallels the story of women becoming workers during World War II. In both cases, men left their jobs to become soldiers and inadvertently opened doors that previously had been closed to women. When men returned from the war, they fought to regain their "rightful" place in the worksite and on the cheerleading squads. In fact, the University of Tennessee banned female cheerleaders in the early 1950s.[13] However, women prevailed, and following World War II, cheerleading squads became predominantly female, especially in elementary and secondary schools. In the last several decades, males have re-entered this so-called feminine domain; gay and lesbian squads have been formed; All-Star squads, which do not support any athletic team, are the fastest growing segment of cheerleading; and senior citizens now boast 15 squads in North Carolina. All of these cheerleading squads disrupt our assumptions about the role and activities of cheerleading. They demonstrate also how individuals and groups of individuals are actively engaged in redefining for themselves cultural practices and what counts as normal masculinity, femininity, sexual orientation, and cheerleading itself.

Third, cheerleading can tell us much about what it means to grow up female in this country today. With the Girl Power movement of the 1990s, girls are now expected to be confident, fit, and athletic. However, they are also still expected to be nice (i.e., chaste), pretty, and heterosexual.[14] Cheerleading in the twenty-first century captures this new vision of ideal femininity. Cheerleading still remains one of the highest-status activities for girls.[15] It is the most visible space for them to inhabit, and being known and liked by everyone continues to be a priority of school life. Cheerleading provides that public visibility. Although Title IX[16] and the athletic exploits of Mia Hamm and Venus and Serena Williams have been the impetus for girls and young women around the country to play and compete in interscholastic and professional sports, cheerleading still retains its status and allure for young girls. Christa Grizzle, former college cheerleader, UCA instructor, and now manager of a private gym for cheerleading training, succinctly explains the perennial appeal of cheerleading: "As long as you have little girls, you will have cheerleaders."[17] With the emphasis on tumbling, building, and stunting along with the proliferation of regional and national cheerleading championships, cheerleading today offers many girls opportunities to demonstrate their athletic prowess through a new kind of cheerleading. This new cheerleading approach no longer includes pom pons, chants, and saddle oxfords; these have been replaced by two-and-a-half-minute routines of intense physical exertion, tumbling feats, pyramid building, difficult jumps, and complicated cheers and dances, all performed in front of judges and in competition with other squads. As one of the girls in the movie *Bring It On* notes, cheering for football games is merely seen as practice for the national cheerleading competition in which her squad participates every year.

Anyone who attends local university or college athletic events already knows that the powerful image of cheerleading is not just relegated to high school and college. Cheerleading uniforms are worn by two-year-old little girls, and pom pons are the toys that keep them occupied during the football or basketball games that their parents are watching. Throughout the United States, pee wee and midget leagues of cheerleaders include girls as young as four years old, and typically they are helped in learning a few cheers from cheer coach moms, often former cheerleaders themselves, and local high school cheerleaders. One 12-year-old girl who was selected for an eighth-grade cheerleading squad told us, "I've been waiting for this all of my life."[18] Indeed, she had certainly been prepared for it all of her short life through cheerleading camps, tumbling lessons, and private cheer classes.

Fourth, exploring cheerleading can give us insights as to the contradictory and inconsistent ways that racial and ethnic integration occurred in our nation's schools and gymnasiums. Long before desegregation in the South, historically black colleges and high schools had cheerleading squads. Typically, these squads had very different cheering styles than their white counterparts.[19] Reminiscing about his high school football days prior to desegregation at Eastman High in Corinth, Mississippi, Dr. Harold Bishop recalls the powerful influence of the blues and of the Baptist Church on the all-black cheerleading squad. "The cheerleaders at that time still did not do things by rehearsal. It was still by spirit. I always felt that they were based on our culture in the churches so that you might hear a young lady take the words of a hymn and put it into a cheer."[20]

After the 1954 Supreme Court decision in *Brown v. Board of Education of Topeka,* which mandated the end of school desegregation, athletic teams began integrating mainly for the purpose of increasing the pool of athletes from which to select team members.[21] However, the integration of cheerleading squads in both collegiate and secondary schools did not follow that pattern. With the feminization of cheerleading, cheerleaders came to represent ideal femininity. Repeatedly, African American girls and women were denied opportunities to hold the esteemed position of cheerleader. In fact, Pamela Grundy argues that "the selection of cheerleading squads would, in fact, become one of the most volatile issues of school de-segregation issues around the South." [22]Throughout the United States, protests and riots occurred as a result of the selection of cheerleading squads, and these protests were not limited to African American communities. The creation of the La Raza Unida Party movement in Texas is partially attributed to a school- and community-wide protest of the lack of Chicano cheerleaders in a school whose demographics were 85 percent Mexican. In Crystal City, Texas, Chicano students at the local high school led a historic walk-out for their right to have more than one Mexican American on the cheerleading squad. They also demanded the right to speak Spanish, to have more Chicano teachers and a more culturally sensitive history curriculum.[23] Today, cheerleading squads remain disproportionately white in many parts of the country, provoking parents across the United States to file lawsuits against school districts and grievances with the Office for Civil Rights (OCR), with the goal of attaining more racially diverse cheerleading squads.

Fifth, studying cheerleading, which is a big business in this country, offers insights into American capitalism and American entrepreneurship. Lawrence Herkimer, often called the "Father of Cheerleading," recognized its profit potential and was instrumental in taking what was a recreational activity and turning it into big business. In 1948 he began offering cheerleading camps; in 1953 he formed the first cheerleading association, the National Cheerleading Association, and he also invented pom poms (later renamed pom pons),[24] proving that cheerleading had to be taken seriously by the corporate world.[25] Cheerleading may have disappeared in the 1970s had not one of Herkimer's protegees, Jeff Webb, recognized that the times called for a remaking of cheerleading in order to keep it a money-making business. His keen entrepreneurial skills coupled with his vision of cheerleading as an athletic endeavor and not a popularity contest radically altered the image of cheerleading and led his company, Universal Cheerleading Association, to become the chief rival of his former mentor.[26] Today, approximately 50 companies and businesses catering solely to cheerleaders have also tried to get a piece of the very profitable cheerleading pie.[27]

Finally, exploring the meaning of cheerleading can tell us something about the monumental importance our histories as adolescents play in our identities as adults. It seems that almost everyone has a cheerleader story to tell. Cheerleaders represent something to a variety of people, and that "something" becomes deeply ingrained within their psyches. Marlene Cota understands this well. As vice president of marketing for the Universal Cheerleading Association, one of the biggest obstacles she has to face in her job of acquiring sponsors for various cheerleading events is the negative personal experiences countless individuals have had with cheerleaders in their adolescent years. Thirty years after being shunned by a cheerleader in high school, many account managers want nothing to do with anything remotely associated with cheerleading.[28]

So, what exactly is there to cheer about in cheerleading? Plenty. In researching this book for the last four years, we have heard hundreds of cheerleading stories, documented dozens of references to cheerleaders in popular culture, recorded numerous TV segments on cheerleading, read every article we could find about cheerleading over the last 100 years, attended cheerleading camps, cheerleading practices, cheerleading competitions, and high school and college football games, interviewed people in the cheerleading industry, and talked to countless cheerleaders, former cheerleaders, cheerleader wanna-be's, and those who despise cheerleading. We have even judged cheerleading tryouts.[29] Natalie's 12-year-old daughter also became a cheerleader during this time period, which offered the opportunity to spend hours talking informally with mothers of young cheerleaders. What we have come to realize is that the meaning of cheerleading goes well beyond simply a group of girls wearing short skirts and leading fans in "Two bits, four bits, six bits a dollar." In this book, we undo the simplicity in which cheerleading has been approached and explore this beloved and maligned activity by examining cheerleading through the lens of history, sociology, popular culture, and the stories of those who love cheerleading and those who disdain it. We hope this book will provoke both critics and enthusiasts to see cheerleading in a more multifaceted light. We also hope to convey some of the fun we have had in researching this book and the pleasure enjoyed by the 3.8 million individuals who participate in cheerleading every year in this country.

CHEERLEADING

As American as Apple Pie and Customized Synthetic Wiglets

Hey! Hey! What do you say?
We're proud to live in the USA![1]

During the summer of 2002, we followed a discussion on a cheerleading listserv in which cheerleaders and their coaches grappled with how to choreograph sensitively a routine that was to be a part of a memorial observance for September 11, 2001. One coach replied in detail about her squad's performance during a November holiday parade following the attack. The squad is located near New York City, and members and their families had personal connections with those lost in the tragedy. In reflecting on how she had conceptualized the entire performance and selected the music, she wrote:

> Using the flag only brought the symbolism visually to the front. Auld Lange Syne always causes reflection of the past year—past events—it was different—except for what was being reflected on. . . . Going into the "Born in the USA" for us was a symbol of—this is where we are—We're Americans, we're strong. By ending with the Jingle Bells, it was our symbol of "We will survive and continue on"—even though we have seen great tragedy, we can still celebrate and continue on.[2]

According to the sponsor, audience members wept during the routine, and the announcer kept repeating "beautiful" as the squad performed.

After first reading these exchanges, we were struck by the seeming strangeness of cheerleaders performing a memorial tribute to such a terrible national tragedy. However, reflecting on how the activity of cheerleading represents much of what is our uniquely American character and identity, the inclusion of cheerleaders at such a memorial service began to make sense to us. Combining a new-age version of a traditional New Year's Eve song with Springsteen's rock 'n' roll patriotic lament of the Vietnam War and economic decline in the United States, and capping these with "Jingle Bells," in some ways represents the complexity of an American identity.

Photographer Eddie Adams also thought that cheerleaders say something about American culture and identity. He included a picture of high school cheerleaders in his pictorial display "Our American Spirit," commemorating the first anniversary of September 11 in the nationally syndicated Sunday *Parade* magazine. Adams' task was to present images that demonstrated American resiliency in the face of adversity. The cheerleading picture he included was labeled "Sheer Energy" and was placed next to a photograph of a young civil rights marcher in the 1963 march on Washington, D.C., and above a portrait of a family who was on vacation.[3] How American such a disparate range of images is. And cheerleading was among them.

For many Americans, cheerleading is, indeed, as American as apple pie. Maybe it's because cheerleading began in this country and has not caught on in other countries as much as other American cultural and corporate institutions, such as McDonalds and jazz. Perhaps, it's because female cheerleaders are often described as the "all-American, girl next door" and are still considered, by many, to represent the ideal American girl. Or maybe it's because cheerleading is so closely associated with the American spectacle of football, the sport beloved by so many Americans of every race, ethnicity, age, and social class. Maybe it's because "cheerleading" is used with such regularity in our American vernacular, often in contexts having nothing to do with sports, that it's part of our cultural lexicon as reflected in a recent newspaper headline, "Workers blame corporate cheerleading for huge retirement losses with BC-Enron - Investigation."[4] Cheerleading represents, for many, the American virtues they embrace: loyalty and devotion to a cause; perseverance even in the face of insurmountable obstacles; and a confidence and optimism that sometimes defy explanation.

Granted, cheerleading may be as American as apple pie for some. But for many others, it's definitely a store-bought frozen apple pie with too much sugar and not enough apples. Take, for example, Marty Beckerman, the teenage author of *Death to All Cheerleaders* and former editor of his Alaska high school newspaper, who agrees that cheerleading does indeed represent something about our American character: its worst traits. "Cheerleading is nothing more than a perfect example, an incontestable paradigm, of what is horribly wrong with our generation. . . . Our generation, as a whole, has so much capacity, but we toss it all away on vacuous brand name loyalties and the superficial corporate blueprint for our lives that is unceasingly shoved down out throats."[5] Many would agree with Beckerman's assessment of cheerleaders as shallow in character, disingenuous, egocentric, and materialistic, and would point out that these character flaws are often the same criticisms aimed at Americans as a whole.

Whether we think cheerleaders represent the best of American culture or the worst of American culture, the fact is cheerleading is a uniquely American cultural institution that reveals much about the diverse and contradictory values of the American people. Cheerleading's origins are found in this country. Further, cheerleading has persevered through massive cultural changes since its beginnings in the late 1800s, and its popularity continues into the twenty-first century. So what can this activity tell us about some of our strengths and weaknesses as a people? What can it tell us about the American identity? More important, since cheerleading in this country is a mainly a youthful activity, what can it tell us about how we socialize our young people?

Cheerleading: An American Invention

On November 6, 1869, Princeton and Rutgers met for the first intercollegiate football game. At this time, 25 players from each team were on the field at the same time; they could not throw the ball or run with it; they couldn't trip or hold the other players. Their main goal was to "kick or bat the round, inflated rubber ball toward goals eight paces wide. . . . The first team to score six goals was to be the victor"[6] At the end of the contest, Rutgers beat Princeton with a score of six goals to four.[7] During the game, a group of Princeton spectators, residents of Nassau Hall, broke into a rocket cheer, known as the Princeton Locomotive:

> Ray, ray, ray
> Tiger, Tiger, Tiger
> Sis, sis, sis
> Boom, boom, boom
> Aaaaah!
> Princeton, Princeton, Princeton

Hence, cheerleading was born—so the story goes.[8]

But the Princeton boys weren't the sole inventors of the cheer they yelled on that blustery November day. Rather, they borrowed it from a skyrocket cheer performed by the New York 7th Regiment when it passed through Princeton during the Civil War. Indeed, cheering has long been part of the military tradition, as this 1842 description of a U.S. Navy cheering spectacular illustrates:

At the command, "Clean yourselves!" the pig-tailed tars donned fresh uniforms; At "Lay aloft!" the crew clambered to the top-gallant masthead and the topmast crosstrees; at "Lay out upon the yards!" they scampered like monkeys to spaced intervals along the rigging, and at "Cheer!" they took off their caps, waved and shouted as lustily as possible. Regulations defined the length of the yell . . . : After three cheers have been given, if the Commodore returns the same number, it must be answered by one; if he returns but one, no further notice is to be taken and the people called down.[9]

When the Princeton students yelled the Princeton Locomotive at the 1869 game, it probably consisted only of the "sis, boom, aah" part. The tiger line may have been added in the 1880s, when the tiger was adopted as Princeton's mascot. Or the tiger used in the cheer may not have referred to an animal; rather it may have simply meant a "howl, yell, or shriek at the end of a round of cheering" or "the action at the end of a yell in which the cheerleader leaps into the air with arms and legs outstretched"—two common usages of the word "tiger" in the vernacular of the time.[10]

Although football began as a game initiated and played by white male students on elite college campuses throughout the country, by the late 1800s many black colleges and universities also had football teams. The first football game between two black colleges was on December 27, 1892. Two North Carolina schools, Livingstone and Biddle, played, with Biddle winning 4–0 (at this time a touchdown was worth 4 points).[11] By the early 1900s, football was the most popular sport on most college campuses and a revenue-producing activity. For example, from 1891 to 1894, receipts from Harvard football totaled nearly $19,000; by 1899–1902, that had risen to over $52,000.[12] In 1903, with fewer than 5,000 students, Harvard built a stadium that could seat 57,000.[13] By the early 1900s, football had become so dangerous (in the 1905 season alone, 18 deaths and 149 injuries related to football were reported) that President Theodore Roosevelt threatened to ban football from college campuses unless major changes were made. He formed the Intercollegiate Athletic Association, whose purpose was to make such changes. In 1910, this association changed its name to the National Collegiate Athletic Association (NCAA).[14]

This institutionalization of sports into the administration and curriculum of colleges and universities was a signal that the role of sports in colleges and universities had changed. No longer was it seen as a student-initiated, -led, and -regulated leisure activity that kept unruly college men occupied while not studying; rather, sports was touted by its advocates as one of the best ways to socialize youth into the values and norms that bolster national unity and patriotism.[15] As more and more colleges offered intercollegiate football, the need for institutional identity and proving one's loyalty to one's schools became intensified. Mascots, school colors, and local cheers helped to solidify this identity and loyalty to one's local school. So did cheer leaders, whose purpose was to organize spectator response to the games. In the early years, these first yell leaders or rooters were the players themselves, who, when not on the field, would let loose a yell. Beginning in the late 1890s colleges began officially designating yell leaders, rooter kings, or cheer leaders. Johnny Campbell of the University of Minnesota in 1898 is usually given credit for being the first officially recognized collegiate cheer leader.[16] Typically, these first formal yell leaders were the captains of other sports at their university, such as baseball or track.[17] By the early 1900s most colleges and universities had cheer leading squads or rooters who led the fans in such cheers as the following by the 1910 Southwestern Louisiana Industrial Institute Rooters:

Boomalacka, Boomalacka, Bow-wow-wow!
Chickalacka, Chickalacka, Chow-chow-chow!
Boomalacka, Chickalacka, Who are We?
Lafayette Institute, Don't You See?[18]

At the same time that some college administrators were institutionalizing cheerleading on their campuses, others expressed concern over this form of school spirit, which sometimes resulted in "yelling oneself into the hospital or rattling a pitcher."[19] Harvard President A. Lawrence Lowell asserted that organized cheering was the "worst means of expressing emotion ever invented."[20] The editors of *The Nation* responded to Lowell with the following: "the reputation of having been a valiant 'cheer-leader' is one of the most valuable things a boy can take away from college. As a title to promotion in professional or public life, it ranks hardly second to that of being a quarterback."[21] This last line of *The Nation's* overly enthusiastic retort to President Lowell does indicate the importance assigned to cheerleading in terms of its public prominence and its association with college leadership. It was during this time period that cheerleading also became affiliated with high-status fraternities on campus. Greek organizations came to be the major suppliers of collegiate leadership in all of its variations, from athletics to student government to cheerleading.[22]

Cheerleading remained a predominantly male activity well into the 1930s for a variety of reasons. During this era, men still outnumbered women on university campuses; further, traditional feminine emotional and physical traits did not seem appropriate for cheerleading; and the belief that women could even be harmed by the activity kept most women from participating. Thus, the two earliest manuals on cheerleading, written in 1927, refer exclusively to cheerleaders as "man," "chap," and "fellow."[23] Prior to

World War II, yell leaders formed Gamma Sigma, a national honorary fraternity for yell marshals, and with the help of sportswriters and sportscasters, they selected an annual 11-man All-American cheering squad. As late as 1939, female cheerleaders were excluded from the All-American cheering squad, and even in the 1950s, the head cheerleader was still typically referred to as the "rooter king."[24] Thus, although young women in the late 1920s and 1930s began entering collegiate organized cheering in small numbers, until the late 1940s cheering was still considered to be a male activity, associated with masculine characteristics of athleticism and leadership.

This brief early history of cheerleading demonstrates its unique relationship to the eminently American institution of sports, specifically football during this time, and the military. Cheerleading's origins, therefore, lay in the making of men, and not just any men, but American men. Through the regimen of physical contests that football provided in its more bloody days and the hardships and discipline encountered in early American military life, cheers and cheerleading were an acceptable part of the socialization of American men.

Cheerleading: Pride, Patriotism, and Tradition

Two bits, four bits, six bits a dollar
All for the Wildcats stand up and holler.

V-I-C-T-T-O-R-Y
That's the Wildcat Battle Cry![25]

Winnsboro, Louisiana, sits in the northeast corner of the state, 40 miles from the Mississippi River. Highway 15 runs through the middle of town, and anyone driving that way remembers Winnsboro because of its 325 18-feet-high American flags adorning a 2-mile stretch along that highway. For a while, the largest flag to fly on a pole outside of Washington, D.C., flew in Winnsboro's Patriot Square. The wind whipped it so badly that after 18 days it was almost in shreds and, unknown to many in the community, had to be replaced by a smaller one. Winnsboro is a frequent winner of the Cleanest City Contest. It's home to the Catfish Festival, which in 2002 drew more than 40,000 people. Fred Carter, Jr., accomplished Nashville studio musician and father of country music singer Deana Carter, grew up there. Booger McFarland, defensive tackle for the Tampa Bay Buccaneers, is a Winnsboro native. It's also the home of Debra Kay Robinson, 1979 Miss World Rodeo and World Barrel Racer, the 1967 state runner-up football champs, and the 1992 AAA state basketball champs. These are fairly impressive facts for a town of only 6,000.

Similar to most small towns in the United States, tradition is important in Winnsboro, and much of the community's traditions are centered around Winnsboro High School, particularly Winnsboro High School sports. Local talk says that the first football coach was B. S. Landis, Jr., who attended school in the Northeast, where he witnessed a football game, was enamoured with the game, returned home and began a team in Winnsboro, around 1925. By the 1940s, football was firmly established in Winnsboro, with cheerleaders being integral to the football rituals, which included pep rallies, afternoon parades, and Friday night games. For over 50 years, WHS cheerleaders have made decorations for the halls, gym, and bleachers of Winnsboro High, organized pep rallies, painted signs for football players to run through, greeted the opposing team's fans and cheerleaders, and led the sometimes large but often small crowds of football fans in cheering for the team.

Betty Price Sewell, a WHS cheerleader from 1947 to 1950 and, before her death in 2002, an ardent supporter of her All-American cheerleader granddaughter, recalls the simplicity of cheerleading in the post-WWII era: "It was a happy time for us. World War II was over; our brothers, cousins and older friends were home. . . . Being a cheerleader was the epitome of being popular. It was 'self esteem to the max!'—before we knew anything about self esteem and self confidence!"[26]

Friday afternoon pep rallies are an enduring tradition of Winnsboro High. For over 55 years, the entire student body has met in the gym for the pep rally to get the team and fans motivated for the Friday night football game. Cheerleaders from the 1940s through the 1980s coordinated the pep rally, relatively free from adult intervention or supervision. They were responsible for not only planning the agenda but also for creatively "firing up" the student body. One way was through skits, usually made up by the cheerleaders themselves. Mary Zoe Snyder Brasher, cheerleader from 1950 to 1954, recalls a homecoming pep rally when the Wildcats were playing the Neville Tigers. "I helped make a tiger which was brought in on a stretcher. Johnny Guice was dressed as a doctor with a doctor's bag. He examined the tiger and pronounced him dead from a wildcat attack." Jo Ann Boutwell, cheerleader from 1977 to 1979, recalls the "Get Fired Up" pep rally in which the cheerleaders arranged for the student body to meet in the football bleachers rather than in the gym. The cheerleaders then got the local fire department to drive them onto the field on a fire truck.

Until the 1960s, a parade was held in downtown Winnsboro on the Friday afternoons of local games. Shirley Renfrow Taliaferro, cheerleader from 1949 to 1953, recalls the community support shown at these parades:

Winnsboro High School had an excellent band. The pep squad and the cheer-leaders marched with the band. The sidewalks were lined with people. The community was very supportive. The parade would stop about half-way down Main Street. The cheerleaders would do a yell. Everyone yelled—the towns-people, the pep squad and the band. I really loved these parades and I loved prancing, clapping and twirling our skirts as we paraded downtown!

Winnsboro High cheerleaders attended their first camp in 1953, travel-ing to Texas to one of the newly created cheerleading camps offered by Lawrence Herkimer. In 1954, they attended a camp sponsored by the newly formed cheerleading organization, the National Cheerleading Association, at Northwestern State College (later University), a tradition that lasted over 30 years. Unchaperoned for most of this time, the cheerleaders from the 1950s to 1980s recall similar camp experiences: sore muscles, cigarette smoking, boyfriend talk, and bonding as a squad.

Sandi Eley, a cheerleader from 1975 to 1978, expresses a sentiment shared by many WHS cheerleaders throughout the years: "We were whole-some respectable girls that came from hard working families. Being a WHS cheerleader, made you feel like you were chosen and special." Peggy Elrod Nations, a cheerleader from 1968 to 1971, agrees and laments what she sees as the changes that have occurred in cheerleading in the last 30 years: "Being a Wildcat cheerleader was a tradition and quite an honor. We truly felt an immense responsibility to set and maintain the standard of excellence that we all enjoyed. The cheerleaders today don't seem to have the same morals and scruples." Natylon Lee, a cheerleader from 1998 to 2001, would dis-agree with Peggy's assessment of today's cheerleader. Natylon notes that "WHS cheerleaders are considered role models. People who set a good ex-ample for the school and those whom little future cheerleaders can look up to and admire." Cassie Gilbert, who cheered with Natylon, agrees but points out that the cheerleaders received "boo's" at several of the pep rallies—some-thing with which Peggy Elrod Nations, Betty Sewell Price, and Jo Ann Boutwell never had to contend.

In many ways, the WHS cheerleaders are fairly typical of most cheer-leading squads in the United States. In their 55 years, the Winnsboro High School cheerleaders have never competed in, much less won a national cheerleading competition. They've never been the squad that others envied at summer cheerleading camp. For many, many years, they passed down their uniforms from one squad to the next; until the 1980s, camp clothes were made from Simplicity patterns, and they wore saddle oxfords long past the time cheerleading tennis shoes were introduced. At every pep rally, the cheerleaders still lead the singing of the alma mater, written in the 1920s, and at every game they lead the fans in "Two bits, four bits, six bits a dollar," even though no one has any idea what a "bit" is. There are "Winns-boro High School cheerleading squads" in just about every town and city in the United States. Businesses comes and go, high school students come and go, mayors and school board members come and go, but the cheer-leader, like the sports team, endures, and in that endurance is something very American—small-town traditional patriotism.

Cheerleading operates at the interesting intersection of small-town local pride and national patriotism, both of which promote civic rituals and pub-lic spectacles. Americans love a parade and public spectacle, and local sports competitions provide that spectacle. Similar to why sports were institution-alized into American college culture, part of the original rationale for pro-moting extracurricular activities in the early high school was to encourage school pride and loyalty. Early policymakers and educators believed that these activities, such as sports and student government, would encourage so-cial unity among different ethnic groups and between the rich and the poor. Such activities would also teach cooperation and teamwork. Athletics, espe-cially team sports such as football, was considered a perfect vehicle to incul-cate these virtues in our high school students. It was believed that the loyalty and school pride engendered by these activities would naturally transfer to the nation at large when the youth matured into adults.[27] The cheerleaders were the ones responsible for ensuring that school spirit, loyalty, and pride transcended differences. Cheerleaders came to represent the model citizens whose values and actions were to reflect the ideals of the community.

Most middle and secondary school cheerleading constitutions speak di-rectly to this small-town traditional patriotism with their emphasis on com-munity over self. In this eighth- and ninth-grade cheerleader constitution for a Midwestern middle school, the "philosophy" of membership on the squad, includes the following: "A cheerleading squad has the responsibility to up-hold, to reflect, and to project the goals and ideals of the school community. A cheerleader shall represent the school by acting as a positive role model and demonstrating good leadership. He/she should promote positive school climate." In the 2002 *UCA Advisor/Coach Manual Building Traditions,* this national cheerleading organization makes the following statement about the purpose of cheerleading: "While recognizing the benefits of athletic compe-tition, the primary function of a cheerleading program is to support inter-school athletics and to uphold, reflect, and project the goals of the school community."[28]

It is a difficult endeavor to unite a diverse array of people and help shape them into something larger than they are as individuals. Yet, this is precisely what cheerleaders are expected to do—to promote school pride and loyalty in a diverse group of students and fans who come together, at least for a short period of time, for a common goal: to support their athletic team. As

Jim Lord, executive director of the American Association of Cheerleading Coaches and Advisors, asserts, "When you say I'm a Bearcat or a Wildcat, it pulls you into a bigger community than just your little niche."[29]

Further, cheerleaders must galvanize group members to remain supportive and part of this larger whole, even when the team faces challenges that it may not overcome. This can test school loyalty and pride and the group's ability to focus on similarities and not their differences. School pep rallies exemplify this unity of purpose and group resolve. Typically, the football team or the basketball team members sit together but are separated from the fans and cheerleaders. The cheerleaders are in front of the school's student body, which is often segregated by grade level. Different classes will often create different chants or cheers, which the cheerleaders of that grade lead. Ultimately, the job of the cheerleaders is to rally all of the school citizens to support the team against the week's opponent. This is the heart of patriotism—to galvanize people to come together to support a common goal through the use of symbols, rituals, and traditions.

Living in a Cheerocracy: American Optimism on Display

When local cheerleaders hold their fingers up and yell "We're number 1!" they bear a remarkable resemblance to the countless displays of patriotism that were seen in the immediate aftermath of the 9–11 attacks, as Americans from all walks of life proudly proclaimed, "We're still number 1!" Americans are an optimistic people, and cheerleaders represent this optimism because they are expected, above all else, to be perky and cheerful. In fact, if there is anything ubiquitous about any cheerleader, anywhere, it is their ever-present smile. That smile has been labeled in a variety of ways—as the toothpaste smiles and velcroed-on smiles. But smiling is part of the standard cheerleading uniform. Also part of the standard cheerleading look is pom pons, which also help with the cheery appearance. As Kline Boyd, vice president of Varsity Spirit Corporation, the world's most successful producer of cheerleading paraphernalia, says, "people just like pom pons. It makes people smile and makes them happy."[30] The spirit stick, the most coveted award at hundreds of cheerleading camps throughout this country, is also associated with cheerfulness and only given to those squads who most demonstrate cheerful optimism and energy. And consider the colors of the original National Cheerleading Association (NCA) spirit stick—red, white, and blue.

Repeatedly in our interviews with cheerleaders throughout this country, they referred to themselves as ambassadors for their schools. While football players may growl and shout obscenities to the opposing players, cheerleaders, as ambassadors of the school, are expected to be model citizens who are even cheerful to the opposing cheerleaders and fans. In fact, a common practice at many junior high and high school football games is that the home cheerleaders visit the other side of the stadium to greet the opposing team's cheerleaders and fans. Typically they perform a "Hello Cheer" on the opponent's side, and then their opponent's cheerleaders come back with them to be introduced to the home crowd. Shelia Angalet, spirit coordinator of Metuchen (NJ) High School, explains the importance of this ambassador role in maintaining a civil competitive environment, even when the atmosphere around the cheerleaders is less than cordial:

> It [the football game] has been a big rivalry—and sometimes a nasty one. I had warned my cheerleaders to be on their best behavior—that if anything was going to be sparked—it would be from the opposition, not us. After the game began, and things were rolling, the home team's cheerleaders came over to do their cheer. Our crowd was not overly cordial, but they were not rude either. As the other cheerleaders got closer, I encouraged my girls to welcome them and they started applauding! It caught on a little bit in the stands. The girls did their cheer nicely and there was applause for them—not rousing—but applause nonetheless. Shortly after that, we went to their side to do our Hello cheer. As we got close to the stands, the boos and cat calls started. I told my girls walk proud. Their cheerleaders were sitting waiting and applauding and cheering us! Their crowd may have been rude, but their cheerleaders were awesome and welcoming! While we lost the game, I feel the cheerleaders gained a bit of new respect and some cheer friends within our local community.[31]

This cheerful ambassador role, for many squads, extends beyond simply greeting the other team with a "hello cheer," as we discovered in a conversation on a cheerleading listserv about the importance of cheerleaders "spreading good cheer." The Mascoutah High Cheerleaders from Illinois, after hearing that many of the surrounding cheerleading squads hated them because they were so good, decided to rectify that situation by taking the following action: "The girls decided they would rather be remembered as the 'nice squad', rather than a squad people hated. So they came up with this idea. At each home game, we fill up a 1 gallon plastic jar with candy & goodies for the opposing cheerleaders. We decorate the jar with paint pens in their school's colors and initials. It takes very little time, but spreads some cheer!"[32]

Even when the chips are down—when all obstacles are stacked against us—when we're losing 66–3, the cheerleaders are expected to continue to yell "F-I-G-H-T, Fight, Eagles Fight!" Kline Boyd believes this cheerleading "can-do" mentality is at the heart of American idealism. "Cheerleaders go out there and say dad gum it, we support our team, we're going to cheer for them to win and believe they can win even if they don't have a chance."[33] In her reflection of what it was like to cheer during a miserable losing season at a small rural school, Ginger Hopkins admits that it was difficult to yell when the basketball team trailed by 58 points and their players were six inches shorter than the opposing team. However, her squad shifted to some innovative cheers such as, "Mayonnaise, mustard, relish—catch up!" and "Gimme a G, an R, an O, a W. What's that spell? . . . GROW!" And Ginger has a typical cheerleading spin on that season: "In fact, we'll probably remember that unchampionship season after other seasons are long forgotten. During it, we tried our hardest and kept our dignity, pride, and our sense of humor. The team may have lost, but we cheerleaders went undefeated!"[34]

Such a portrayal of cheerleaders may sound corny to many people, but these sentiments are shared by many in the cheerleading world. Indeed, cheerleading has almost become a synonym for eternal optimism and is used regularly in our American vernacular to convey the ability to look on the bright side even in the midst of travails. After the economic summit called by President Bush in the summer of 2002, the *Tuscaloosa News* in Tuscaloosa, Alabama, introduced its editorial for the day with the headline, "President leads cheers at summit." The article goes on to say:

> President George W. Bush's heralded economic summit in Waco, Texas Tuesday resembled nothing if not a pep rally meant to reassure a shaken stock market and public. And Bush, true to his roots as a prep school cheerleader, was out front leading the cheers. At times it almost seemed that he wanted to break into a rousing, "Give me an A! Give me a M! Give me an E . . ." "Even though times are kind of tough right now, we're America," Bush said. "I'm incredibly optimistic about the future of this country because I understand the strength of this country. . . . We've got a lot going for us."[35]

In the aftermath of the September 11 tragedy, the American character attributes that have been highlighted by the press and in conversations across the nation include our strength to pull together during a crisis, our faith in the future, and our optimism. In many ways, the activity of cheerleading embodies all of these qualities. We think that is why diverse groups of Americans with diverse causes and ways of presenting themselves have adopted cheerleading as the vehicle for their message. So, even radicals from the left, whose politics, one might think, would preclude their use of cheerleading, still become cheerleaders, albeit "radical cheerleaders."[36] Although their protests are bereft of short skirts and football chants, they shoulder the burdens of environmental degradation, globalization, the threat of war, patriarchy, and homophobia through clever cheers and chants such as the following:

I don't know but I've been told
SUV's have got to go
They smell bad, take too much space
They pollute all over the place
That beast's just a passenger car
No more two-tiered emission laws
They think driving in a mall parking lot
Is going off-roading, but it's not
Sustainable transit's what we want to see
So join me on a bike, yuppie!

As one of the groups explains on their website, "Radical Cheerleading is protest and performance! It is activism with pom-poms and combat boots! It is non-violent direct action in the form of street theatre."[37] Cheerleading, somehow, seems just as appropriate for those wearing combat boots and shaking milk jugs filled with pebbles as for those in kicky skirts who shake pom pons. Whether it's optimism for the end of global pollution or optimism for a winning football season, both groups of cheerleaders embody enthusiasm for whatever their passion. As Torrance, the captain of the Torro High School cheerleading squad in the popular cheerleading movie *Bring It On,* says, "we don't live in a democracy but a cheerocracy."[38]

Cheerleading: As American as Consumerism, Shallowness, and the Worst of American Culture

Two, four, six, eight
Go for a look you'll appreciate
Body in shape and looking great
Hurry, don't procrastinate![39]

If most people considered cheerleading only in light of the preceding discussion, there would be few, if any, criticisms of this activity and its participants. But all of us know that this is certainly not the case. In fact, cheerleaders are continually maligned in this culture, in very vicious as well as humorous ways, and are often used to highlight the worst of American culture, particularly conformity, mindlessness, and confused priorities. As Marty Beckerman notes, cheerleading is "an activity that attracts a lot of people with a lot of capacity, a lot of really energetic people who are throwing that energy away on this meaningless, pom-pom, jumping-around activity that doesn't really stand for anything. Clearly, that energy could be devoted to something more meaningful."[40] For Marty as well as countless other Americans, cheerleading represents a shallowness in intelligence and character as parodied by the Spartan Cheerleaders on *Saturday Night Live* and the innumerable "dumb cheerleader" jokes such as: "What did the Trojan cheerleader say when she learned she was pregnant? Is it mine?"[41]

Marty's book title, *Death to all Cheerleaders*, is certainly not so far removed from reality when we consider the case of the Texas cheerleader murder plot. In 1991, a Channelview, Texas, housewife named Wanda Holloway was arrested for solicitation of murder. When the reason behind the murder solicitation was revealed, the case made national and international headlines and confirmed countless people's beliefs that the activity of cheerleading is filled with narcissistic and shallow people whose mothers are even worse. Wanda had attempted to find someone to kill her former close friend, Verna Heath, because in the past Verna's daughter had beaten out Wanda's daughter for a slot on the cheerleading squad. Wanda believed that if Verna died, her 13-year-old daughter Amber would be so distraught that she would be unable to try out for cheerleader, which would then ensure that Wanda's daughter, Shana, was selected.[42] This sensational story led to a book, 2 made-for-television movies, innumerable talk show discussions, and countless gossip magazine stories. Further, the story was publicized around the world; for many outside the United States, the Texas cheerleading murder plot confirmed what they had seen in the popular TV show *Dallas:* that Americans were superficial people who will do anything to win. In 1996, Wanda, Texas housewife, school and church volunteer received a 10-year sentence; 6 months of the sentence would be served in jail while the remaining time would be spent on probation. Verna's family received $150,000 compensation from Wanda's insurance company.[43]

The Texas cheerleading murder plot illuminated much of what many critics complain about cheerleading—that it is a mindless activity fueled, in part, by unfulfilled mothers who live their meaningless lives through their daughters. Indeed, the entire scheme and the subsequent trial was full of small-town petty jealousy and intrigue. Wanda complained that Verna was always kissing up to those who had some authority in the cheerleading selection. Further, the tape-recorded conversations of Wanda and her former brother-in-law, whose job was to secure a hit man to carry out Wanda's wishes, revealed the worst in "cheerleader moms." In the book *Mother Love, Deadly Love,* Wanda considers whether the hit man should take out her daughter's rival, Amber. The quotes are from the audiotape recording of their conversation that was played during Wanda's trial: "'And to be honest with you, Wanda,' Terry said. 'Doing kids is just, you know.' 'Yeah, but Terry, you don't know this little girl!' Wanda interrupted, her voice dripping with venom. 'If you knew her! Ooooooh! I can't stand her. I mean, she's a bitch! Makes me sick! I mean I could knock her in the face, you know?'"[44]

Although most parents of cheerleaders are not plotting to murder anyone standing in their daughter's way, the California Newport Harbor High School controversy provides further ammunition for critics who blame overzealous parents for the misguided priorities taught to our young people. In 1995, the parents of a student not selected as a Newport Harbor High cheerleader filed a lawsuit against the school district, claiming the selection process had been unfair. The school district settled out of court for $50,000. As a result, a new selection process was implemented: three paid external, expert judges, votes tallied by a certified public accountant, and a representative of the League of Women Voters standing by to make sure nothing went amiss. Despite all of the precautions to ensure a fair selection process, when the squad was selected at the November 2001 tryouts, the coach, who was not a faculty member and was paid by the boosters, complained to the principal that the judges were inconsistent and showed partiality. The principal decided to reverse the judges' decisions and allow all 48 girls to be on the squad. This action incited several of the parents whose daughters had been selected; one filed a formal complaint with the school district. An investigative team was convened and determined that the selection process had been fair. Thus, the principal had to reverse his earlier decision—only the 30 originally selected would be able to cheer, but, as a compromise, tryouts would be held again and four additional cheerleaders selected.[45] The subsequent letters to the *Los Angeles Times* reflected a general disbelief that cheerleading can garner more serious attention that an economic recession, failing achievement scores, and even the war on terrorism. David Perez of Irvine wrote tongue-in-cheek: "Forget the Taliban, Al Qaeda, and Osama bin Ladin's whereabouts. No, what is of most urgency is getting to the bottom of 'pompomgate' at Newport Harbor High School."[46] Similarly, Julie Hudash, who graduated from USC on a full athletic scholarship, wrote:

I have a few suggestions on the cheerleading "crisis" in Newport Beach. First, the administrators should skip cheerleading this year and invest their money in a way that actually benefits students. Open the High School of Second Chances for pushy and overly involved parents. Here moms and dads can pay to relive, or re-create, their own high school fantasies. Moms can be cheerleaders and homecoming queens. Competitive dads can try to be the superjock they think their kids should be. While their parents are busy, their kids can finally concentrate on what is really important: growing into responsible and mature adults.[47]

But it is not just cheerleading parents whose shallowness is highlighted in the above commentaries. Cheerleaders themselves are often associated with shallowness and narcissism. Supposedly, they are so egocentric that they even lose track of the game for which they are cheering, as the following critical cheer reflects:

> Totally, for sure, I just got a manicure.
> The sun, up there, is bleaching out my hair.
> My makeup is smearing; I just lost an earring.
> 33–44, I don't know the stinking score.
> Go, go, fight, fight!
> Gee, I hope I look alright.

This same complaint has been made about professional cheerleaders. Scott Ostler, writing in 1994, considers the role of professional cheerleaders who are so caught up in being the center of attention that they actually detract from the game:

> When it's a good game, the cheerleaders get in the way. At the Forum years ago, the Lakers went on a hellacious 14–0 run, and the other team's coach frantically called timeout. The crowd, worked into a frenzy by Magic and Showtime, went nuts. For about four seconds. Then the disco music started and the Laker Girls ran onto the court, an acre of womanhood in two square yards of Spandex.
>
> The forum fell silent, except for the pounding disco beat and from the stands, the occasional growl or whimper. The fans not only stopped cheering, they almost stopped breathing. There's an irony for you: cheering stopped cold by cheerleaders.[48]

"Give a cheer for good looks. Plan your beauty routines as carefully as you plan your routines on the fields and look your best from kick-off until the clock runs out!"[49] This advice from an article in *Teen* magazine is what leads many critics of cheerleading to hold such disdain for the activity. They argue that cheerleading, despite claims made to the contrary, has less to do with athleticism and more to do with projecting a particular "look." That look can be seen at any regional or national cheerleading competition where spiral curl ponytails and red lipstick are part of standard uniform wear. As a recent article for coaches in *American Cheerleader Junior* reflects, achieving the right cheerleading look requires not only such essentials as uniforms, bodysuits, bloomers, and healthy snacks but also hair ribbons, bows, makeup, glitter sprays and curlers "for those crazy competition curls."[50] And if you can't get those "crazy competition curls" just right, you can now purchase them from Cheer Curls, a company that specializes in creating customized synthetic wiglets. Made to match each girl's natural hair color and texture, these synthetic curls ensure that the entire squad has the exact same curly ponytail. According to its makers,

"THEY WILL NOT FALL OFF no matter how active you are. Tumble, stunt, fly . . . Your curls will stay firmly attached until you are ready to remove them."[51]

Besides narcissism and shallowness, cheerleading is also denigrated because of the enormous cost to participate. Many families make substantial (and some would say, foolish and selfish) financial sacrifices for their daughters to participate in a $1,000-a-year activity that many consider superfluous and more akin to wet T-shirt contests and karaoke. Why not spend money, critics ask, on violin, art, or equestrian lessons—activities that can be continued throughout one's life and represent a higher form of cultural activity? It is certainly disconcerting to many that whereas school orchestras are almost non-existent today in many small towns, 85 girls may show up to try out for 12 slots on a cheerleading squad. These misguided financial priorities are what many would say is the most American facet of cheerleading and perhaps most representative of American culture at large.

Cheerleading: Something so American

After watching *Bring it On* and the ESPN National Cheerleading Championships, a cheerleading online participant, Celso, from Brazil, thought cheerleading looked really cool. However, he notes that in Brazil, "we don't have such a thing. I don't know why. I believe that there you cheer the audience, here for a long time we have our own shouts and everything. It's also something so American that it wouldn't look good as it looks there."[52]

We agree with Celso that cheerleading is "something so American." Yet what is "so American" about it can be read in both positive and negative ways. On the one hand, cheerleading is seen, by many, as a positive representation of the patriotic American, the good citizen, who exudes optimism even in the face of adversity. On the other hand, cheerleading, for many, represents the worst of American culture with its shallow, consumer-oriented, misguided emphasis on crass entertainment over intellectual, cultural pursuits. However, as we all know, the American identity is not monolithic, nor is it fixed. It changes and adopts new ways of being American while still clinging to some of the older American markers. American institutions that can tell us something about ourselves, like jazz, baseball, and cheerleading, are also not static but being created anew with each generation. These shifts, these reconfigurations are very American. Further, Americans are known for their inventiveness—their ability to take an already existing object or activity and change it to meet a different purpose. Throughout this research we have found diverse groups of Americans doing just this—reinventing cheerleading. As we present in the next chapter, feminist cheerleaders, gay and lesbian cheerleaders, senior citizen cheerleaders and radical cheerleaders all open up the meaning of cheerleading as well as an American identity in new and interesting ways. Perhaps this ingenuity in remaking cheerleading is what is the most American about cheerleading.

CHEERLEADING WITH A TWIST

Transformative Cheerleaders

U-G-L-Y
Corporate scum you cheat you lie
You UGLY—uh, uh—you ugly
G-R-E-E-D
Corporation don't fool me
You greedy—uh, uh—you greedy
E-V-I-L
Money won't save you from hell
You evil—uh, uh—you evil.
R-U-I-N
All this shit has got to end
You ruin—uh, uh—you ruin.
Y-L-G-U
You are ugly backwards too
You UGLY—uh, uh—you ugly.
F-R-E-E
That is what we need to see
Our freedom—uh, uh—our freedom.[1]

As part of American culture, we expect to see cheerleaders in many different places: at ribbon-cutting ceremonies, in basketball gyms, at football stadiums, in parades, on television, and even in movies. What we don't expect to see are cheerleaders at social protests such as the World Trade Organization protest in Quebec City in 2001. But when the police and members of the media arrived, that is exactly what they saw: social protesters dressed in combat boots and holding pom pons made of shredded garbage bags held together with duct tape, and chanting the cheer above.[2]

Radical Cheerleaders are not the only ones who don't fit the traditional image of cheerleaders. Around the nation gay and lesbian squads collect money for local organizations providing care for those suffering from HIV or breast cancer. Feisty X-Cheerleaders from New York motivate 6,000 Chicago working women with their chant, "73 cents to the dollar, makes me want to shout and holler." Japanese cheerleaders act as hostesses for Japanese Airlines (JAL), and the Wilmington Golden Pom Pom Cheerleaders, a senior citizen squad, perform cartwheels and splits for a nursing home audience. Certainly, these are not the traditional images of cheerleading portrayed in *Seventeen, American Cheerleader,* or in mainstream movies such as *Bring it On.* Different from each other in many ways, these groups do share one common feature. They all challenge, disrupt, or call into question who can be a cheerleader, the purpose of cheerleading, and the stereotypes of cheerleaders.

Those "Frog Throated Lassies"

The very first disruptive cheerleaders were women who dared to encroach upon what was seen as a firmly established male activity. As discussed in the previous chapter, the first cheerleaders were male, and they dominated the activity until the 1940s. The first females began entering cheerleading in the 1920s, but it was not until the 1950s that cheerleading came to be regarded as primarily a feminized activity.[3] But women's entrance into cheerleading was not easy, and it disrupted what were considered to be the traditional role and activities of cheerleaders at the time. As girls and women joined cheerleading squads, concern was expressed that they were inherently incapable of performing the difficult acrobatic stunts that had been the mainstay of cheerleading for the previous decades. In his book *School Yells,* Brings (1944) cites an educator who, although he wanted to incorporate as much tumbling as possible, felt constrained: "Such actions as cartwheels, forward and backward rolls, flips, head and hand stands, and diving, are about all we can use now, for the trend is more and more toward girls."[4]

Other concerns besides their supposed tumbling inabilities were also voiced about women cheerleaders. In 1938, John Gach from Janesville High School in Janesville, Wisconsin, spells out why there was such resistance to female cheerleaders.[5] These "frog-throated lassies" don't have the masculine voices needed to lead the yells, and they don't have the athletic skills to perform the acrobatic stunts. Further, girls may become loud, rough and rowdy, even perhaps picking up some slang and profanity, through their association with the male cheerleaders; and they may become conceited. Gach goes on to refute many of these points by arguing that girls can be taught the simpler acrobatic stunts, and with proper coaching they could be taught how to use their voices in ways that would not strain them nor irritate the fans. Further, Gach contended that boys shouldn't be using profanity anyway, and girls who cheer don't become any more or less conceited than do girls who participate in other extracurricular activities. Gach then adds that, in some cases, girls may be more suitable for the activity than boys. First, they are more rhythmic, due to their years of taking tap lessons. Second, they are more magnetic in their appearance, thus able to captivate the audience more easily than boys. And, third, because the most "enthusiastic rooters [read fans] are members of the weaker sex, . . . it is logical that one of their own kind should be able to lead them."[6]

Besides Gach's 1938 arguments about what the "weaker" sex was capable of, several cultural phenomena were taking place during the 1920s that would help set the stage for women to cheer. Women students comprised 47 percent of the undergraduate population, and during this decade became central to the social life of coeducational institutions. On many campuses, the Greeks controlled the school's leadership positions, which certainly included cheerleading. Thus, sororities became involved in cheerleading. It was also during this time period that the Miss America pageant was instituted, and the public was exposed to the glamour of beauty pageants. Further, the fledgling advertising industry began to use female images in their ads, and female movie stars such as Mary Pickford also made the idea of women performing as cheerleaders in front of large crowds more palatable.[7]

By the 1940s, more than 30,000 American high schools and colleges had cheerleaders, many of whom were females.[8] A 1941 article in *Life* reported that the "girl cheerleader is establishing her ability to evoke unprecedented vocal energies from any grandstand she confronts"[9] In this article, three female cheerleaders from a high school in Indiana are featured performing new cheer techniques called "rhythm-nastics," which combined both dance and gymnastics, incorporating the latest in swing. The photographs of the girls do not, however, feature any gymnastics as typical of similar photographs picturing male cheerleaders. Rather the girls are shown kicking their legs into the air, snapping their fingers, swaying their hips, and jumping into the air.

The trend to include girls in what had been a male activity was greatly enhanced in part by World War II. As young men fought in the war, girls were offered entrance into spaces once relegated solely for males. Cheerleading was one of those spaces.[10] As men returned from the war, they sought to reclaim their place in the public spheres. Quite naturally, one such public sphere was cheerleading. In fact, by the 1950s several college (e.g., the University of Tennessee) and high school squads began to ban girls and women from the cheering squad. The student council of Union High School in Redwood City, California, rationalized its decision to ban girl cheerleaders with these four arguments: (1) girls' voices were too shrill, (2) girls don't understand the intricacies of sports to have the ability to lead cheers, (3) girls cannot control spectators who might get out of hand, and (4) boys want to get back into cheerleading.[11]

Some colleges clung to the tradition of male-only squads. For example, Harvard didn't allow women cheerleaders until 1971.[12] However, by the 1950s cheerleading, by and large, was seen as a feminine activity, especially at the junior high and high school levels. Today, one would assume that female cheerleaders are the norm throughout the country, and they are, except in a few places, where women cheerleaders are still considered disruptive. One of those places is in College Station, Texas, home of Texas A & M, which was the first public institution of higher education in Texas. A & M began as an all-male, all-military institution. It did not admit women on an unconditional basis until 1972. It was also the first to have cheerleaders in Texas, a state that takes cheerleading very seriously. These first yell leaders were freshmen cadets who led the Aggies in Army yells. Today the tradition continues at A & M, with five male students, called yell leaders, leading cheers more akin to Army yells. At midnight before each game, they rehearse with the student body (called the 12th Man) the hand signals and yells that will be used in the next day's game.[13]

However, in 2001, Shannan Johnson challenged this tradition of male-only yell leaders by proposing a coed competitive-only squad, the "Fighting Texas Aggie Competition Cheer Squad." Initially, the university granted the squad of 30 women and one man a "provisional" status and established the following rules: no university funds, no cheering at A & M events, no using the A & M logo, and no holding practices on campus.[14] However, opposition to the new squad was fierce, with students and alumni decrying the loss of tradition, as illustrated in this e-mail received by the student newspaper: "The Yell Leaders are enough, there is no room for cheerleaders. And if Johnson and her group doesn't like it, Highway 6 runs both ways!! I'm sure t.u. [a derogatory term for the A & M rival, the University of Texas] would be happy to have them!!"[15]

Another place where female cheerleaders, at least particular female cheerleaders, are not welcomed is at the Virginia Military Institute. Traditionally, the females for the VMI squad were selected from nearby Mary Baldwin College and Southern Seminary. However, when the Virginia Military Institute became coeducational in 1997, female cadets were invited to try out for the squad. But when the first female cadet cheerleaders tried to motivate their fans, they were booed by many of their male peers. Male cadets argued that the short-haired female cadets "don't even look like cheerleaders." Others said that having fellow female cadets on the cheerleading squad was creating undue sexual tension.[16]

With the exception of a few places, such as Texas A & M and VMI, female cheerleaders are certainly no longer seen as being disruptive. Rather they are the norm. It is male cheerleaders, particularly at the high school level, that seem to disrupt people's ideas about cheerleading as something girls do for the boys playing the sport. Heterosexuality is assumed for both the female cheerleaders and the male athletes. In many places, male cheerleaders (whether they are straight or gay), as we discuss further in chapter 4, must deal with the stigma of being labeled "fag" or "sissy." However, a group of cheerleaders who can be found in New York, Seattle, San Francisco, and other cities throughout the United States and Canada challenge the pervasive idea that only straight females can be cheerleaders.

Unstraightening Cheerleading: Gay and Lesbian Cheerleading Squads

At first glance, CHEER San Francisco appears to be a very well-trained collegiate squad. Squad members radiate energy with traditional head nods, pointing index fingers, and miles of smiles. Their stunts are impressive as well. For example, they are known for forming human pyramids that move and for back tuck basket tosses, in which one member is launched 20 feet in the air, does a complete rotation, and is caught by 4 supporters. Their uniforms have a clean crisp look, and their movements are the same. Often the squad is accompanied by a band. On closer inspection, one might note that some of the squad members appear to be older than college age (actually the average age is 35 years) and that there is great diversity of the squad in terms of race and ethnicity. Finally, the number of men versus women on the squad would probably cause some consternation, since male cheerleaders typically do not dominate cheerleading squads. Although traditional in so many ways, CHEER San Francisco is not a typical cheerleading squad.

Begun in 1980 as the first professional openly gay cheerleading squad in the country and probably the world, and now the longest-running openly gay squad, CHEER San Francisco was originally called the Hayward Raw Rahs. The five men who composed the squad at that time performed a mostly dance style of cheerleading. As the squad grew and became more professional, members decided to change their name to reflect that. "We didn't want to sound like a drag cheerleading team, which is the image the old name meant to a lot of people," said Morgan Craig, long-time team member.[17] Over the last 23 years, CHEER San Francisco has evolved into a professional cheerleading squad that performs a combination of dance, tumbling, stunting, and cheering. The group received nonprofit status, and in 1999 established its mission statement and the Cheer for Life Fund that supports organizations providing care for those facing HIV/AIDS and cancer.

The group performs for such local events as lesbian football games and the San Francisco Pride Parade; for national events such as President Clinton's Inaugural Parade in 1997, and has made appearances at every single Gay Games since 1982 which have been held in such places as New York, Amsterdam, and Sydney. Captain Steve Burke explained what he loves about being a long-time member of CHEER San Francisco and a 45-year-old cheerleader:

> CHEER San Francisco doesn't have a specific team to cheer for and we don't exist to compete, so my favorite part of cheerleading is stepping into new venues and seeing the crowds fall in love with us as we fall in love with them. As a unique team of 35 men and 10 women, we are like a magnet when crowds hear us announced. They are curious to see what we are going to do and go wild once we start performing. We are doing things that normally are done by people half many of our ages. The energy that happens between us and the crowds is real life-giving and makes me keep cheering after all these years.[18]

During their twentieth anniversary they were asked to perform for a pregame show for the Golden State Warriors professional basketball team in a game against the Denver Nuggets. Recently, the team was selected to represent the United States in the 2002 Singapore Chinese New Year's Parade, where over 250,000 witnessed American cheerleading, most for the first time. The team has also been recruited to perform at cheerleading camps where most squads are heterosexual. Burke comments that, "When we first walk into places like that, people are kind of looking at us sideways, but by the time we're leaving, everybody wants to get their picture taken with us. If you don't love us at first, you'll love us eventually."[19] Currently, the squad numbers 45 and members are asked for a one-year commitment of weekly practices plus fulfilling a busy performance schedule.

CHEER San Francisco's Mission Statement speaks to the traditional and not so traditional facets of this organization: "To execute extreme stunts and powerful dance routines as a means to entertain, inspire and motivate audiences to strive for personal excellence while celebrating the beauty and unity of diverse people."[20] The first two-thirds of this mission statement could be found in almost any school or college or All-Star cheerleading squad's constitution. However, the phrase "while celebrating the beauty and unity of diverse people" is not commonly considered a priority of cheerleading. CHEER New York's (an affiliate gay cheerleading squad) mission statement also includes sentiments not likely articulated by cheerleading squads: "reaching new heights with love, spirit, strength, and understanding."

CHEER San Francisco welcomes straight, gay, and lesbian members. Although the squad does require tryouts, members hold workshops to help those who have never cheered before. In fact, the most important criteria for making the squad are commitment and willingness to learn. CHEER San Francisco often wins trophies at college level competitions, even with 30-year-old members who have never cheered before. For example, for the third year in a row at a college cheer camp at the University of Southern California, CHEER San Francisco took away the Leadership trophy, which is voted on by all the competing teams and awarded to the team that people would most like to be a part of besides their own.[21]

Obviously, CHEER San Francisco and affiliate teams such as CHEER New York, CHEER Seattle, CHEER San Diego, Colorado Spirit, CHEER Los Angeles, Vancouver LGBT Cheerleading Society, and CHEER Sacramento disrupt some of the assumptions about cheerleaders. Most members of these squads are gay and lesbian, and they are no longer college age. However, in many ways, these squads are the epitome of American cheerleading. Their goal is "to entertain, inspire, and motivate," which is probably the most fundamental goal of cheerleading. Further, they are very optimistic and express a form of local patriotism. Their Cheer for Life Fund raises money for local charities, and their weekly practices and full performance schedule demonstrate a commitment to local civic and social rituals. And, when asked about what retired cheerleaders do, Steve Burke, in true cheerleading fashion, responded, "Probably at age 80, we'll be doing pompom routines from our electric wheelchairs."[22]

Wanted: Ex-Cheerleaders with an Attitude

Hey, We've got the squad
That's close to god
And she told us
To make a fuss, Hey.[23]

The above cheer is one of the first chanted by a group of former cheerleaders, appropriately named the X-Cheerleaders and based in New York City, in a performance art piece that has been called a "post feminist pep rally" by one commentator.[24] Although most members are older than the typical cheerleader, the X-Cheerleaders present themselves in traditional cheerleading fashion. Dressed in short pleated skirts and V neck tops with a large "X" across their chests, the X-Cheerleaders provide spectators with a feisty reinterpretation of traditional cheerleading. The entire performance art piece is conveyed through cheers and mostly typical cheerleading movements. It's what the X-Cheerleaders say, and how they say it, that is surprising.

Kim Irwin, a New York City–based conceptual artist, tried out for cheerleading every year of her high school career and finally made the squad during her senior year. By then, she says, she was over her desire to be a cheerleader. However, while in her forties, she reflected on the influences that had shaped her as a woman, and recognized that cheerleading, or rather the stereotype of cheerleading, had contributed much to her socialization as a female, albeit in contradictory ways. She asked, "Why am I still tied to a cheerleader image of myself—needing to be attractive, popular, have a good figure, be a 'good' girl or someone 'he' would want to marry, socially adept, a good performer, outgoing, happy, bouncy, active, cute, pretty, loving, etc?"[25]

In order to explore the power of cheerleading on women's lives (and she believes that cheerleading as a female icon is just as powerful for those who did not cheer), Irwin advertised for former cheerleaders, recruited a choreographer who was a former cheerleader, Judy Oberfelder, and held tryouts. The selected group composed their own cheers, constructed an entire performance, and went on the road. The performance was entitled "The WANTED: X-Cheerleaders Project."

The cheers that the X-Cheerleaders chant and at times lead the audience in, speak to the contradictions that cheerleading holds for American girls and women. Take the following crowd-pleasing cheer, for example.

> Perky (10 times)
> Pretty (10 times)
> Pleasing (10 times)
> The secret's Vaseline for our
> Pretty, pleasing style
> We put it on our gums
> To keep our perma-smiles

No doubt, the ubiquitous cheerleading smile is an essential element of cheerleading. Any cheerleader will tell you that. But what the X-Cheerleaders do is draw explicit attention to that fact and note how it is done. But the perma-smile is not all it takes to be the ideal female in this society, as the following cheer points out:

> Abs, thighs, buns of steel
> Puking after every meal
> Tummy tucks, liposuction
> Gotta get a breast reduction
> Legs too short, butt too big

Get fake nails, buy a wig
Weight Watchers, Lean Cuisine
I gotta be what's on the screen.
Perfection! Perfection!
Perfection!

Although this cheer mocks the unhealthy ways that women try to achieve the impossibility of physical perfection, the audience knows that for many young girls especially, cheerleaders represent that feminine perfection, that feminine ideal. College cheerleaders are often asked to sign autographs for young idolizing female fans. But this X-Cheerleader cheer asks about the price that one pays for achieving that feminine ideal body and look. Although they are railing against a society that encourages female perfection, they are also very aware that women and girls willingly participate in these oppressive practices. Through their performance, the X-Cheerleaders make explicit the contradictions, constraints, and joys of girls' and women's lives in this society.

No ifs ands or buts, we're the virgin sluts
No ifs ands or buts, we're the virgin sluts

The topics of their cheer performance include feminine hygiene products; violence against women; the pleasures of masturbation; birth; and the perennially popular Kegel exercises that women of all ages practice ("Gimme a K, Gimme a E . . ."). However, don't let the topics fool you into envisioning this performance and these women as somber feminists. The cheerleaders and the performance are fun-loving and playful. It is a joy to watch as Jody Oberholder completes a headstand and kicks her legs in a frog-like position while the squad yells the birth cheer ("Push it out, push it out, way out"). It is a pleasure to watch these former cheerleaders high-kick, cartwheel, and perform some fairly athletic moves. While laughing, spectators must contemplate the truths of the cheers. For Kim Irwin, "To cheer these words is transformative."[26] For the audience, it is the same.

Committed to the feminist principles of collective social action, the X-Cheerleaders did not want to transform only themselves through their cheers. Since 1998, they have been conducting "Cheering for Ourselves" workshops with public school girls, aged 9–12, who live in the Lower East Side of New York. In conjunction with the Institute for Labor and the Community, the X-Cheerleaders use cheerleading as a vehicle to explore issues such as girl power, media images, discrimination, sports, body image, and teasing. The girls and their teachers conduct research around these issues, discuss them, and then create their own transformative cheers.

Cheering for Social Justice: Radical Cheerleaders

"A cheer can lift people's spirits."[27] These words might have been spoken by just about any one of the millions of individuals who participate in cheerleading. However, Alize Zorlutuna is not your typical, traditional cheerleader. Rather, she is part of a growing number of Radical Cheerleaders who cheer as a form of social protest against everything from globalization to the suppression of women's rights and gay/lesbian-bashing.[28]

Cheering as a form of social protest is not new. In the 1960s several individuals used it as a vehicle of social protest and disrupted traditional notions of cheerleading. Jeff Sokol, a long-haired Vietnik campaigning on an antiwar platform, ran for head yell leader at the University of California at Berkeley. He beat his closest opponent by 1,100 votes.[29] His first order of business was to select his 50-member squad, which included, much to the chagrin of many, "a boy with a cowboy hat, another long haired friend, and two others who hadn't even shown up to try out."[30] Other changes he implemented included the use of antiwar songs and cheers created by a local radical theatrical group, the adoption of blue sweaters with gold peace signs and Levi jeans as the official uniform, and employing Country Joe and the Fish to play a half-time gig. After leading the crowd at several games in such chants as "End the War, End the War" and "Ban the Bomb," he was forced to retire through a vigorous recall petition headed mainly by fraternities and sororities. Somewhat surprised at the publicity he received, Sokol stated, "I thought it would be easy to ease the spectators' aggressions away from school spirit to more worthy causes, like the peace movement. Instead, they've directed them toward me."[31]

After the Watts Riots in 1965, UCLA student Eddie Anderson decided to run for the head yell leader position with the intention of using cheerleading as a vehicle to deliver his antiracism and antiwar messages to a larger audience. He was elected. At one game, he performed a parody of Bill Haley's "Rock Around the Clock" and called it "Bomb Around the Clock." When UCLA was playing Duke, one of the Duke fans became quite upset that Anderson, an African American, was dancing with one of the white UCLA song girls. Anderson is reported to have stopped what he was doing, grabbed the microphone, and announced "This woman is trying to be heard, but we can't hear what she's saying through her white sheet."[32]

Similar to these earlier cheerleaders, the Radical Cheerleaders (sometimes called "jeerleaders" or "queerleaders") are using the medium of cheering as a form of social protest. "It's activism with pom poms and middle fingers extended. It's screaming F*CK CAPITALISM while doing splits."[33] They are part of a larger youth movement that combines nonviolent protest and social activism with a little bit of fun. They show up at such events as Take Back the Night, Southern Girls Conventions, Taco Bell protests, the World Trade Organization meetings, and pro-choice rallies. Typically dressed in skirts, combat boots, and sporting pom pons, often homemade from garbage bags, they yell such cheers as "2–4–6–8. We're the ones who ovulate. Not the church, not the state. We will decide our own fate."

Radical Cheerleading groups have popped up all over North America, in such cities as New York, Toronto, Atlanta, Memphis, New Orleans, and Athens, Georgia. Radical cheerleaders can also be found in Sweden, Czechoslovakia, Poland, the United Kingdom, and Brazil. But just like traditional cheerleading, the origins of radical cheerleading are American. The story goes that three sisters, Aimee, Cara, and Colleen Jennings, began radical cheerleading in 1996 on their way to a Youth Liberation conference in Sarasota, Florida. Bored with traditional protests and concerned about the lack of response to protesters' messages, these girls donned cheerleader-like uniforms, created pom pons out of garbage bags, and began circulating their cheers on flyers to call attention to their causes.[34] Aimee, who makes no claim that she and her sisters were the first Radical Cheerleaders, explains why this form of social protest has been so successful: "Radical cheerleading is a wonderful testament to collaborative art and decentralized organizing."[35]

Radical Cheerleading attracts a large number of people who have deep concerns about social injustices such as corporate greed, sexual harassment, dangerous dieting, and environmental degradation, but who have been reluctant in the past to participate in traditional forms of protest. Similar to traditional cheerleaders, Radical Cheerleaders yell chants, perform stunts, dance, and sing songs. Rachel Engler-Stringer, a member of a Toronto Radical Cheerleader squad, describes a Labour Day march in Toronto: "It was really fun because it's filled with union people who are not necessarily radical activists. The people in the unions were marching with their locals, and we ran up to the front of the march and individually cheered for each local, and that made a lot of the people who were marching happy. We also made up cheers for the spectators sitting on the side of the street."[36] Their job is to enliven a protest, to keep the momentum going, and, in some cases, to diffuse some of the raw emotions that transpire at many protests, as illustrated in the following: "In Quebec City, for example, we used cheering as a tool to channel anger. When you are gassed consistently for four days, your tolerance levels definitely get tested. When we felt that energies were running high and people were upset and running in every direction, we would form a circle and do a cheer."[37]

In some cases, Radical Cheerleaders attend traditional cheerleading camps to learn cheers, but more often, they learn from each other, from conferences and workshops, and from listservs. They also publish their own

posters and zines listing dozens of radical cheers.[38] Although loosely organized, they held their first convention in Ottawa in March 2001. At this
convention, in addition to having workshops on stunts and safety, they offered workshops on radical choreography, starting a zine, legal training for
protests, wooing the media, and nonviolence training.[39]

However, some Radical Cheerleaders have started to disband because of
the publicity they have received, claiming they get more attention for their
medium than for their message. They are concerned that their politics have
gotten lost amid the hype about cheerleading. Reporting why Las Sinfronteras, a women's activist and performance group from Tucson, Arizona,
stopped radical cheerleading, Graig Uhlin, reporter for the *Arizona Daily
Wildcat*, noted: "On the one hand, they have to entertain their audience, but
at the same time, they risk losing their message behind the pretty package."[40]
In other cases, the reasons for the protests (e.g., police brutality) are such
powerful and emotional issues that cheerleading is simply not the appropriate medium for displaying outrage, anger, and a call for radical social change.

For Radical Cheerleaders like Mary Christmas, when reporters "focus
more on the fact that we are a bunch of mostly young women in little
skirts," she quickly points out to them that "we work hard to get the radical political message across. We're RADICALS. We openly oppose the current government; we speak out against injustice, and we're not going to
stop." She also notes that cheerleading is but one facet of radical activists'
work; many are employed as labor organizers and rape crisis hotline workers
as well as protest coordinators.[41]

Ultimately, Aimee Jennings sees many similarities between traditional
cheerleaders and Radical Cheerleaders. "Radical cheerleaders and traditional
cheerleaders have lots in common. We are strong and loud; we shout our messages; we want to be acknowledged for our accomplishments; we multitask; we
are tough; we are scene stealers."[42] More ambivalent about the similarities,
Brad Oremland, who participated as a Radical Cheerleader protesting the
chain store Staple's use of old-growth paper products, says that radical cheerleading is "sort of like making fun of [the cheerleading persona] and embrac-
ing it at the same time."[43] However, some radical cheerleading squads are
much more adamant about pointing out the immense differences between
their group and traditional cheerleaders. There are no tryouts for being a Radical Cheerleader; anyone, regardless of race, class, gender, sexual orientation,
body size, or physical appearance, is welcomed; and there are no expensive
uniforms, competitions, or long, structured practices. Lindsay Telfer explains
further how Radical Cheerleaders are different from traditional cheerleaders:

> I really do not like the comparison to traditional cheerleaders. I recognize that
> this may very well be a natural comparison, but I think that it needs to be un-

derstood that many squads are fighting really hard to say, Fuck the image of the sexy cheerleader—we are not happy-go-lucky, flaky women. We're not even all women. We are angry, we are mad, and we have a real message behind what we are doing. It's not just "Go Team," it's "Let's win!"[44]

Radical Cheerleader Koren Manning, a member of the Tucson Radical Cheerleaders, explains how their use of cheerleading is both disruptive of traditional notions of cheerleading and representative of American ingenuity: "It's a great cultural pun, in a way. We're taking cheerleading which I don't think most people would call radical feminist ideology, making it our own, and using it for our own purposes."[45]

Cheering for Themselves: Competitive Cheerleading

Repeatedly in our interviews with cheerleading coaches and individuals involved in the cheerleading industry, we have heard the statement, "If it wasn't for the athletes in the building, there would be no need for cheerleaders." Obviously, squads such as CHEER San Francisco, the X-Cheerleaders, and Radical Cheerleaders would find such claims suspect. But so would All-Star or competitive cheerleaders, who, although much more traditional in look and style to the cheerleaders presented in the previous chapter, do not believe that the sole purpose of cheerleaders is to support the athletic endeavors of others. These competitive squads (often called All-Stars) don't cheer for any team; they compete strictly for themselves in local, regional, state, and national championships against other teams.[46] The CANANM International Cheer & Dance Championships are just one of the hundreds of competitions held every year in the United States. Here squads and individuals from all over the world "compete for more than $25,000 in cash scholarships, trophies, championship jackets, Summer Camp/Cheer Shoppe discounts and more."[47] These competitions typically require squads to perform an intense, highly athletic 2 1/2-minute routine that includes a combination of cheers, music, dance, stunts, and pyramids. In some national championships that cater specifically to these competitive squads, performing a cheer is not even a requirement for the routine.

Competitive-only squads began in the 1990s and have experienced dramatic growth. One of the reasons for their growth is that so many girls wanted to be cheerleaders but schools simply could not provide enough spaces for those girls. Another reason has to do with the decrease in interest in gymnastics. Since many private gyms began as training camps for budding gymnasts, the decline in the number of gymnasts left owners of private gyms with the reality of either having to close their gyms or find a new customer base. Their new clientele became cheerleaders. Beginning initially with offering cheerleading training for middle and high school cheerleaders and cheerleader hopefuls, these gyms soon discovered that they could increase their numbers and fill their pocketbooks by creating their own cheerleading squads, which could range in age from 5 to 18. Today, more than 1,500 private gyms or clubs sponsor competitive-only All-Star squads, charging from $100 to several hundred dollars a month for cheerleading training and/or team membership.[48]

The National Federation of State High School Associations reported that "competitive cheerleading" is the fastest-growing sport for girls. In the 1997–98 school year, approximately 59,000 girls participated in competitive cheerleading—an increase of approximately 25,000 since 1995–96.[49] Georgia All-Star Cheerleading coach Julie Parrish notes that cheerleading has "evolved in recent years into more of a dangerous sport than recreation. . . . Everything has changed so much in this sport. These kids are athletes. We don't even own a pair of pompoms or megaphones."[50]

All-Star squads have begun to lure male cheerleaders, particularly at the high school level, back into cheerleading. In 1994, only 213 boys competed on All-Star squads; by 2000, 1,212 were involved in competitive cheerleading.[51] Many of these competitors are former football players, such as John Luce, whose Cheer Athletics squad (from Dallas, Texas) won first place at the United Spirit Association nationals in 2001. His response to the ribbing he gets for being a cheerleader: "If you think cheering is for sissies, see if you can handle it."[52] But it's not just late adolescent boys who cheer on these squads. In the "Megastar" feature of *American Cheerleader Junior,* a magazine catering to pre-adolescent cheerleaders, boys as young as 9 are showcased for their competitive cheerleading skills.

Still, like traditional cheerleading, the majority of All-Star cheerleaders are females who are drawn to this type of squad because of the athleticism involved. As Amy Argetsinger explains, these new kinds of squads "exist solely to fulfill the competitive urges of a newly liberated generation of girls."[53] On All-Star squads, girls do not perform any of the traditional cheerleading duties, such as painting signs for the athletes to run through, preparing treat bags for the players, or decorating gyms and lockers. The focus is strictly on being the best squad in order to win one of the many highly competitive championships held all over the country. Jennifer Carranza, who was a cheerleader for her high school in California, is typical of today's All-Star cheerleaders. Disturbed by what she saw as the "miniskirts and makeup" emphasis of high school cheering, she quit her school squad to join an All-Star squad. Speaking of the difference between her "old and new" cheerleader peers, she notes: "They don't want to be classified as rah-rahs. They want to give it their all and show that they are just as tough as the guys out there playing sports."[54] Indeed, it has been largely through these competitive-only squads that the image of the cheerleader athlete, which we discuss more fully in the next chapter, has been cemented.

Universal Spirit: Cheering Around the World

As discussed in the previous chapter, cheerleading began as a uniquely American invention. However, with the introduction of professional football leagues overseas as well as the international broadcast of American cheerleading championships, cheerleading has now grown into a global phenomenon, and in doing so has challenged many of the "American" facets of cheerleading. Today 50 countries outside of the United States boast cheerleading squads, including Russia, Ukraine, France, Sweden, Norway, Germany, Switzerland, Finland, Scotland, England, Ireland, Wales, Malaysia, Singapore, Japan, Australia, New Zealand, South Africa, Costa Rica, Ecuador, Bolivia, Peru, Chili, Mexico, Canada, and Puerto Rico.[55]

In some ways, cheerleading overseas closely resembles cheerleading in the United States. Take, for example, Katarina Ericsson, a Swedish cheerleader, whose cheerleading story is closely akin to many of her American counterparts. When the men at Kalmar University decided to start an American football team, the women decided they would begin a cheerleading squad. At first, Katarina was opposed to the squad, thinking that cheerleading was antifeminist; however, once she started participating, she was "hooked." She cheered for several sports, spent two semesters in Japan practicing 30 hours a week on a competitive squad, and participated in the European Championship, winning a double silver. At 32, she is still involved in cheerleading— as vice president of the Swedish Cheerleading Federation and a coach (along with 16 assistant coaches) of 70 girls, age 7 to 15.[56]

Similar to the trend in the United States, more and more cheerleaders overseas are involved in the competitive part of cheerleading, participating in regional, national, and international competitions. In the recent International Championships, the largest in Europe, 1,661 cheerleaders from 10 different countries competed. The World Cheerleading Association (WCA), which began in 1995, held its 2002 WCA Europe Cheerleading and Dance Championship in Scotland. Competition was fierce, with 850 cheerleaders from over 50 squads from 7 countries. The Campeonato Nacional de Animadoras (National Cheerleading Championship) held in Acapulco, Mexico, attracts thousands of cheerleaders each year from Latin American countries.[57]

Several United States cheerleading companies have tried to sell their products and services to cheerleaders in other countries; however, in many ways, their attempts have not been successful. Company representatives claim that cheerleading is just too American, thus making it difficult to make the translation to other cultural contexts. A top-level executive associated with cheerleading in the United States explains: "We're not really nurturing the market overseas. We tried to, but it's too disorganized. You go to Germany and the fans at the championships are in the stands with their beer and it's rowdy. The cheerleaders are ages 15 to 32. Every break they're sitting down and smoking. It's a funny thing to us."[58] Mike Fultz, director of camp administration and special events for UCA and a New Orleans native, concurs, using the following analogy: "Taking cheerleading overseas is like going down to New Orleans and taking a kid on the football field and handing him a Lacross thing and say here's the ball, here's the bat, go at it. He's very talented in football, very athletic, but you're probably going to hear some Cajun curse words. It's the same thing over there. They're very talented in the sports they've done, but cheerleading is just a whole other thing."[59]

However, the overseas cheerleaders with whom we have spoken don't necessarily share the sentiment of the Americans cited above. Rather, they claim that they are remaking cheerleading so that it fits within their own cultural context. Hence, there are many differences between cheerleading in the United States and in other countries. One of the biggest differences is that the squads elsewhere are neither "varsity" nor "All-Star" (the two most common kinds in the United States). Since few countries overseas have sports in their secondary schools and universities, as in the United States, cheerleading squads are not associated, sponsored, or funded by schools and universities. In Great Britain, for example, less than 10 percent of their squads/clubs are school based. Rather, they operate, according to Bob Kiralfy, chairman of the British Cheerleading Association (BCA), as "self-funded, independent squads that support the local community in a varsity-like manner. Around half regularly support a local sports team (pro soccer, pro basketball, pro rugby football, American football)."[60] Many of these cheerleading clubs have as many as 180 cheerleaders of various ages on various squads. The Carlshalton Cheerleaders in Surry, England, are an example of such a squad. Formed in 1993, they now have 130 cheerleaders. In 1995, they became the officially recognized cheerleading squad for the professional Crystal Palace Football (soccer) Club. However, they are not supported financially by the Club; thus, they have to raise their own money to cover expenses, including the cost of a uniform. They cheer for all home games in a stadium that seats 26,000. Because there is no place for the cheerleaders on the field, they cheer directly in front of the fans 30 minutes before the game begins. At half-time they perform a dance and stunt routine.[61]

In Sweden, sports are organized in clubs that cover both recreational and elite activities. These clubs have cheerleaders who cheer for their games. Some gymnastics clubs have begun cheerleading squads, primarily for the purpose of competition. In Japan, there are both school cheerleaders (similar to the United States) and club teams (similar to All-Star squads in the United States) that are formed primarily for competition. Another common type of squad in Japan are company cheerleaders. Corporations, such as Asahi, Fujitsu, Onward, Matsushita, Japanese Airlines, and Tokyo Marine support teams who play in the Japan-based X League, an American football league. Each of these teams has cheerleaders who cheer for their athletic competitions, but they also perform public relations duties for the company.[62]

One major difference between cheerleading in the United States and cheerleading in Europe is that in most European countries, a unified governing body for cheerleading has been established. For example, the British Cheerleading Association (BCA) is the officially recognized body for cheerleading in the United Kingdom. It was formed in 1984 and was formally recognized as the governing body in 1990.[63] Similarly, the Swedish Cheerleader Federation (SCF) was formed in 1995.[64] Like other European governing bodies, the SCF's and BCA's main priority is to develop cheerleading in the country and to develop and ensure the implementation of uniform safety standards. In the United States, no such governing body exists. Bob Kiralfy, chairman of the BCA, sees this neglect as a serious drawback for American cheerleading: "Unfortunately, America still has no governing body, being a free market of competing commercial cheer companies who seem unable to work together. We find this very strange!"[65] Because of the absence of a single, unified governing body, no uniform standard of safety exists to govern cheerleading competitions in the United States although, as discussed in chapter 3, there is some movement in this direction. This is confusing for cheerleading squads as they compete in some championships that follow one set of guidelines and another one that follows a different set. Additionally, in countries such as Great Britain with a national governing body for cheerleading, strict policies exist about who is eligible to coach any sport or recreational activity, including cheerleading. For example, in Great Britain cheerleading coaches must certify through the Criminal Records Bureau that they have no criminal record that would make them unfit to work with children and youth.[66]

Certainly the exportation of cheerleading overseas by American companies and organizations could be read as just another example of America's thirst to impose its culture, even popular culture, on every country in the world. Indeed, many countries have resisted this Americanization and have refashioned American-style cheerleading to suit their own needs, values, and interests. Additionally, cheerleading associations overseas believe that American cheerleading has something to learn from them, particularly in the area of governance and regulations. However, Bob Kiralfy offers another take on the globalization of cheerleading—not surprisingly a much more positive perspective of the possibilities of cheerleading to eradicate boundaries and bring different cultures together: "I believe that the spirit of cheerleading is universal, transcending all team league and national boundaries. When you are a cheerleader you have friends all over the world, sharing the same hopes, goals, and dreams."[67]

Golden Poms and Silver Hair: Senior Citizen Squads

In Wilmington, North Carolina, the Wilmington Golden Pom Pom Cheerleaders are local celebrities. They appear at the County Fair Cheerleader Show, in the Christmas and Easter parades, and at the University of North Carolina - Wilmington's basketball halftime. They also cheer at nursing homes, Senior Games, and their grandchildren's elementary schools. Dressed in the latest Varsity Spirit cheerleading apparel, these cheerleaders are different in only one respect from the millions of other cheerleaders around the country. Unlike selection criteria for many other cheerleading squads, the Wilmington squad only has one, and it is not a back handspring. You must be at least 55 years old to join. In a culture that worships youth and recognizes the cheerleader as representative of youthful female sexuality, the Wilmington Golden Cheerleaders call into question many of our preconceptions about cheerleaders, providing a different image: attractive and physically fit mature women who enjoy having a good time.

The Wilmington Golden Cheerleaders were the brainchild of the city of Wilmington's Parks and Recreation Department in 1985. At the time seniors could participate in a wide variety of sports and activities, ranging from badminton to football to croquet, but not cheerleading. When Parks and Recreation offered the activity of cheerleading, seven women signed up. The squad's first performance was at the opening ceremonies of the By-the-Sea Senior Games. Their skill levels varied, from some members having limited mobility due to strokes, heart bypasses, glaucoma, and arthritis to others who could do cartwheels and splits, backbends, and headstands. In 1986, the squad gained a cheerleading coach, Nancy DeGrant, who had cheerleading experience, and consequently, they became more organized and more akin to traditional cheerleaders. Performing pom pon routines to music, building stunts and pyramids, and even tumbling, the Wilmington Golden Cheerleaders were crowd pleasers for audiences of all ages. As they became more athletic, their uniforms changed and they traded their saddle oxfords for tennis shoes. By 1992, the squad had grown to 15, and in 1993, they competed in the North Carolina Senior Games, where the squad won the gold medal.[68]

Since the formation of the Wilmington Golden Cheerleaders, 14 other senior citizen squads have been formed in North Carolina. In fact, the competition at the state Senior Games has become quite fierce, with ten senior squads participating in last year's competition. In 2002, Wilmington brought home the silver medal, losing the gold to their fiercest opponent, the Carteret County Cheerleaders from Beaufort, North Carolina. According to the current coach, Mary Jones, the squad is intent on winning back the gold and has already begun planning a routine that will incorporate a moving pyramid.[69]

Today's squad consists of five members: Martina Lipsey (70, captain, and known for her cartwheels and splits), Irma Baker (74), Sylvia Auten (66), Barbara Napier (70), and Joy McCormick (69). These are not your sit-at-home, rock on the front porch, and do needlepoint kind of grandmothers. Squad members take cheering seriously, as Sylvia Auten, who is proud that she can still do a headstand at age 66, explains: "ours is similar to traditional [cheerleaders] in the fact that we are 'cheering' someone on and uplifting their moods and inspiring them to live their own lives a little better." [70]The squad practices twice a week for 90 minutes; they polish old routines, create new ones, schedule their appearances, and critique each other's moves and dances. Before competitions, they may practice up to four times a week. Outside of practice, they celebrate birthdays together, have an annual "pot luck" Christmas dinner, and go to lunch quite often. They are also frequent guests at the University of North Carolina - Wilmington gerontology classes, where they perform their cheers and speak about aging as a rejuvenating process.

For all of them, cheerleading is an activity that keeps them physically fit, mentally alert, confident, and enthusiastic. It's also about having some fun and sharing laughs with your girlfriends. For instance, when asked how they would respond to critics who say cheerleading moves have gotten too sexual, one of the current squad members replied, "At our age, we are just glad we can move and perform!" For many of them, becoming a cheerleader later in their life is the fulfillment of a desire they had 50 years earlier, as explained by former Golden Cheerleader, Evelyn Taylor: "When I was younger, I did not make the cheering squad because they told me my legs were too big. I am thrilled to finally fulfill a life-long dream to become a cheerleader." Evelyn died several years ago and asked to be buried in her cheerleading uniform.[71]

Transforming Cheerleading

Disruptive, interruptive, and dangerous are adjectives that are frequently used by some academics in the social sciences to describe something that doesn't quite fit the normalized or generally accepted everyday version of something. Hence, our first inclination was to coin all of the cheerleaders in this chapter "disruptive cheerleaders." In this sense, a disruptive cheerleader would be one who breaks some unspoken rules about who a cheerleader is. However, "disruptive cheerleaders" is not a term many of these groups would use to describe themselves. For example, CHEER San Francisco and the Wilmington Golden Pom Pom Cheerleaders would argue that if the fundamental purpose of cheerleading, to motivate and energize, is retained, then personal characteristics such as age and sexual orientation are irrelevant. And if you ever have the opportunity to observe the extraordinary athleticism, precision, and classic uniforms of CHEER San Francisco, the issue of their sexual orientation would be secondary, just as age is when you see the joy and spirit of the Wilmington Golden Cheerleaders. Other groups like the X-Cheerleaders and the Radical Cheerleaders embrace the label of disruptive since one essential goal for each of these groups is to challenge the normalized view of cheerleading. For instance, the radical cheer with which we began this discussion is illustrative of the Radical Cheerleaders' reconfiguration of traditional cheerleading. They have rewritten a well-known, traditional cheer for their own explicit political agenda. Further, dressed in black skirts and combat boots, these cheerleaders interrupt every typical image of cheerleading.

But all of the groups described in this chapter are disruptive in that they challenge or disrupt the normal way of thinking about cheerleaders as being able bodied, heterosexual, young, and athletic spirit boosters. In their disruptions, they open up a space for thinking about cheerleading in a way that is more inclusive and, many would add, more positive. Certainly, feminist critics of cheerleading may be persuaded to think about cheerleading in a different way once they saw Radical Cheerleaders, X-Cheerleaders, and gay and lesbian squads using the medium of cheerleading to critique the status quo with "Cheer Loud, Cheer Proud." Others, who believe cheerleading offers nothing positive to the new generation of young women, may be challenged to rethink their position after viewing the highly competitive All-Stars cheering solely for themselves and a chance at a national championship. Those who associate cheerleading only with youthful bodies may be heartened to know that senior citizen squads are reminders that fun, joy, and pleasure in the physical and in bonding with others is something that is timeless and should be enjoyed by all—regardless of one's age. Perhaps a more apt label for these squads would be "tranformative" cheerleaders, since they seem to be transforming the possibilities of what cheerleading could be, and through their disruptions, they are also remaking cheerleading as a cultural icon with new meanings for new groups of people.

PUMP IT UP

Sports, Athleticism, and the New Cheerleader[1]

Pump, Pump, Pump It Up!
Pump that Patriot Spirit Up!

Chanting this sideline cheer, a varsity squad attempts to lift the spirits of the football team that is losing 20–7, but the muscled arms and legs of the cheerleaders attest to the fact that they spend lots of time pumping themselves up—in the gym, pumping iron. The knee brace on one, the taped wrist on another, and the one on crutches sitting out speaks further to the athleticism involved in being a cheerleader today. As several bases lift their fliers into a liberty heel stretch and then catch the fliers in a cradle, the "aahhhs" of the crowd is further testimony that these stunts are a far cry from pony mounts, shoulder sits, and splits of the earlier years of cheerleading. The opening poem of the 1999 Varsity catalog captures this contemporary face of cheerleading:

I am not arrogant.
I am confident.
I am not a daredevil.
I am daring.
I am not a beauty queen.
I am an athlete.
I am not a stereotype.
I am my own person.
I am not interested in the past.
I am living for the future.
I am not afraid of success.
I am afraid of nothing.

I am not another face in the crowd.
I am the ones others wish they could be.
I am not just any cheerleader.
I am the one in the Varsity uniform.[2]

Confident, daring, athletic, future-oriented, fearless, and worthy of envy are the characteristics ascribed to the new breed of cheerleaders. These are also traits once reserved solely for males. One popular T-shirt often worn by cheerleaders sports the slogan: "Cheerleading—if it were any easier it would be called football." As many coaches can attest, more and more males and females want to be involved in cheerleading, not only to lead cheers on the sidelines but to tumble, stunt, and pyramid build. Weight lifting, running, strength training, year-round practices, and extensive hours in the gym working on tumbling, jumps, and stunts are all part of the life of many cheerleading squads throughout this country.[3] But how did this shift from pretty girls to serious athletes come about?

From Pom Pons to Power Lifts: Cheerleading in Transition

The 1960s and 1970s brought about a second wave of feminist activism that provoked such policies as Title IX of the Education Amendments Act (1972), which prohibited any program receiving federal aid to discriminate on the basis of sex.[4] This meant that public schools, colleges, and universities had to provide more opportunities for girls and women to participate in athletics. During this time, new ideas about the roles and expectations of women emerged, and the image of the cheerleader yelling chants and cheers from the sidelines for the male athletes while occasionally performing a cartwheel or split seemed out of touch with the general pulse of the day. Unsurprisingly, corporations associated with cheerleading and national cheerleading organizations, faced with potential loss of profit due to this outdated image of cheerleading, sought to reshape cheerleading as an activity congruent with newer images of the ideal woman. "In post - Title IX, cheerleading might have vanished but it harnessed the spirit of the time, evolving into a melange of highflying acrobatics and show-biz flair that required more athleticism than before."[5] With greater opportunities for girls to play a wide variety of sports, cheerleading had to compete for the status that had been accorded to it in the past because it literally had been the only game in town. Tight athletic motions, difficult jumps, pyramid building, and fast-paced, crowd-pleasing dances to music began to be emphasized in the hundreds of cheerleading camps offered throughout the country. These new cheerleading techniques required girls who were not only strong but who were also agile, well-coordinated, and possessed athletic prowess.

This new image of cheerleading brought about a different approach to selection. Prior to the 1970s, the typical process of selecting cheerleaders for most junior high and high school squads and many university and college squads consisted of the student body voting for squad members. Due to parental complaints that questioned the fairness of the process along with the growing influence of national cheerleading organizations wanting to change the image of cheerleaders from that of pretty popular girls to "entertainers" and "athletes," schools moved away from student body selection to employing external judges to select the squad members. Hence, the requisite criteria for becoming a cheerleader changed from popularity to the ability to execute physically demanding cheer routines, tumbling stunts, jumps, and dance moves.[6]

Part of the transformation of cheerleading also centered on the introduction of national, state, and regional competitions in the 1970s.[7] Cheerleaders suddenly moved from the sidelines where they were motivational spectators to the center of the field to become the competitors themselves. With the introduction of these popular annual cheerleading championships, cheerleading became a commercial venture on its own with commercial sponsors, television air time, national exposure, and eventually international exposure. To create an audience, the viewers had to be given more than simply a group of girls yelling "go, fight, win!"; the new cheerleaders had to perform strenuous athletic feats that would awe an audience.

Today, national cheerleading championships garner a TV audience of close to 450,000 viewers, and competing in state, regional, and national championships is the main priority of many squads throughout this country.[8] But the competition starts months, even years, before any TV appearance. In many places, making the squad itself is a highly competitive event. As described by one Texas high school cheerleader: "It's survival of the fittest."[9]

Wanted—Cheerleaders: Only Athletes Need Apply

It's recess at Monroe High School, 1975, and about 100 of the school's 500 students amble into the gymnasium to watch cheerleading tryouts. Twenty girls dressed in new shorts outfits await their name to be announced. "Anna Smith," yells the physical education teacher in charge of tryouts. Anna runs to the middle of the gym floor alone and performs a 30-second cheer that ends with a cartwheel and a split. The crowd claps unenthusiastically. The other 19 girls follow suit, performing the cheer of their choice. Some end their cheer with a split; others simply rely on their dazzling smiles to capture the audience. Fifteen minutes later, the bell rings; recess is over, and tryouts for another year are complete. The next morning the students are given a ballot listing the names of the girls trying out for cheerleader. They dutifully circle the names of eight girls and return their ballot to the homeroom teacher. Later that day votes are tallied by the cheerleader sponsor, and the girls' names are announced on the intercom at the end of the day. As the sponsor reads the names, no one is too surprised. After all, besides the two new freshmen girls, it's the same girls who were elected cheerleader last year. And, Anna Smith, the girl who flawlessly executed a cartwheel and a split, once again did not make cheerleader.

Flash forward—cheerleader tryouts, Monroe High School, 2003. Ms. Grayson, the cheerleading coach, holds an informational meeting for parents of students expressing a desire to try out for cheerleader. She tells them:

> Cheerleading is a huge time commitment. So, if your daughter doesn't make good grades, you really need to discourage her from trying out. It's basically a 24/7, 12 months a year commitment. We go to competition two days after Christmas, so basically that blows Christmas holidays if you plan to go out of town. Hopefully we'll be going to nationals again this year. The cost is $1,000 a year, payable in three installments over a five-month period from April to August. This doesn't include what it will cost to go to nationals. We'll begin our clinic on Monday after school, where they'll be taught the cheer, the dance, and they'll get to choose their stunt partners to begin practicing their building. Pretty much, you have to be able to tumble to make it. There's a standing back handspring incorporated into the cheer. The cheer is worth 25 points; if you can't do the back handspring, you automatically get deducted 5 points. We'll have mock tryouts on Friday night, which you can come to. The real tryouts will be Saturday, which are closed to the public. I'll have three cheerleaders from different colleges to be the judges. I have nothing to do with the selection process, and please remember that just because your daughter doesn't make it, doesn't mean she isn't a wonderful and adorable person or a good cheerleader. The competition is stiff and I take the best 16, regardless of what grade they're in. Also, just because someone made it last year doesn't guarantee a spot this year. In fact, last year, I had two girls who didn't make it their senior year. I know it sounds tough, but cheerleading is a sport today and only athletes need apply.

The cheerleading tryout described in the first scenario is one that many of us growing up in the 1960s and 1970s remember. The popular girls were elected cheerleader, and preparing to be a cheerleader meant little more than buying a cute outfit, learning a cheer (probably from an older cheerleader), and having the courage to try out in front of your classmates. But those are the old days. Today, preparation for being a cheerleader often requires years of practice perfecting jumps, tumbling, and stunts, as the second scenario attests. It also requires, for many families, financial finagling to afford the hefty costs associated with junior high and high school cheerleading. And, the athletic preparation begins early. All over this country, independent squads, Pop Warner squads, and pee wee squads provide girls, as young as four and five, an opportunity to begin honing the skills they will need to win a spot on their junior high, high school, and All-Star squads.

Natalie got a taste of the new face of cheerleading this year when her daughter, Rebecca, tried out and made a competitive cheerleading squad for fourth through sixth graders. Two days a week (with an occasional Saturday and Sunday practice as well) these nine- to eleven-year-olds participate in a one-hour practice that is more akin to a football practice, all in preparation for the regional competitions held in December. Miss Ashley, a petite University of Alabama cheerleader, leads them in grueling conditioning exercises complete with push ups, crunches, and sprints, followed by pyramid building, stunts, dancing, and tumbling. On the first day of practice, one girl, who was serving as a base, received a bloody lip from a flier's foot. After suffering scrapes on her neck and shoulders from holding the foot of another flier, one girl quit after the first night. At the end of practice, Miss Ashley told the girls, "I hope you don't think I'm being too tough but you got to be tough to be a cheerleader."

Cheerleading at the high school and college level is even more strenuous. To be a serious contender for most collegiate squads, you must be a physically fit athlete, as the following requisites to try out for the Middle Tennessee State University Blue/White Squad, illustrate:

- Standing back handspring
- Standing back tuck
- Standing back handspring back tuck
- Running tumbling series
- Toss extension/pop off
- Toss liberty/regular cradle
- Pop & go heel stretch/full down cradle
- Optional stunt of your choice (must be a combination stunt)
- Cheer: incorporating a tumbling skill and stunt (will be taught at tryouts)
- Fight song (will be taught at tryouts)[10]

Once you make the team you have to commit not only to stay in shape through weight training, stamina building, and endurance exercises, but you must also commit to, in some places, daily cheerleading practices almost year round. A glimpse into one collegiate practice demonstrates the athleticism involved in collegiate cheering.

The Washington State University cheerleading squads begin their two-hour practice at seven A.M. After pulling out the heavy mats and listening to coach Barby Ingle detail their upcoming activities, junior varsity and varsity squads split up. To one side, members of the junior varsity squad, some of whom have never stunted, practice the elevator, which involves one or two men lifting a standing woman by her feet into the air. Several of the male cheerleaders say that the elevator is like learning other cheerleading stunts; you have to just keep on doing it until it catches. Then, the skill, like riding a bike, is never forgotten. These young women and men are fully focused; their concentration is revealed in their lack of smiles and tactical observations about weight shifting or sloppy falling. On the other side, the varsity women rehearse over and over their new dance, which combines jazz dance and more traditional cheer movements; their captain demands detailed changes after each performance. For the last hour, everyone stunts. Watching these stunts from 20 feet away, you can see the twitching arm muscles of the men, the concentration of the flyers who are trying to keep perfect balance, and the anticipation of the spotters, whose arms are taut with strain to catch the flyer. As the practice wears on, flyers fall, bases collapse, and knees buckle with the strain. A student athletic trainer (AT) comments that cheerleaders are very different from other athletes in their response to injury. At this practice, one young woman is accidentally kicked in the mouth while she and two other women act as bases. Although her lip is obviously smarting, since she keeps touching it, she doesn't ask for ice from the AT. Instead, she continues to work with her group on the stunt. It is not until the group takes a rest (ten minutes after the accident) that the young woman approaches the AT for some help. The AT says this is typical; cheerleaders are tenacious in their will to perform and stunt—no injury, certainly as minor as a swollen lip, is going to prohibit them from doing so.

Obviously, once you make it to the collegiate level of cheerleading, where the time and physical commitment can be extremely demanding, it is rather difficult to play any other sports. However, at the high school and middle school level, many cheerleaders are accomplished athletes in other sports, something many critics of cheerleading fail to recognize. In a Universal Cheerleading Association survey of 2,500 cheerleaders, 50 percent of those polled participated in other athletic activities at their school.[11] Particularly in rural areas and small towns, the cheerleaders, like those in Lapwai, Idaho, are often the stars of the basketball, softball, and track teams as well. With a student population of only 230, the 11 members of the Lapwai High School cheerleading squad are needed on sports teams. Thus, three quarters of the cheerleaders play either for their number-one-ranked girls basketball team or the volleyball team.

Because of the very athletic nature of contemporary cheerleading, many males who participate in cheerleading at both the high school and collegiate level were former baseball, football, and basketball players.[12] Others cheer during their off-season, like Carlos, whose "cheerleading injuries have convinced his football colleagues that stunting can be as masculine as running down a field. In both sports, he gets kicked, hit, fallen on, and otherwise mangled."[13] In Tuscaloosa, Alabama, where football couldn't be any bigger (remember, this is "Bear" Bryant country), many of the football players at the local high schools compete with the cheerleaders in their off-season and for national competitions. The coed cheerleading squad of Christian Brothers High School, an all-male school in Memphis, has won the UCA national championship 11 times in the last 17 years. Coach Chris Darby attributes their success, in part, to the male cheerleaders' persistence in proving to their football and basketball friends that cheerleading is just as demanding and athletic as their sport.[14]

It's not just the physical challenges of cheerleading that advocates want noncheerleaders to contemplate when considering the athleticism required of cheerleaders. It's also the incredible amount of time that squads spend to perfect their skills for state, regional, and national competitions. Much more time, they would argue, than any other sport spends on preparation for competitions. For example, the Washington State University spirit coordinator, Barby Ingle, estimates that for a nationally competitive two-and-a-half minute routine, her squad will practice somewhere between 700 and 900 hours.[15] The Louisiana State University Tiger Cheerleaders spend three months perfecting their national routine, and Christmas break is unheard of for the University of Kentucky cheerleaders, twelve-time winner of the UCA national championship, who spend their semester break on campus preparing for January's championship.[16]

Cheerleading Injuries

Because of the almost year-round nature of cheerleading as well as the physical difficulty of many stunts and pyramids, injuries have become an expected part of the cheerleading culture. Attend any high school or collegiate game and you will invariably see at least one or two cheerleaders jumping, building, and tumbling with knee braces, ankle wrappings, or taped wrists. In fact, when debates arise about the athleticism required in cheerleading, the discussion inevitably leads to the number of injuries cheerleaders suffer as compared to other sports. Barby Ingle, collegiate coach, provides what some might consider a typical resume of injuries, including a broken leg during gymnastics training, a broken wrist during university cheering, as well as a concussion while she was stunting.

Interestingly, both critics and supporters of the athletic turn in cheerleading often emphasize the risk and danger associated with cheerleading.

Those who argue that cheerleading is more dangerous than football and hockey usually point to the 18th annual report of the National Center for Catastrophic Sport Injury Research. This report states that from 1982 to 2000, high school and college female athletes suffered 74 direct catastrophic injuries and 30 indirect catastrophic injuries. Direct catastrophic injuries are defined in the report as "those injuries resulting directly from participation in the skills of the sport." Indirect catastrophic injuries are "those injuries which were caused by systemic failure as a result of exertion while participating in a sport activity or by a complication which was secondary to a nonfatal injury."[17] Of the 50 direct injuries at the high school level, 25 were cheerleading injuries, which accounts for 50 percent of all high school direct catastrophic injuries to female athletes. Of the 26 indirect fatalities occurring at the high school level, three were related to cheerleading. Of the 24 college direct injuries, 17 were related to cheerleading, accounting for 70.8 percent of all direct catastrophic injuries to female athletes at the college level. Overall, cheerleading accounted for 42 (56.8 percent) of the total number of direct catastrophic injuries to high school and college female athletes from 1982 to 2000. The authors of the report note that the substantial increase of catastrophic injuries to female athletes over the years is a direct result of the change in cheerleading to a more athletic endeavor involving stunts, gymnastics, and pyramid building.

Others, who believe that the risks associated with cheerleading have been greatly exaggerated, point to the research of Dr. Mark Hutchinson. He asserts that compared to other sports, cheerleading is a safe sport with a relatively low risk of injury, the most common involving the ankle. Hutchinson reports that the injury risks in high school cheerleading per 1,000 exposures is .17, compared to 9.40 for wrestling and 8.60 for gymnastics. He further states there is little research documenting the number of severe injuries from cheerleading, but he does report that cheerleaders lose more days to injuries than participants in any other sport (28.8 compared to 12.8 for women's basketball, 12.3 for wrestling, and 5.6 for football). This may be due to the fact that cheerleaders, unlike football players, require "all extremities to be completely functional for stunts and tumbling runs. . . . Cheerleaders must often lift a partner, perform a tumbling run, do a dance routine and balance atop a pyramid—all within the span of a few minutes." On the other hand, football players can play with a sprained ankle, finger, or wrist without detrimentally affecting their ability to play their position. Cheerleading also differs from other sports in that it is a year-round sport that does not allow time for recuperation and conditioning, thus magnifying the risk of continuous injuries.[18] As Shelia Angalet, coach of the Metuchen Pop Warner squad and the Metuchen New Jersey High School squad says, "Whoever coined the phrase 'off season' wasn't a cheerleader."

Due to the growing concern over cheerleading injuries, the American Association of Cheerleading Coaches and Advisors (AACCA) published its first safety manual in 1990.[19] Now in its second printing, the manual provides safety rules and guidelines, according to the organization's executive director, Jim Lord, that allow for a reasonable amount of risk while not compromising the safety of the athletes performing the athletic feats.[20] However, because no officially recognized governing board for cheerleading exists in the United States, as is the case in European countries, adherence to safety guidelines varies greatly not only from squad to squad but also from state to state and from competition to competition. Additionally, there are no certification requirements for sponsors or coaches. Thus, in many places, the cheerleading sponsor/advisor has received no cheerleading training or safety training. To help alleviate this problem, the Universal Cheerleading Association (UCA) and the National Federation of State High School Associations (NFHS) formed a partnership in October 2002 with the goal of educating cheerleading coaches and advisors/sponsors about cheerleading safety.[21] Several months later, 5 other cheerleading companies, the National Cheerleading Association (NCA), Cheerleaders of America (COA), Cheer LTD, AmeriCheer, and United Performers Association (UPA), formed The National Council for Spirit Safety and Education (NCSSE) with the goal of providing more uniform safety standards and a safety training and certification program for cheerleading coaches and sponsors.[22]

The response from various school districts, college divisions, and universities to cheerleading injuries demonstrates the tenuous position cheerleaders occupy in the athletic hierarchy. In 1996, Tracy Jensen, a cheerleader at the University of Nebraska - Lincoln, was seriously injured during cheerleading practice. In April 2001, the university settled with Jensen for $2.1 million ($600,000 to be paid in a lump sum and $150,000 to be paid annually for ten years).[23] Bill Byrne, then athletic director at UNL, announced in March 2002 that he was ground bounding the cheerleading squad beginning in the fall 2002, meaning they could not perform pyramids or stunts.[24] The policy prohibits cheerleaders from performing any "exercises in which both feet and both hands leave the floor."[25] Not only does such a policy prohibit the squad from building pyramids, performing partner stunts, and doing advanced tumbling; if taken literally, it also prohibits them from even jumping.[26] Duke University is the only other Division I school that has enforced such a severe policy, although many states, school districts, and college divisions have banned certain stunts and pyramids. For example, in 1998, the Atlantic Coast Conference outlawed high-flying stunts at all their basketball tournaments, and the Illinois State High School Association banned the basket toss and pyramid formations higher than two levels.[27]

Many cheerleaders see bans against tough stunts and complex pyramids reflective of the sexist and paternalistic attitudes of many athletic directors, administrators, and governing bodies, who still view cheerleaders as supporters of athletes rather than as athletes themselves. Then University of Nebraska athletic director, Bill Byrne, argued that after researching the dangers associated with stunting, he decided to ban it; but cheerleaders and cheerleading coaches are quick to note the duplicity in that sentiment. All they have to do is point to football players who routinely practice in hot temperatures considered medically unsafe. In 2001 alone, a total of 23 football players (from Pop Warner leagues to professional leagues) died; 8 as a result of direct injuries on the field; 3 from heat strokes, and 12 from natural causes brought about from vigorous physical activity associated with practices and games. From 1995 to 2000, 19 football players died from heat strokes and other heat-related causes. Yet, despite the rash of deaths of football players at the high school and college level in the last few years, not one school district or college division has banned practicing in the summer heat.[28] Further, pole vaulting is considered one of the most dangerous sports with, on average over the last 20 years, one pole vaulter dying every year. However, pole vaulting has not been eliminated from high schools and colleges.[29] Certainly, any time a tackle occurs, a potential for serious injury exists; yet, tackling has not been banned from football. In fact it is considered integral to the game. One aspiring Nebraska cheerleader from Texas, Josh Rangel, maintained that the ground bound rule would be comparable to the Nebraska football team being forced to play flag football.[30] Responding to what she considered the sexist nature of restrictive Atlantic Coast Conference sanctions, Susan Pyle, a cheerleader at North Caroline State, claimed that ruling out stunts from cheerleading is like "ruling out the slam dunk for the basketball players at the tournament. The dunk is a big part of their games. Stunts are a big part of our games."[31]

This transition from the popular cheerleader to the athletic cheerleader has placed cheerleading in a catch–22. Certainly, when the most complicated move a cheerleader did was a cartwheel and a split or a shoulder-high mount, the risks were minimal. But certainly at that time, cheerleading was not given much legitimacy as an athletic endeavor, nor were the participants seen as athletes. As it has changed over the years to incorporate physically demanding stunts, tumbling, and pyramid building, thus gaining some legitimacy as a sport, the risks and dangers involved have increased. When accidents occur, just as they do with other sports guided by safety guidelines, often the response is to put cheerleaders back in their pre-1970s place—on the sidelines yelling cheers in support of their team. But such a move also takes away much of the status and legitimacy cheerleaders have fought to attain over the last 30 years.

Is Cheerleading a Sport?

THE SUPPORTERS

All of this discussion of injuries and competitions and hours of practice have led inevitably to the question of whether cheerleading should be categorized as a sport. Within the world of cheerleading, the response to whether or not cheerleading should be considered a sport is a mixed one. Many owners of gyms who sponsor All-Star competitive squads and coaches for these teams feel that competitive cheerleading already fits the generally agreed upon definition of a sport: that its primary goal should be that of competition. Believing that the acknowledgement of cheerleading as a sport will bring about a concomitant increase in status and legitimacy, these advocates recognize the cultural, economic, and social power of sports in this country.

Many high school and university advisors and coaches are also supportive of the move to make cheerleading a sport; they believe that categorizing cheerleading as a sport will put cheerleading on the same level as football, basketball, baseball, and wrestling in vying for resources, use of facilities, allocation of funds, and scholarships. Currently 250 colleges and universities provide some kind of financial support to their cheerleaders.[32] However, the amount of scholarship money given to collegiate cheerleaders varies greatly across the United States. Typically, they do not receive the types of scholarships that team athletes do. A notable exception to this is the University of Kentucky, where Blue squad members are compensated with a full tuition scholarship.[33] The average scholarship for a PAC 10 university cheerleader is $250 per semester.[34] Ohio State University, home of the 2002 national college football champions, offers their varsity cheerleaders a $1,200 scholarship. The University of Texas - Austin cheerleaders receive $100-$300 a semester. At Louisiana State University, freshmen cheerleaders receive no financial help. If they continue with the program, senior cheerleaders receive a scholarship ($2,000) that pays for almost half of their tuition. [35]Members of the Crimson squad at the University of Alabama, which cheers for men's football and basketball games, receive a $1,500 scholarship per semester.[36] However, a large number of collegiate cheerleaders receive no scholarship; their compensation may be a letter jacket at the end of the season along with a notation on their transcripts.

Unsurprisingly, when university and secondary school cheerleading coaches' compensation is compared to salaries of coaches for sports teams and to the number of hours these coaches actually work, the compensation is minimal. The University of Idaho spirit coordinator is so poorly compensated that it is unofficially considered a volunteer position. Similarly, the volunteer coach for the Wilmington College Quakers cheerleading squad receives a mere $150 a month stipend.[37] At the University of Alabama, the salary of the head football coach in 2002 (at the time of this writing) is $1,050,000; the head men's basketball coach is paid $650,000; the women's gymnastics coach $154,999.92. The cheerleading coach who has the responsibility of coordinating two cheerleading squads (nationally ranked), the dance line, and Big Al, the mascot, is paid $24,680.88. A fact that would probably surprise many is that the University of Alabama cheerleaders, who contract their services to UCA to facilitate all the cheerleading camps at their university, are the second-largest revenue producers of any sports team on the campus, second only to the football team.[38] Many believe that categorizing cheerleading as a sport would bring more equity to cheerleader coaches' salaries and cheerleader scholarships.

Cheerleader coaches also contend that if cheerleading were a sport, then they would be able to compete more effectively for other resources as well. During our interviews with secondary and university coaches, they expressed frustration with their position as "low man on the totem pole" when it comes to having space in the gym or time in the weight room. One collegiate squad practices during dinner time, causing many of the cheerleaders who use the university dining services to miss their evening meal. Another cheerleading coach said they couldn't begin practice until 8:30 P.M., after all the other athletes had finally gone home. Another university coach told us that her squad has to raise a large part of the funds needed to attend national competitions (even though they are ranked nationally), and sometimes squad members have even been forced to fund their travel when performing at the request of university officials. One coach of a collegiate squad opened her own private gym primarily so her cheerleading squad would have a place to practice on a regular basis. Other resources that are not readily available to many cheerleading squads include access to athletic trainers, mats (imperative for stunting), storage for cheerleading supplies, and such mundane but important perks as power bars. When teams practice stunting, safety becomes an important issue, and whether universities and colleges provide athletic trainers and appropriate mats can make a difference in what stunts the squad may attempt.

Still others, including several state high school athletic associations, consider the move to recognize cheerleading as a sport a sound economic decision. In fact, 20 state high school associations have already made that move, and others such as Washington and Illinois are currently considering it.[39] Hosting state championships in cheerleading, similar to those held in basketball, football, and other sports, would entice local cheerleaders to compete in those championships rather than travel out of state to national championships. Of course, this means added revenues for businesses and merchants who cater to these championships as well as to the state high school athletic associations.

THE OPPONENTS

However, the position of most cheerleading associations and organizations, the Women's Sports Foundation, many state high school athletic associations, and countless coaches and athletic directors at the high school and collegiate level is that cheerleading should not be categorized as a sport. One reason relates to the regulations that govern any activity considered a sport at the high school level. Rules about practice times, eligibility of transfer students, and how many miles one can travel to compete would place restrictions on cheerleaders and their ability to compete at national championships. Others fear that categorizing cheerleading as a sport is but another way to subvert the intentions of Title IX. Currently, under Title IX guidelines, cheerleading is not a sport, although the U.S. Department's Office for Civil Rights has been asked to reconsider this.[40] If schools (trying to comply with Title IX) are suddenly able to take an existing funded extracurricular activity, such as cheerleading, and count it as one of their female sports and include cheerleaders in their numbers of female athletes, many are concerned that traditional women's sports, such as volleyball, soccer, and softball, would be eliminated from many schools' athletic rosters. We would also no longer see male cheerleaders, since coed sports cannot be counted as a female sport. The formal position of the Women's Sports Foundation is that cheerleading is an extracurricular activity, conducted in conjunction with sports contests, and involves some degree of physical activity, but it should not be considered a sport. In their position statement, the Foundation cites a 1975 Office for Civil Rights Memorandum to School Superintendents, which explicitly states that cheerleading is to be considered an extracurricular activity rather than part of the school's athletic program. Even when cheerleading squads compete in a few championship-type competitions, the "existence of a competitive opportunity does not qualify the extracurricular activity as an athletic activity or sport." The Women's Sports Foundation position statement does offer an exception: "if they [the cheerleading squad] have a coach, practice as frequently as a regular varsity team and compete against other cheerleading teams on a regular basis and more frequently than they appear to cheer for other teams, they may meet the definition of a varsity team."[41]

Those who oppose any move toward formally considering cheerleading a sport would prefer that cheerleading be considered an athletic activity—the position taken by the largest national cheerleading association, the Universal Cheerleading Association. Such a move ensures that cheerleaders can enjoy many of the privileges associated with sports as well as the privileges associated with other school activities, such as the band, debate team, or choral group. They believe that categorizing cheerleading as an athletic activity rather than a sport allows cheerleaders to enjoy the best of both worlds.

Although there are mixed responses to the activity versus sport debate within the cheerleading world, the world outside of cheerleading is fairly unanimous in its belief that cheerleading is in no shape, form, or fashion a sport. Three days after *USA Today* ran a feature story on the changing face of cheerleading in America, the Dan Patrick Show, an ESPN-produced show aired to 6,000 radio stations, asked its listeners to call in and express their opinion on the question: "Is cheerleading a sport?" Not surprisingly, the majority of the call-in's thought the question was ludicrous. From their mainly male audience, responses such as the following were typical:

"Cheerleading is a sport for the men who watch it."
"Cheerleading can't be a sport because the scoring take places after the game is over."

Certainly, one could argue that these responses are what one would expect from a radio talk show geared specifically to men who love traditionally male sports, but these responses demonstrate the struggle cheerleaders have in gaining legitimacy outside the world of cheerleading itself.

However, listeners of the Dan Patrick Show are not the only outsiders who object to designating cheerleading as a sport. Many feminists, parents, sports participants, and coaches of girls' and women's sports see cheerleading as a continuation of a pre-Title IX culture that limits girls' and women's opportunities. Prior to Title IX, in many places in the United States, cheerleading was one of the only ways for girls to be at least affiliated with sports. It was also one of the only activities in many high schools affording girls the opportunity to participate in a physical activity. Yet, Title IX was begun as a response to these limited opportunities for girls, and the mantra of moving girls off the sidelines (implying cheerleaders) to the game itself inevitably situated cheerleading in opposition to girls' sports. In the height of the women's movement of the 1960s and 1970s and the passage of Title IX, cheerleading, like beauty pageants and Playboy bunnies, represented all that feminists were working against. Feminists might be sympathetic to women who participated in cheerleading prior to the passage of Title IX, but when the athletic fields opened to girls, Why, they ask, would anyone want their daughters to be cheerleaders? In the age of Mia Hamm, the WNBA, Serena and Venus Williams, and Marion Jones, why would athletic girls choose to be a cheerleader rather than a basketball player, soccer player, or tennis player? "Why do we encourage girls to cheer the boys, to idolize the boys?

Why do we want them on the sideline when most of them could be between the sidelines?"[42] We turn to some seventh-grade cheerleaders and their coach to answer that question.

Don't Burp, Don't Fart, Just Build: Being a Lady and an Athlete[43]

Cheerleading coaches throughout this country have the responsibility of ensuring that their cheerleading squads attain the delicate balance of being serious athletes while performing the traditional duties of a cheerleader. Louise Stone, a 48-year-old former high school and college cheerleader and long time cheerleading coach, explains: "Cheerleaders are still very feminine, and we work on those characteristics. We have rules, no burping, no farting. You are young ladies. But we build, we jump, we try to get a balance because cheerleading does prepare them for later on in life." Mrs. Stone is employed by Wichita Middle School (WMS), which is located in a Midwestern town with a population of 26,000. Wichita Middle School is a fairly typical middle school. Students are organized into teams that travel together for their core classes. They can take drama, art, computer literacy, and foreign language as exploratory courses. They go on field trips, put on plays, perform choir concerts, participate in essay contests, and go about the usual doings of school. Like most middle schools, various cliques exist—the Preps, the gangsters, the Sex-Mob, the outsiders—and the cafeteria is a space where the cliques mark their territory. There are fights at the school periodically, the Winter Dance is something to which most seventh graders look forward, and cheerleading is considered the highest-status activity for girls. Unusual about WMS is that the school offers a cheerleading preparation class as a physical education elective. In fact, so many girls sign up for the class that the administration has to offer two classes in the spring semester to accommodate the interest.Every year during March, girls endure the trauma and excitement of cheerleading tryouts for the approximately 20 coveted spots on the mid-high cheerleading squad. Louise Stone, as the instructor for the two cheerleading preparation classes, has the formidable task of taking these seventh-grade girls at various skill levels and preparing them for the strenuous and closed-to-the public tryouts. One of her main tasks is to get these girls in shape so they can be serious contenders for the highly athletic mid-high squad.

Watching Mrs. Stone at work is similar to watching a drill sergeant. Her language is replete with powerful, masculine, militaristic language:

Attack those jumps.
Punch forward.

Smash through the floor.
Power off the toes.
Command the room with your presence.
Chins up, shoulders back, smiles. Hit the motion. Hit. Hit. Hit. 1, 2, 3,
Hit. 1, 2, 3, Hit. When I say Hit, do a V. When I say, Hit, do a down V.
Hit-L; Hit V; Hit Down V.

Understanding that the judges would be looking for athletic, physically fit
girls, Ms. Stone reminds the girls of the importance of showing off their muscular bodies: "Alright, girls, make your muscles tight so the judges can see
them. Tight across the shoulders. Tomorrow you should hurt. Come on, legs
are tight. This is a great time to show off your muscles." Mrs. Stone knows
that loose arms, shrill "woos," and floppy movements have no place in today's
cheerleading. Thus, she stresses to the girls constantly the need for tight motion technique. "Punch forward," she yells to the girls. " Don't swing your
arms. Keep everything close to your body. Think close. Tight, tight, tight."
Lisa, a petite but muscular blonde who made the mid-high team, explains the
importance of being "tight": "Like, when you cheer, your arms have to be
tight, and your emotions are like aggressive, not like to where you're going to
punch someone, just like when they're tight. Like when I get up there, I'm
like [hard snapping noise] push my arms down and slap them."

Part of Mrs. Stone's work in preparing the girls for tryouts is teaching
them self-discipline, particularly in how to control their emotions and out-
ward actions. She tells the girls that it is inappropriate to "go ballistic" if they
do not find their names on the list of girls selected. Rather, they are to learn
to win with grace and to lose with grace. But she also warns them that if they
do see their names listed as the chosen squad members, they should not
flaunt their success nor should they think they are suddenly better than
those who did not make it. She tells them, "Cheerleaders have a tendency to
become snobs," and for most of these seventh-grade girls, being labeled a
snob is the second worst and feared label one can have attached to her. Only
being labeled a slut is worse.

However, cheerleading is not just about controlling one's emotion; it is
also about learning how to control the body. As any athlete will tell you, a
key component of participation in athletics is the ability to discipline the
body, to push the body beyond its normal limits, to train the body to with-
stand pain and injury. Cheerleading is no different, as explained by Lisa,
who earned the highest number of points at tryouts, but was able to accomplish this only by pushing her body beyond its normal limits, even in
the face of pain and injury: "On the day of tryouts, I had 104 degrees fever;
I had pneumonia. I had been sick for days and lost six pounds before tryouts. At tryouts, I fell on my head during my back handspring. It was like

my wrists just collapsed. But I scored #1. I couldn't even come to school the next day because I was so sick. My dad said he was proud of me because I showed determination." Lisa's story is not unusual. The cheerleading literature is replete with such stories. Take for example the recent *Dateline* feature "Personal Best," which highlighted a girl from Florida, who was so intent on making the highly competitive varsity squad at her high school that she insisted on performing a round-off, back tuck with a broken finger and against doctor's orders. The fact that the cheerleading coach and judge knew she was not supposed to put any pressure on her broken finger but still allowed her to do it, not only once but twice, is typical of the new cheerleading culture.[44] Cheerleaders across this country regularly cheer and compete with sprained ankles, broken wrists and fingers, and torn ligaments. In fact, as we discussed earlier, these injuries are often worn as a badge of honor signifying that cheerleaders too are warrior athletes capable of overcoming any obstacle on the journey to victory.

But the girls at WMS are constantly reminded also of their traditional role as supporter of others' wants and needs. The Wichita Cheerleading Constitution, which all cheerleaders must sign, clearly states this: "The primary purpose of cheerleading is to promote unity, sportsmanship, and school spirit at school and school events. . . . The primary function of a cheerleading program is to support interscholastic athletics." It is this traditional role of cheerleader as supporter that upsets many who see cheerleading as a throwback to a time when women were expected to be subservient to men. Mrs. Stone shares the view that cheerleaders should remember their role of loyal supporter of others, but she sees this as preparation for their future role of wife and mother—a role, she contends, that requires all women to be strong, particularly in the face of adversity:

> My school spirit comes from the heart, and these young women need to learn how to be loyal. They need to learn how to take the eyes off of themselves. We're there for other people; we're not there for ourselves. . . . If it weren't for the athletes in the building, there would be no reason for us; we're to give of ourselves; we are serving our athletes. But cheerleaders have got to be strong. They've got to bear pain to have children. . . . They've got to be able to stand on their feet and make decisions when it may be mom, or dad, or husband, who's laid out there and you've got to do what is the right thing to do. You've got to support. You've got to lift up. That's the whole role of being an adult woman.

Interestingly, however, many of the girls trying out for the mid-high team did not share Mrs. Stone's idea that the purpose of cheerleading was to demonstrate loyalty to their school and the team for which they were cheering. Many simply wanted to cheer because it was fun; others saw it as a venue for them to show off their skills, thus becoming the center of attention as explained by Lisa, Julie, and Patti, three of the girls chosen for the mid-high squad:

> I thought cheerleading's just neat, cause you get to tumble and you get to be some of the stars of the game. . . . It's just you want to be one of the main focuses of the game instead of the players. And you want to get people's attention. (Lisa)

> I LIKE getting up in front of people and, like, being the one in charge. I like showing off and being with the guys. (Julie)

> Most of us are loud and we like to cheer because we like to draw attention to ourselves. (Patti)

When the points were finally tallied for the 20 spots on the mid-high cheerleading squad, most of the girls selected were accomplished athletes. Many of them participated in other sports, such as track and basketball. They were also thin, cute, and confident. When asked whether or not cheerleading was a sport, their responses were ambivalent: "not really," "kinda," "it gives you a good workout, so I guess so." However, Lisa's response was the most telling: "Cheerleading is just different from soccer and other sports because cheerleading lets you be tough while also being a girly girl."

The Cheerleading-as-Sport Controversy: Why Does the Debate Matter?

Obviously, as the girls' comments illustrate, there are conflicting responses to the value and legitimacy of categorizing cheerleading as a sport. Perhaps a more important question is, Why does it matter? What does the debate itself tell us about gender roles and expectations, both past and present? To understand that, we must turn in brief to the larger history of women's entrance into sports and societal resistance to any such attempts for women to be considered true athletes.

From the very inception of institutionalized sports in this country, men have resisted women's attempts to participate in sports. Begun as a way for males to demonstrate their masculinity and to socialize young boys into the proper way to be a man, sports served for the nineteenth century and the early twentieth century as a sacred arena where men could bond with each other without the influence of women. By the early 1900s, sports were viewed by many as the ideal way to cultivate character, moral integrity, and leadership in boys and men.[45]

By the early 1900s women began to make inroads into the world of physical activity, mainly through the efforts of physical education specialists.[46] Although poor women and women of color had engaged in physically demanding labor throughout history, at this time powerful Victorian beliefs prevailed about the debilitating effects of strenuous activity on women and their general physical frailty. Female academics in physical education were successful in encouraging the general public to recognize the health benefits of exercise and physical activity, even for girls and women. Thus, upper-class women attending college in the early 1900s began to participate in lawn tennis, croquet, bicycling, archery, and rowing. However, the same women academics who encouraged the public to recognize the health benefits of physical activity for girls and women were the ones opposed to competitive sports for women.[47] Their argument, which was supported by some male academics, most notably Charles Eliot, president of Harvard University from 1875 to 1909, was that competitive athletics emphasized the most base elements of American character and society.[48] These included the crass commercialization of sports, the unacceptable belief that only the strongest athletes should compete, and the display of excessive emotions during competitive events. Thus, in their attempt to shape women in different ways than men were being socialized, these female physical educators promoted intramural activities and encouraged the values of harmony and order instead of the chaos and competition found in male sports.[49] As late as 1951, Louise Weisiger, director of research at Richmond High School, reported in *School Activities* that the majority of educators do not recommend interscholastic competitive athletics for girls. Rather, the emphasis should be on promoting sports through an intramural program that is open to all girls. The emphasis, she reports, should be on developing a new attitude toward competition: "As long as the playing of the game has augmented the health not endangered it, has strengthened old and built up new friendships instead of destroying them, has refreshed and restored the spirit of the players instead of harassing them, the competition engaged in has been educative."[50]

Slowly, competitive sports were introduced and became central to the lives of many high school and collegiate female athletes. But those numbers were few, and in many cases, women athletes were required to play by very different rules than their male counterparts, even if they were playing the same sport. For example, many women basketball teams played half-court basketball well into the 1960s. Additionally, to gain public approval, women athletes always had to prove that once they were off the court or field, they were indeed true ladies. In the late 1940s, Babe Didrikson, who had won both gold and silver medals in track events at the 1932 Olympics, took up the more socially appropriate sport of golf. In the 1950s she was recognized as the best female golfer in the United States. But, it was not until she married

George Zaharias, a professional wrestler, let her hair grow, and started wearing makeup and dresses that she gained social acceptance by the mass audience.[51] In fact her transformation from athlete to wife was as highly publicized as her athletic accomplishments. For example, in 1947 *Life* magazine ran an article about her marriage with the headlines: "Babe is a Lady Now: The World's Most Amazing Athlete Has Learned to Wear Nylons and Cook for her Huge Husband."[52]

Fifty years later, thanks in large part to the Babe Didrikson's and to Title IX, we do see more girls and women playing sports, although we see fewer women coaches and athletic directors than in the previous era.[53] However, women athletes today are still expected to maintain a balance between their athleticism and their feminism, or as Palzkill calls it, "the inner strife between gymshoes and high-heels."[54] Often labeled the "Babe Factor" in sports, female athletes are constantly reminded that they can play the game as long as they adopt the rules and norms of the males who created and are the real owners of the sports while also demonstrating an appropriate dose of heterosexual femininity. They are to be heterosexy athletes.[55] The Ladies Professional Golf Association (LPGA) knows the importance of conveying that image. In fact, they hired an image consultant who worked with the women golfers on such areas as their hair, fingernails, and skin care. Such image control paid off: "the tour has experienced an increase in corporate sponsorship and prize money, a 50 percent gain in revenue, and twice as much television coverage."[56] The coach of a British Columbia women's volleyball team, in an attempt to make her players appear more feminine, required them to wear long hair that could be pulled back in a ponytail with a ribbon.[57] In 1999, female professional beach volleyball players were informed of new regulations, which had them wearing tiny sports bikinis, while the male players were to wear baggy shorts.[58]

As many female athletes can attest, their sexual orientation is constantly being questioned, and threats of being labeled a lesbian lead both gay and heterosexual athletes to emphasize their femininity.[59] After all it wasn't that long ago that tennis star Martina Navratilova lost her sponsorships after identifying herself as a lesbian or that Rene Portland, the head coach of Penn State's women's basketball team, implemented a policy of "no drugs, no alcohol, no lesbians." Veri argues that this threat of being labeled a lesbian serves two purposes in women's sports: it keeps heterosexual women from pursuing sports, since they do not want to be accused of what is seen as deviant sexual behavior; and it reminds lesbian athletes that they should keep quiet about their sexual orientation or run the risk of losing public favor, sponsorship, or publicity.[60]

How then does cheerleading play into this historical and contemporary debate about the role of sports in society and gendered roles and expectations? From the feminization of cheerleading in the 1950s to the 1990s, cheerleaders have not challenged the well-established dichotomy between masculine and feminine spheres or male and female roles in society. Men play the sports; girl cheerleaders (and the occasional male collegiate cheerleader) support them in their athletic endeavors by motivating the fans to root for their fearless warriors. Cheerleaders have never threatened the status quo. In fact, they have served too well, many feminists would argue, in perpetuating the status quo. Further, unlike girls and women participating in sports, female cheerleaders' sexual orientation is simply assumed to be heterosexual; they do not have to face what some would consider the negative consequences of their activity being labeled as a "lesbian haven." But as cheerleaders have become more athletic and less interested in cheerleading because of its traditional role of spirit booster and supporter of the athletes, anxieties about the appropriate and normal role of men and women surface once again and can be found simmering in the undercurrents of the cheerleading-as-sport debate. If cheerleaders are one of the last bastions of traditional femininity, what does it mean when they too want to leave their poms and megaphones behind to be tough athletes who are competitors themselves?

Cheerleaders: We Just Want Some Respect

Clearly, cheerleading has changed tremendously from its origins in the 1860s, and the days of cheerleaders being the BMOC (Big Man on Campus) or merely popular girls with pretty faces are long gone. However, cheerleaders continue to occupy a tenuous position at their schools and universities. Many would say it is because cheerleading has not been unanimously recognized as a sport. The last to receive gym time, no access to physical trainers, few scholarships, lack of proper equipment, glaring pay differences between athletic coaches and cheerleading coaches, and little coverage in local newspapers are the realities of many squads throughout this country. Others would say that the media continues to perpetuate an outdated image of cheerleaders that is detrimental to cheerleading's quest to be recognized as a legitimate sport or athletic activity. Take, for example, the January 25–31, 2003 *TV Guide.* On the cover is Jimmy Kimmel with two long-haired blonde cheerleaders looking at him adoringly. The text reads: "Why is this man smiling? A) It's Super Bowl Sunday, B) He's Surrounded by Cheerleaders, C) He's Jimmy Kimmel and He's Got a New Show, D) All of the Above!" The Spokane *Spokesman-Review* presented cheerleaders in a similar way in their recent feature of the 2002 Apple Cup football contest between Washington State University and long-time rival, the University of Washington. The only picture of the cheerleaders is that of two female WSU cheerleaders curling their hair. This is part of the accompanying narrative: "By 10:30 Saturday morning [Ashley] Courtial and Brianna Pope had been primping for an hour. They dipped repeatedly into two drawers, pulling out hair ribbons, makeup, fake lashes, face glitter and assorted brushes, curling irons and hair spray."[61] No mention is made that the WSU cheerleaders are, in fact, a NCA nationally ranked collegiate squad known for their physically demanding stunts and pyramids.

At the same time, many administrators do not like the athletic turn cheerleading has taken, seeing their emphasis on preparing for competition as either too dangerous or time away from their real duty as a supporter of athletics. Many administrators, as was the case at the University of Nebraska, have forced cheerleaders back to being only sideline entertainers by enforcing "ground bound" rules and limited competitions. Hence, cheerleaders, more so than any other athlete, are constantly struggling to receive the respect they believe they deserve.

Although we have attempted to argue that cheerleaders are athletes, we recognize that many skeptics will still see cheerleading as a dinosaur of the past best remembered by a display of pom pons and saddle oxfords in a museum somewhere in the Deep South. One of the primary reasons for this argument is that cheerleaders are still perceived by many as sexual objects. We saw evidence of this in our study at Wichita Middle School. In stark contrast to the sharp, military-like commands for girls to attack their jumps, smash through the floors, and prove they are athletes, Mrs. Stone reminded the girls that when they make their turn in front of the judges, "give them a sexy look. Dazzle them. Give them goosebumps." Many would argue that until cheerleading is able to completely shed its highly sexualized image and its association with the erotic, cheerleaders will continue to receive little respect as serious athletes. It is to the persistent theme of sexuality and eroticism in cheerleading that we now turn.

CLEAVAGE, BUNS, AND POMS

Cheerleading and Eroticism

Give me an S
Give me an E
Give me an X
What do we want?
S-E-X[1]

Although the above cheer may be a fantasy for many teenagers and Dallas Cowboys Cheerleader fans, it wasn't for the crowds at the University of California at Berkeley during the 1960s. This cheer was actually used to redirect the crowd when California was losing. Robert Ellsburg, the 1969 yell leader for Berkeley, explained, "You've got to give them something risqué," and went about doing just that.[2] The dancer he hired for a pep rally wore a Cal sweater and she was to take it off during the rally and supposedly reveal a bikini top. However, when the sweater came off, there was no bikini. What crowd enthusiasm!

Granted the above Trojan cheer is an anomaly among the typical cheers and chants, such as "Two bits, four bits" heard across the country; however, its substance is not. Sexuality and cheerleading often go hand in hand. In 1978, when the Dallas Cowboys Cheerleaders had themselves become national celebrities, Bruce Newman asserted, "goodness knows, the only thing anybody talks about anymore is S-E-X and the Dallas Cowboy Cheerleaders."[3] In 2000, the now defunct XFL sought to use cheerleaders and sexuality to boost sagging ratings by promising their audience a peep into the locker rooms where the cheerleaders dress and undress.[4] Apparently, it's not only television audiences that may be interested in peeping into cheerleaders' dressing rooms.

In 2001, two members of the Philadelphia Eagles cheerleading squad, later joined by over a 100 of their former Eagles peers, charged 23 National Football League (NFL) teams with peeping into their locker rooms over a span of 18 years. Supposedly, an added perk to playing at Veterans Stadium, in Philadelphia, was a real peep show in which visiting team members could observe cheerleaders dressing and undressing prior to the game as well as showering and dressing after the game. The lawsuit seeks $150,000 from each of the 23 teams.[5] However, some critics found a bit of irony when the 2002–2003 Eagles cheerleading squad members posed for a Philadelphia Eagles Cheerleaders Lingerie Calendar. Current Eagles cheerleader Christina Fuller commented that the calendar was "something beautiful, very tasteful" and that "It's not some kind of low-class calendar."[6]

Sports Illustrated makes explicit this connection between cheerleading and peep shows in its derisive commentary on cheerleading: "Consider, too, that as you move up the cheerleading pyramid—from college to the professional ranks—all of those high-concept acrobatics are tossed in favor of dance moves and naughty roller skate routines. Cheerleaders may call themselves teams, but they are essentially a sideshow and, in some cases, a peep show."[7]

Recently cheerleaders have become more than a sideshow, with the introduction of *Debbie Does Dallas* to Off-Broadway. If you don't already know the tale, Debbie is a teenager and captain of her high school cheerleading squad. Dallas is the home of the Dallas Cowboys Cheerleaders, which at the time of the original movie was the hottest professional cheerleading squad in the country. The mission of Debbie and the rest of her perky and libidinous squad members is to raise enough money, through gainful and, if necessary, other kinds of employment, so they can afford to travel to Dallas and try out for their favorite squad. The 2002 play follows the original plot but does not include all of the details of the movie—most remarkably, no female nudity.[8]

Admittedly, the examples presented above center on professional cheerleaders, and many would argue that professional cheerleaders should not be considered cheerleaders at all. Rather they are more akin to Las Vegas showgirls, as one commentator explains: "The Rams Cheerleaders show owes less to high school games than it does to *Flashdance* and the Bal du Moulin Rouge."[9] Certainly most secondary and college cheerleaders do not see themselves as sex objects, and work hard to distance themselves from professional squads. However, from short stories such as *Cheerleaders from Gomorrah* to pornographic movies such as *Debbie Does Dallas,* the cheerleader continues to represent in American culture a "disturbing erotic icon."[10]

Thus, one cannot talk about cheerleading in American society without talking about the sexuality associated with it. It is, in fact, the sexual nature of cheerleading that contributes to why it is such a controversial yet perennially popular activity.

Cheerleading as a Disturbing Erotic Icon

> We're the Cosmic Cheerleaders
> And we're hornier than Hell
> We want you
> To ring our bell.[11]

This cheer chanted by the sexually frustrated Cosmic Cheerleaders in the adult movie *Flesh Gordan 2* makes explicit the erotic facets of cheerleading. But the eroticism of cheerleading is not confined solely to pornographic movies. As George Kurman claims, "the cheerleader incarnates in a word, a basic male-voyeuristic fantasy."[12] The cheerleader represents in one package the ultimate male fantasy: a woman who is both a virgin and a vamp.

The virgin part of the package was definitely a product of the early years of female cheerleaders. With the feminization of cheerleading in the 1940s and 1950s, cheerleaders came to represent wholesome, good girls. They were typically portrayed as models of virtue, good behavior, and feminine leadership as illustrated in this 1955 list of desirable traits for cheerleaders: "manners, cheerfulness, good disposition, character of high standing, leadership ability, scholarship of high standing, good personal appearance, citizen of high standing, and [lastly] good co-ordination and voice."[13] The cheerleader represented a certain kind of girl—the kind Olivia Newton-John portrays in the movie *Grease*. The kind of girl the Pink Ladies made fun of (but secretly envied) and the boys, even hoodlums like Danny, played by John Travolta, wanted to marry. It's not that guys weren't lusting after the cheerleaders (remember, Danny repeatedly makes sexual advances toward Sandy), but cheerleaders represented the good girls—the girls you want to bring home to meet the family. The kind of good girl cheerleader Ruth MacDougall described in this 1973 novel, *The Cheerleader:*

> He stared at Snowy [the cheerleader]. When he'd been going steady with Bev, Snowy had been simply Bev's little friend, Bev's shadow, and when this year he'd considered the freshmen-turned-sophomore girls, he had dismissed her, mistaking shyness for snottiness. Her quick hi's at the traffic post, sometimes

no hi at all but just a self-conscious smile, and her leaving when he was kidding around with Bev, and the way she was so starched and ironed, all her clothes appearing new, the way she looked as if someone touched her she'd get wrinkled, the way she walked with her chin up gave her such an air of hauteur that he figured she wasn't worth any bother.[14]

Maxine Paetro, a writer from New York, describes the good cheerleader girls of her high school days in the early 1960s: "Back then we really, really wanted to be good. This is why we looked up to cheerleaders. They were athletic in a ladylike way. They got good grades, but they weren't considered 'brainy.' They observed the rules. They always had Saturday night dates. And they were very, very nice. They were our moral standard-bearers; the best that girls could be."[15] Today cheerleaders are still used in popular media, such as Toby Keith's "How Do you Like Me Now?," Old Navy's "Rugby Bunch" ads, and Steve Wariner's "I'm Already Taken" to convey a wholesome feminine image.

But the other part of the erotic fantasy is the vamp—the one all guys want because they know once she gets behind closed doors she is the ultimate hottie in bed. As the middle-aged, paunchy Mr. Greenfield in the infamous film *Debbie Does Dallas* says as he is chasing Debbie, captain of the high school squad, through his store, "I've always dreamed of being quarterback and making love to the captain of the cheerleaders."[16] The popularity of *Debbie Does Dallas* has spawned a series of follow-ups featuring Debbie's continuing sexual escapades (*Debbie Does Dallas 2, 3,* and *4* along with *Debbie Does Dallas 99; Debbie Does Dallas: The Next Generation;* and *Debbie Does Iowa*), yet it is just one in a series of adult and mainstream videos in which cheerleaders provide a variety of sexual images and activities. *Revenge of the Cheerleaders, Cheerleader Diaries (1,2,3,4), Fast Times at Deep Crack High, Sorority Cheerleaders, Ripe Cherry Cheerleaders,* and *Busty Pom Poms* are just a few of many adult videos that feature cheerleaders as either sexual objects, nymphomaniacs, or the object of male fantasies. Further, the range of adult cheerleading videos is wide, to appeal to a variety of viewers' tastes, including *Ebony Cheerleaders* and *Hip Hop Cheerleaderz* which provide a "taste of chocolate goodness" and "all-girl action."[17] And as anyone who has ever typed in "cheerleader" for an internet search can attest, pornographic images of cheerleaders of all kinds (e.g., Jewish cheerleaders, "big fat" cheerleaders, teenage cheerleaders, lesbian cheerleaders) abound for those who have fantasies of making it with a cheerleader via virtual reality.

Male fantasies about cheerleaders are not just relegated to the realm of adult videos. Lester Burnham in the critically acclaimed *American Beauty* (1999) fantasizes about engaging in sexual activity with Angela, his teenage daughter's best friend who happens to be a cheerleader. Even older men still fantasize about cheerleaders, as a card we found demonstrates. Two elderly men, one with a walking cane, are sitting on a bench. One of the men is sobbing and says, "I'm married to a 21-year-old cheerleader who is gorgeous and hot and all over me!" The other replies, "Then why are you crying?" He responds (as you open the card), "I can't remember where I live." Robert Shaw, writing in *Esquire,* says, "Cheerleaders rank right up there with lever-action Winchester and the stock Chevy in young men's dreams. You can even find a few old men dreaming about cheerleaders long after the carbine and the coupe have lost their luster."[18]

In the adolescent movie *Bring It On,* the captain of the high school squad, Torrance, is accused by a few members of her squad of having "cheer sex" with her newly made boyfriend, meaning that while she performs her very athletic and simultaneously very erotic cheer/dance routine, she maintains a fixed gaze upon him as he sits in the bleachers and returns that gaze. This notion of cheer sex speaks to another reason why cheerleaders are the objects of male fantasies: besides being the good girl, cheerleaders are generally unobtainable. Only a few chosen men will be allowed to actually touch cheerleaders. For the rest of the male viewers, watching the cheerleaders while creating and enjoying their own fantasies, may be as close as they get. One former professional cheerleader explained how the Dallas Cowboys Cheerleaders offered entertainment similar to the action in *Debbie Does Dallas* on every game day: "Every Sunday after church there was a whole stadium of private viewings of *Debbie Does Dallas* going on in the fecund mind of the male fan with his binocs zoomed in on those luscious bazooms."[19]

Making it with the cheerleader is apparently a mainstay of adolescent male culture, as exemplified in "The Promiscuous Cheerleader," a popular urban legend. Gary Fine and Bruce Johnson collected 29 versions of this tale, and although regional variants exist, the legend in its many forms has some basic ingredients: after a big game, a lone cheerleader performs fellatio on an entire team. She is then rushed to the hospital for her stomach to be pumped.[20] According to Fine and Johnson, the legend works only if the girl performing the act is a cheerleader: "The dichotomy between the 'good girl' and 'the easy girl'" is the emotional crux of the story. The cheerleader is the image of the good girl—sexually virtuous and highly desirable. She is the object her male contemporaries fantasize about and lust after."[21]

The Sexualization of Cheerleading

Differential Y, Differential X
To hell with differentials
We want sex![22]

As early as the 1920s, one can find cheerleaders (who would have been primarily male at the time) being described in very sensual terms, as illustrated in this editorial from the *New York Times:*

> A contemporary of Pericles, strolling into one of our football stadiums, would . . . delight in those lithe, white-sweatered and flannel-trousered youths in front of the bleachers, their mingled force and grace, their gestures at the same time hieratic and apparently jointless, that accompanied the spelling out of the locomotive cheer. And even an ancient Greek pulse would halt for a moment at that final upward leap of the young body, like a diver into the azure, as the stands thundered out the climatic "Stanford!"[23]

"Like a diver into the azure" ascribes to male yell leaders almost mythic characteristics, and halting "an ancient Greek pulse" is quite a feat. (Today, a Lakers Girl routine, replete with blood-pressure-raising cleavage and hip thrusts, would probably have a similar effect on the pulses of many Laker fans.) Thirty years later, in 1956, Arturo Gonzales, after describing the typical male cheerleader as a "Big Man on Campus," gives the following report about female cheerleaders: "no report on cheerleaders over the past three decades could be complete, of course, without reference to the coeds. Pretty young things in vestigial skirts, amply-filled sweaters and wearing baby shakos, they've burbled and twirled to the intense enjoyment of those fans easily distracted from the male carnage at the midfield by a few well-placed curves."[24]

But, it was not until the 1970s, with the introduction of professional cheerleading squads, that the sexualization of cheerleading became overt, and cheerleaders blatantly began being situated as sexual objects to be consumed for the pleasure of men. Probably the squad most responsible for this transformation of cheerleader from wholesome, good girl next door to the sex object is the Dallas Cowboys Cheerleaders (DCC). Prior to 1972, Dallas Cowboys fans were entertained at half-time by 30 high school students, consisting of both males and females. However, by 1972, football itself had drastically changed from simply a sporting event to a major media and entertainment spectacle. Tex Schramm, general manager of the Cowboys, decided to capitalize on this by offering Cowboys fans a flashier, more entertaining half-time. To accomplish this, he hired local choreographer, Texie Waterman, to create dance routines for an older female squad, to be called the Dallas Cowboys Cheerleaders. One hundred women tried out in front of five judges for that first squad.[25] Clad in short shorts and go-go boots while performing sexually provocative moves, these women were to be "sexually alluring in the abstract but not in actuality."[26] Seven women made that first squad, and at the 1976 Super Bowl in Miami the Dallas Cowboys Cheerleaders became a national craze when one of the cheerleaders winked at the cameraman and that wink was broadcasted to 75 million viewers. By 1979, they were so popular that 48 percent of the viewing audience watched a made-for-TV movie about the Dallas Cowboys Cheerleaders.[27]

In reality, being a Dallas Cowboys Cheerleader was and is hard work with little pay, and one has to agree to abide by certain strict rules—no jewelry, no gum, no smoking in uniform, and no dating the players.[28] As one of the original Dallas Cowboys Cheerleaders, Dixie Smith Luque, said, "These were the Tom Landry days, and he was a very respected and classy man. We were expected to uphold that class."[29] But, it wasn't classy behaviors that the DCC came to be known for; rather it was that celebrated Dallas Cowboys look: the cleavage-revealing tops and high-cut hotpants.

In a reflection on the importance of the Dallas Cowboys cheerleading squad, Patoski comments on their wider role in society: "The Dallas Cowboys Cheerleaders are international icons. They were the first pinups of modern sports, the sizzle on the steak that established the Cowboys as America's team as much as the players on the field did. They're also the reason Dallas women are perceived as some of the most gorgeous creatures on earth—big smiles, big hair, big makeup, big cosmetic surgery, and all."[30]

Patoski's point that the Dallas Cowboys Cheerleaders are the first pinups of modern sports links these contemporary professional cheerleaders with a historical context, that of World War II, where pinups were one of American womanhood's most recognized contributions to the war effort: that of keeping the morale up for U.S. troops. Pinups were not only about individual men looking at individual photographs of beautiful women; pinups became a topic of conversation that all men, officer or enlisted, could enjoy together equally, in the harsh conditions of war.[31] Therefore, pinups came to be understood as a form of feminine patriotism, and reinforced the need for men to fight: to protect what was waiting for them at home.

The Dallas Cowboys Cheerleaders have nurtured this patriotic connection by their association with "America's Team," their own designation as America's Sweethearts, and their blue and white uniforms. Further, they have performed for United States overseas troops 42 times during their 30 years of existence.[32] And they are known locally for their work with a variety of charities, such as visits to orphanages, nursing homes, and VA hospitals and their help with various fundraising events.

The Dallas Cowboys Cheerleaders' website declares them to be America's Sweethearts, which speaks to the tensions that have nurtured the sexual fantasies surrounding this squad. That title has a long history and includes the likes of silent movie star Mary Pickford, skater Dorothy Hamill, and contemporary movie star Julia Roberts. Mary Pickford was one of the nation's first silent screen stars, and it was her talent in playing innocent and virtuous young girls that helped promote her career.[33] Dorothy Hamill, whose

haircut was imitated throughout the country, was beloved as the skilled athlete and the sweet girl. And of course Julia Roberts has also benefited from
her public persona as the All-American, funny, sweet woman. But these are
the "sweethearts" of which male sexual fantasies are made. The following
passage written by a trio of sisters, all of whom were former Dallas Cowboys
Cheerleaders, speaks to these sexual tensions:

> How do you tap into the paradox of the sexy, wholesome girl, the girl you'd
> like to take home to mother but make love to on the way over there? Well,
> take Miss America and dress her in hot pants and a halter top. Then put her
> out on a football field grinding out a lot of provocative dances, but the whole
> time keep telling the fans that these are good girls, wholesome girls. Barrage
> the fans with the girl-next-door rhetoric while you tease, tease, tease. Tell
> them they're not seeing what they're seeing. Make them feel like they got
> caught in the spin cycle of some giant brainwashing machine. Get them hot
> over these girls, then tell the fans that they can't have them. They're sweet and
> untouchable. Oh, it's the stuff obsessions are forged from.[34]

That obsession is an appropriate term for the Dallas Cowboys Cheerleaders. Part of that obsession has been nurtured deliberately by the squad's
organization. For example, each cheerleader's physical appearance is aimed
at appealing to a different group of men so that no viewer's fantasy goes unfulfilled. There are blond, red-headed, and brunette Dallas Cowboys Cheerleaders; there are short- and long-haired cheerleaders; there are African
American, White, Asian, and Hispanic Dallas Cowboys Cheerleaders; there
are the sweet, wholesome girls and the inscrutable, mysterious girls.[35]

The Dallas Cowboys Cheerleaders were the first professional cheerleading squad that capitalized on the demand for a sexual form of entertainment
during sports events. They are, in a sense, the matriarchs of professional
cheerleading squads. Their status was recently solidified when five of the
original 1972 seven-member squad was photographed for a recent *Sports Illustrated* issue, which asked, "Where are they now?"[36] However, other professional squads have also cashed in on the obsession with sexually alluring
cheerleading squads.[37]

After the success of the Dallas Cowboys Cheerleaders, professional basketball teams decided their franchises could also benefit from a little titillat-
ing half-time entertainment. When the Atlanta Hawks began looking for
cheerleaders for their team, their promotions director made the sexual appeal of cheerleaders very explicit: "We're gonna put them in the skimpiest
uniforms possible that won't be obscene and won't get us arrested."[38] By
1978, professional cheerleaders had gotten so popular that John Madden,
then coach of the Oakland Raiders, predicted that in the near future the professional cheerleaders would attract a larger audience on Sunday afternoon

than the game being played on the field. "After the girls have competed, the football players will come out at halftime for their exhibition, but the press won't notice because they'll be too busy watching replays of the cheerleaders."[39] This, of course, has not come true; in fact, some teams have dropped their cheerleading squads, including the Detroit Lions and New York Jets. But from the Oakland Raiderettes to the Laker Girls to the Rhein Fire Pyromaniacs (NFL Europe cheerleaders) to the Argo (Toronto) Sunshine Girls (Canadian Football League), professional cheerleaders, with their high kicks, skimpy clothes, and sexy dances have become a permanent half-time fixture of professional football and basketball.[40] However, their presence continues to elicit a cacophony of reactions to their role in the sports world. Take, for example, the following denigrating editorial by Scott Ostler:

> There is no question that cheerbabes are politically incorrect, but that's not my objection. My objection is that they are stupid. Not individually. Some of these girls probably are as smart as whips, though you never see them on "Jeopardy."
>
> It's the concept that is stupid. Bouncing, flouncing cleavage and bunage has its place in our world, such as in music videos. But between plays at a football game, or during basketball timeouts? Why?
>
> When did we come to the conclusion as a society, that we couldn't have a ballgame without the presence of lissome babes with massive hair and costumes that appear to be hanging on for dear life? . . .
>
> For the most part, though, people who run sports seem convinced that fans can't work themselves into a cheery mood without spiritual inspiration from slinky, sultry, lip-licking, hyper-perky young women in teensy matching suits.[41]

Many Americans share Ostler's sentiments; however, they are not apparently the sentiments of those who spend large amounts of money on sports. And this is what much of the explicit sexuality of professional cheerleading squads is all about. As Mary Ellen Hanson notes, professional cheerleading squads were created to satisfy the entertainment facets of sports and the promotional needs of the sports organization. Professional football is not just lived one afternoon a week. There are products such as calendars, T-shirts, sports paraphernalia, and an assortment of unrelated sports products that contribute to the organization's coffers. Cheerleaders are a definite part of that promotion since they are employed to not only cheer at games but also make public appearances for charity (in their uniforms typically) and for profit.[42]

Clearly, a sexual tension is embedded in the selection, marketing, and promotion of professional cheerleading squads. They are to be smart, classy, intelligent, and wholesome while also incarnating the ultimate male fantasy. This tension can be seen in several lawsuits. One such lawsuit involved the Dallas Cowboys Cheerleaders and their suit against Pussycat Cinema, which produced the film *Debbie Does Dallas*. The case was heard in the United States Court of Appeals (2nd district) and concerned the use of a trademark, specifically the Dallas Cowboys Cheerleaders' patented uniforms in the film. However, it was the content of the film that was of greatest concern to this national football organization, which did not want their cheerleaders associated with explicit sex. That would take away the sexual tensions that make the DCC so popular.[43] The Dallas Cowboys Cheerleaders organization won the lawsuit.

Another lawsuit involving the Oakland Raiderettes and Microsoft treads some of the same murky water. Oakland Raiders officials were concerned about the sexually suggestive ads on the official Raiderette website (maintained by Boathouse Row Entertainment, Inc.). These ads included lures to "porncity.com" among others. Team officials were worried that these ads would damage the Raiderettes reputation.[44] The ads are like the movie *Debbie Does Dallas*. They unsettle the delicate balance that professional cheerleading squads must maintain in order to be desirable for most American men: to be sexy without being a slut.

As these court cases point out, professional cheerleading as an industry must keep the tensions between virtue and vampishness in place. Many would argue that the XFL failed to maintain this delicate balance. When it was obvious that the XFL was in trouble, the owners and TV producers looked to the XFL cheerleaders to boost ratings. They promised the audience cameras in the dressing rooms.[45] XFL Los Angeles cheerleader Bonnie-Jil Lafin explains how the XFL cheerleaders were portrayed: "What they have shown so far on national TV is girls looking like strippers, and it looks like we may not get all the breaks we thought we would get."[46] Bonnie-Jil is correct in her assessment. For cheerleaders to maintain the sexual tensions that make them sexually provocative, they must not receive too much exposure, both literally and figuratively. They cannot be presented as overly sexual or they become associated with strippers and porn stars, rather than as the secretive, subtle fantasy. Bonnie-Jil understood quite clearly the need to market them differently, although she personally chose to pose nude for an online adult e-zine: "I think that they're gonna have to definitely market us differently and publicity wise . . . so that people know exactly what some of us do. Maybe find out that we have girls on our team who are teachers, who are court reporters, who are massage therapists, girls who are students . . . so people can see that these girls, at least the L.A. team and some of these other girls, you know, aren't [strippers and porn stars]."[47]

In the above instances, sexuality clearly plays an important role in the popularity of professional cheerleaders. Although not exhibited in the same way, sexuality is also a part of the lives of school-age cheerleaders. We found this out in our study of middle school girls who were trying out for their mid-high cheerleading squad, newspaper stories of school cheerleaders, and in the way that adolescent cheerleaders are portrayed in popular culture and the media.

Trying out for Womanhood: Cheerleading and Sexuality in Schools

I'm sexy; I'm cute.
I'm popular to boot.
I'm bitchin', great hair,
The boys all love to stare.
I'm on it; I'm hot.
I'm everything you're not.
I'm pretty; I'm cool.
I dominate this school.
Who am I? Just guess.
Guys want to touch my chest.
I'm rockin'; I smile.
And many think I'm vile.
I fly; I jump.
You can look, but you can't hump.
I'm major; I roar
I swear I'm not a whore.
We cheer and we lead
We act like we're on speed.
Hate us cause we're beautiful,
But we don't like you either.
We're cheerleaders;
We are cheerleaders.[48]

Many associated with cheerleading at the junior high, high school, college, and university levels have worked diligently to rid cheerleading of its sexual image. At many tryouts and competitions throughout this country, judges are told to deduct points for vulgar, sexually provocative, and inappropriate moves, cheers, or chants. Chris Darby, coach of the Christian Brothers squad in Memphis, says that he wants to ensure that his girl cheerleaders are not seen as sexual objects. There are no "Stunt Naked" T-shirts at his practices, no sexually provocative dance moves, and certainly no bare-midriff uniforms.[49] Debbie Purifoy, coach of the University of Alabama cheerleading squads, was incensed when a local radio show suggested that, to get comfortable with each other, the Alabama cheerleaders stunt in the nude for their first few practices together. "That is ridiculous. Our kids are so conservative. They would never even dream of doing that."[50] Certainly, most nonprofessional cheerleading squads around the country do not imitate the moves of the Dallas Cowboys Cheerleaders or the Laker Girls. However, junior high, high school, and college cheerleaders are enveloped in some of the same sexual tensions that surround the professional squads.[51]

The opening cheer in the popular movie *Bring It On* speaks to some of these sexual tensions. Entangled in this entertaining play on what cheerleaders are really thinking is the vanity of cheerleaders and their snobbishness, along with the acknowledgement of their sexual powers over the boys in school. "Who am I? Just guess. Guys want to touch my chest!" But as the girls of El Torro High, the fictitious school of *Bring It On,* are quick to point out, they are not whores. The cheerleaders we introduced previously from Wichita Middle School made the same claim. Certainly, all adolescent girls understand the detrimental consequences of being labeled a slut.[52] However, the cheerleaders we interviewed were also concerned about being labeled a snob. Nice girls, good girls, the ones that are valued in this culture, are seen as neither sluts nor snobs. Thus, adolescent girls must navigate the narrow pathway between slut and snob on a daily basis. But for school cheerleaders, that pathway is, in some ways, a more treacherous one, partly because of the public visibility of their positions as cheerleaders, but partly because of what cheerleading represents: the wholesome good girl and the sexy tease.

In high schools and middle schools, cheerleading is an adult-sponsored and school-regulated activity that is designed to encourage school loyalty and spirit, nurture self and team discipline, and promote participation in mass culture via dance and cheer routines.[53] That's the official description of this perennially popular activity. Additionally, school cheering is seen as encouraging such characteristics as leadership, time management, and a healthy competitive life outlook. These characteristics are promoted in most athletic teams as well. However, because participants in cheerleading are 97 percent female, there are other facets of this activity not found in male-dominated sports and activities. As mentioned earlier, cheerleaders have a long history of being viewed as symbols of the ideal girl/woman, and are expected to convey this image. Because of this wholesome image, to which many Americans at least partially subscribe, the morals of cheerleaders must be beyond reproach. If they include provocative moves in their cheer routines, that is the only place that those moves should be practiced. Cheerleaders must restrict their feminine sexuality to their cheers only and not use it in the back seats of football players' cars. And they certainly better not get pregnant, as four cheerleaders at Hempstead High School in Hempstead, Texas, discovered.

Hempstead, Texas, is like many small rural communities. School activities, especially athletics, are important to the identity of this town of 3,500. But in Texas, where football is almost a religion, it's even more important. In 1993, the community had to suffer through a losing football season, which was bad enough, but then it had to figure out what to do when four cheerleaders turned up pregnant. The four were dismissed from the squad after the school board hastily instituted a school policy that prohibited students who had achieved an elected office from being pregnant, on the grounds that they were poor role models and their condition provoked health risks. One of the four girls terminated her pregnancy and was offered the opportunity to resume her cheerleading position, which many observers thought sent a contradictory ethical message. Eventually, the board had to rescind its policy for fear of loss of federal funding via Title IX lawsuits.[54] Clearly, the point to the story is that cheerleaders are not to cross a particular moral boundary if they are to represent virtuous girlhood.

Certainly, high school cheerleaders, in actuality, are no more or no less sexually promiscuous than any other group of girls; yet, because of the image attached to cheerleading, cheerleaders are expected to maintain high moral behavior. Middle school, high school, and university squads typically must abide by very strict rules of personal conduct outside of the stadium or basketball court. This strict code of conduct has been a part of cheerleading from its very inception—however, the feminization of cheerleading brought about changes in expected conduct that reflect the expectations society had of how "good" girls should act. If you remember in chapter 2, we point out that one of the reasons why girls were discouraged from being a cheerleader was the concern that they would pick up the profanity that was used by male cheerleaders. Obviously, in the 1930s, it was expected that boys may swear but girls must never engage in such unlady-like behavior. The following guidelines, rules, and comments from cheerleaders of different time periods are representative of the concern with explicit sexuality and the maintenance of wholesomeness in the activity.

> Cheerleaders should never use cheers that are the least bit suggestive, or have phrases that rhyme with swear words. Cheers of this nature discourage many rooters in the stands from cooperating and encourage others to carry on with crude and inappropriate responses.[55] (1962)

> Corny as it sounds, cheerleaders do represent their school, so we have to act properly wherever we're likely to meet anyone who knows us in that capacity. Our squad works under a system of demerits, which are handed out for reasons, ranging from wearing too much makeup to smoking or drinking in uniform. A squad member who gets a certain number of demerits is automatically benched; if she gets too many she's thrown off for good. So the girls become a very respectable bunch, which is sometimes misinterpreted as acting stuck-up.[56] (1977)

> Each 8th grade candidate is to wear a plain white shirt with red shorts and each 9th grade candidate is to wear a plain white shirt with navy shorts. Also, .

hair should be pulled away from the face. The girls will not be able to wear jewelry of any kind."[57] (1998)

Most recently, the Universal Cheerleading Association explicitly attended to the concern with how sexual the moves of cheerleading had become by writing new policy that penalizes cheerleading squads that perform "slashy" moves. Here Bill Seely, vice president of operations and development for the Universal Cheerleading Association, directly addresses parental criticism of the sexual nature of cheerleading:

> It's something we put in our score sheets at competition. Sportsmanship clause, it's 5 percent of their score. If there are suggestive moves, they get penalized. It comes largely from the All Star market; they're real performance oriented, and what we've seen over the last couple of years, you have your traditional cheerleaders that are school based and the All Star thing, and it just comes from the outgrowth of the popularity of the activity, school's just can't have 200 cheerleaders, so all the kids that want to be cheerleaders are going to gyms where all they do is compete. There are some organizations that really don't have good standards that we would like everyone to have; there are some things in the past, like for example, called slashing, the cheerleaders do this. We outlawed this. Within one year it was eliminated. People came to our stance. We have done the same thing with the dances. We all have kids, we are all family oriented. Our camp dances, we screen them for those, but some parents don't like their hips to shake at all, it just runs the spectrum. We try to align ourselves closer to the more conservative side of that spectrum. But it's not conservative enough for some people.[58]

Certainly adults, such as coaches and principals, want to maintain the high moral behaviors of squad members, but the girls themselves also have a stake in making sure that the image of the cheerleader is not tarnished. Cheerleaders who are sexually active, smoke, and drink are expected to keep it a secret. Anthropologist Don Merten explored what happened when a middle school member of the "burnout" clique was selected to join the cheerleading squad, dominated by members of the "prep" group. Burnouts were kids who did not even attempt to meet the adult expectations of adolescent good behavior. They smoked pot, drank alcohol, and were sexually active. More important, burnouts told everyone about these activities. So when Jackie, a burnout, was selected by a panel of judges to be a member of the cheerleading squad, several popular boys immediately claimed that the squad was now made up of losers, and those prep girls who had made the squad were decimated by the remark. The prized activity of cheerleading, which made girls feel special, was now tarnished. The irony of Merten's study is that some members of the prep group were also sexually active and drank and smoked as well. However, they did not publicly advertise these activities.[59]

At Wichita Middle School, the seventh-grade girls elected cheerleader were aware of a code of conduct, but they were also aware and intrigued with the sexual tensions inherent in cheerleading.[60] Certainly, one of the attractions of cheerleading is that it continues to represent in many schools the highest-status activity for girls. It is also seen as a route to popularity and to getting guys. Daneka, a Native American seventh grader who wanted to be a cheerleader but did not try out, told us, "girls want to be cheerleaders because they believe that guys will like them more—they will see them as cute women in short skirts." Daneka's use of "girls" and "women" in the same sentence reflects a primary attraction of cheerleading for many girls: it allows girls to try on a womanly (i.e., sexualized) identity in a school-sanctioned space. And part of that trying on of a womanly identity is through the use of their physically developing bodies.

As we observed the cheerleading preparation class at Wichita, we noted the giddy emotional responses of girls when they were learning dance or cheer movements that were overtly sexual in nature. Part of what they were learning as they practiced these routines was how to move their bodies in new ways in a new arena where they were explicitly being gazed upon. As these seventh-grade girls practiced putting their hands on each side of their pelvic bones and swaying their hips at the same time, they would often exaggerate the movements as if they were practicing their sexuality; then in true early adolescent fashion, they would break out in girlish giggles.

Typically, schools either seek to remove, suppress, or ignore evidence of sexuality, as anyone who has ever yawned through the mechanically based sex education literature can attest. Desire is never discussed, particularly female sexual desire.[61] There are also prohibitions against allowing desire to enter school spaces, even in student-driven avenues such as the student newspaper.[62] But cheerleading somehow has escaped some of this concern about sexuality, which is why so many girls still, in this day of sports and Girl Power, want to be cheerleaders. Cheerleading allows the erotic to enter into school-sanctioned space; in fact, it is one of the only school spaces in which girls can play with or try on the identity of the All-American nice girl next door and the sexually provocative woman simultaneously. In many schools, cheerleaders are allowed to wear short skirts and tight-fitting vests, which often violate school dress codes, while performing sexually provocative dance moves such as pelvic thrusts to popular music—neither of which is typically allowed in school elsewhere. For a white girl Julie, who was selected as cheerleader, this opportunity to play with a sexualized identity was a primary reason why cheerleading was so appealing. She explains, "I'm in it for the short skirts, the guys, getting in front of everybody and making a total fool of myself." Like many of the girls with whom we talked, Julie sees cheerleading as a school-sanctioned space in which to be gazed upon, particularly by boys. Lisa, a white girl who scored the most points during the tryouts, says, "It's just you want to be one of the main focuses of the game instead of the players." Because cheerleading has been one of the only spaces in the past in which females could enjoy high status and visibility, Milea, a Native American girl who made the squad, states, "I've been waitin' for it [cheerleading] my whole life."

The girls themselves put a different spin on the idea that cheerleaders are objects of sexual desire. They readily admit that they are looked at, and that they like that. It's one of the reasons they get so much pleasure from being a cheerleader. However, they believe that this position in the public eye gives them power. Julie comments, "And I like getting up in—I LIKE getting up in front of people and, like, being the one in charge." This sentiment is shared by cheerleaders of all ages and both sexes. In fact, the more people under one's charge, the better. For example, Jim Lord, now executive director of the American Association of Cheerleading Coaches and Advisors (AACCA), talks about being a cheerleader at the University of Kentucky and his work in motivating Kentucky fans to cheer for U.S. troops during Desert Storm:

> Desert Storm we had a lot of people from Kentucky Medical center over in Kuwait. At the basketball game, during half time, I was captain of the squad and also the mikeman, so I got on the microphone. We filmed the game, Kentucky-Louisville game, and during half time led cheers for our troops and people over seas, the cheerleading squad did that with me on the microphone, and here I had 24,000 people in the arena doing exactly what I wanted them to do and then we sent that tape over so they could watch a Kentucky basketball game and at half they got all that stuff.[63]

Debbie Purifoy, coach of the University of Alabama cheerleaders, concurs: "It's a rush to get on the field and see that there are 80,000 people responding to you. That's why people want to be a Bama cheerleader."[64]

Rather than seeing themselves as sex objects, many cheerleaders view themselves as either objects of respect and admiration or as objects of envy and emulation. When asked why she wanted to be a cheerleader, Shanna, a Native American girl, responded: "Well, I want to do it, so, like, other people that aren't doin' it that want to be, but are afraid to, will look up to me and say, 'Well, she can do it, I can do it.' You know, especially Indians . . . a lot of Indians that are very talented. And, you know, they're bashful and they're afraid to admit that they want to be like that." Lisa, who is clearly aware of the sexual allure of cheerleaders in the following quote, ultimately sees herself as a role model for younger children. She answered this way when asked about the purpose of cheerleading:

Well, I guess, they, like, somehow, like, I guess pump up the crowd or something, like, I don't know, like, cheer them guys on which they're probably not
paying attention, any attention to the cheerleaders anyways except looking at
their legs or something. But, I don't know, they, like, if there's kids like girls
there or other kids that aren't into basketball, they can watch the cheerleaders
and, like, "Wow! I want to do that!" and probably think of them as, like, an
example. Like, "Yeah, Mom, there's a cheerleader. I want to be that when I
grow up.' And that's what I did.

Although school personnel typically downplay the erotic elements of cheerleading, it still creeps into their language. At Wichita, Louise, the cheer coach,
occasionally instructed the girls to play up their sexuality, "When you make
that turn, give the judges a sexy look. " She further instructed them, "you
should be oozing out cheerleading stuff. Dazzle me, smile, give me goosebumps. I want to be dazzled." The last advice Ms. Stone gave the girls before
the day of tryouts was, "put Vaseline on your teeth and put on a little extra
makeup but not too much. Don't come looking like someone who could stand
on the street." The combination of these instructions from "give me goosebumps" to "don't come looking like someone who could stand on the street"
bump into each other and literally speak to the sexual tensions with which the
girls are grappling. Dazzling the judges or crowd with Vaseline on your teeth
yet maintaining a distance from being labeled a slut is difficult work for
women, much less adolescent girls. Yet, cheerleading is one of the only school-
and adult-sanctioned activities where girls can learn what it is like to be a mature female, with power and male attraction. For many young girls in their
transition to womanhood, cheerleading provides a space that is exciting, fun,
and full of opportunities to see what womanhood is all about.

Male Cheerleaders and Sexuality: "Basically, the Guy is the Frame. The Girl's a Piece of Art."

However, female cheerleaders are not the only ones enveloped in sexuality.
Male cheerleaders must also grapple with issues of sexuality. But first, they
must be prepared to face questions about their sexual orientation. As we noted
in chapter 2, the proliferation of gay and lesbian squads in the United States
has disrupted our ideas about the assumed sexual orientation of cheerleaders.
But still, for the most part, cheerleaders, particularly at the middle and high
school level, are assumed to be female and straight. With the feminization of
cheerleading, males who participate in this activity must be willing to subject
themselves to countless questions about their masculinity and sexual orientation.[65] The belief that "girls, sissies, and fags" are the only people who cheer

continues to permeate certain facets of American culture, as evident in this story we were told about an ardent, life-long Louisiana Republican. Upon hearing that Trent Lott, Republican Senator of Mississippi, had been elected Senate Majority Leader, he declared, "I don't know if I want a damn cheerleader from Ole Miss running our country." As a Louisiana State University graduate, maybe the problem was with Ole Miss, but we don't think so. In late-twentieth-century American culture, real men and cheerleading just don't go together, especially if the men are Republican.

Today's male cheerleaders typically experience two reactions to their gender-bending endeavors. The most immediate response is to be called a "cheerqueer" or a "cheer fag," as Jason Crostin, a former Eastern Washington University cheerleader, noted.[66] A common assumption is that any male who cheers could not possibly be heterosexual. At the time that Jason was a cheerleader, he was also enrolled in ROTC, which further confused those who questioned his masculinity. The second most common reaction is a series of questions about what it was like to be "handling" the thighs and buttocks of some very attractive and athletic women. At first, Jason was enamored with that part of his role; however, he said that cheering and stunting are so physically and psychologically demanding, that he couldn't think about those thighs until practice was over. But he did use those kinds of questions and comments to thwart any uncertainty about his heterosexuality.

It should be of little surprise that the return of men to cheerleading has paralleled the redefinition of cheerleading as a sport. As the image of cheerleading has changed from pretty popular girls performing cartwheels to the gymnastics-oriented stunting that many teams now incorporate, men have increasingly turned to cheerleading and found a niche. As Michael DellaPenna, captain of both the football and track teams at Eastchester High School in New York in 1999, noted, his cheerleading injuries have ultimately convinced his skeptical football friends that cheerleading and in particular the stunting, can be as masculine as any other sport. He argued that in both sports players get kicked, mangled, and hurt.[67] However, many men still believe that they must pay a price for becoming a cheerleader, and that price concerns their perceived sexual orientation. We even heard one story in which a Japanese gymnast successfully tried out for a U.S. cheerleading squad. When he informed his mother in Japan that he had been selected to a nationally ranked collegiate cheerleading squad, she asked him whether he had changed into a woman. The young man had to fax pictures of coed cheerleading squads to his mother to assure her that men do indeed cheer.

Fortunately, many straight men disregard the continual criticism and develop some very snappy comebacks for those who do question their sexual orientation. When football players give Jesse Nishikawa a hard time, this very athletically built sophomore responds first with a question: How heavy

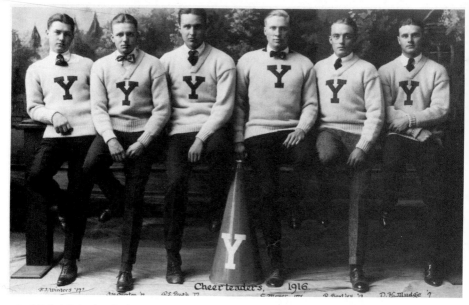

1916 Yale (CT) Cheerleaders—Models of masculinity and future industrial leaders

Fifty years later, Yale Cheerleaders having a bit of sideline fun displaying their acrobatic abilities

Senior cheerleaders at Erasmus High School (NY)—In the 1940s, men still dominated most high school squads

The 1959 Mount Carmel (IL) Golden Aces cheerleading squad participates in the annual civic ritual of the Homecoming parade

(left) Swirling skirts and strong arms—City College of New York Cheerleaders in the 1950s illustrate the "division of labor" commonly found in coed squads

Cheerleaders at the historically black Clark College in Atlanta (GA) enthusiastically sport the typical 1950s cheerleading look with saddle oxfords, bobby sox, sweaters and megaphones

Cheerleading opens the door to fame, fortune, and success. Legendary Alabama coach "Bear" Bryant poses with future actress Sela Ward and Crimson Tide cheerleading coach, Debbie Purifoy.

The 1977 Winnsboro (LA) High School squad gets "fired up" with their big poms and Farrah Fawcett hair. Natalie Adams, author, at top right.

(left) Donning miniature cheerleading regalia, these two little 1983 New Iberia (LA) fans contemplate the meaning of poms.

(below) Hugging and smiling, these two 1990 Marshwood (ME) High School cheerleaders strike the classic cheerleading pose.

(left) Building the corporate pyramid, the staff of the newly formed Universal Cheerleading Association demonstrate the athletic turn in cheerleading in the 1970s.

(below) Competition becomes part of the cheerleading culture by the 1980s. Here the New Iberia (LA) Middle School Yellow Jackets show off their trophies, medallions, and ribbons after winning the 1985 International Cheerleading Federation (ICF) championship.

Competitive-only squads are introduced in the 1990s. The Cheer Authority (AL) All-Star Wizards are headed for a national competition after winning first place at regionals.

Motivating 80,000 fans, the 2002 University of Alabama Crimson Squad demonstrate the mix of leadership and athleticism required in contemporary cheerleading.

Homecoming Court representatives, basketball stars, and class presidents, the Lapwai (ID) High School cheerleaders exemplify the leadership expected of school cheerleaders.

Cheerleading and patriotism go hand and hand. In the case of the Crowville High School (LA) cheerleaders, they knowingly use their left hand to pledge the flag so they can flash their school rings.

Linking local patriotism to nationalism, the Metuchen (NJ) Pop Warner squad commemorates the 9–11 tragedy along with local police and Port Authority representatives.

Even feminists cheer as illustrated by these X-Cheerleaders as they perform the "birth cheer": Push it out, push it out, way out!

REBEL

1. = first group   2. = second group   * = both groups

1. I don't wanna work no more!
                2. What did you say?
1. The system doesn't work no more!
                2. What did you say?

1. I said STOMP, SMASH THE STATE,
   * Let's Liberate! *
Acknowledge me or go to HELL
        Another Woman to Rebel!
2. STOMP, SMASH THE STATE! Let's Liberate!
Acknowledge me or go to HELL!
Another Woman to REBEL!
* STOMP, SMASH the State! Let's Liberate!
Acknowledge Me or
or go to Hell
Another Woman to Rebel!

Radical Cheerleaders take their cheers to the street as they protest a host of social injustices.

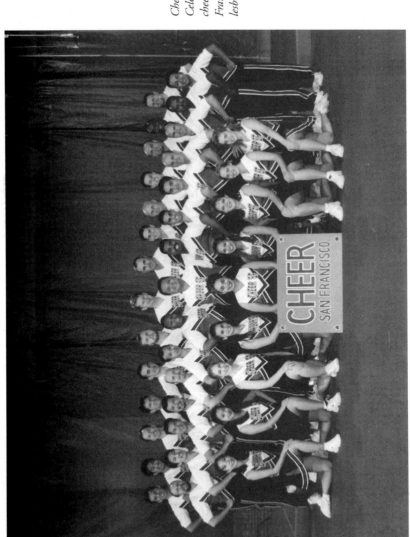

Cheer Loud! Cheer Proud! Celebrating diversity in cheerleading, CHEER San Francisco is the oldest gay and lesbian squad in the world.

You're never too old to be a cheerleader: The Wilmington (NC) Golden Pom Pom Cheerleaders, winner of several gold medals in the North Carolina Senior Games, symbolize the perennial popularity of cheerleading.

Cheerleading is a dynamic, cultural icon that has changed significantly in its 135-year history. What will the future of cheerleading hold for these two little cheerleaders?

is the football? The answer, of course, is about one pound. Jesse then goes on to argue that football is no big deal, since all the players do is carry around a one-pound ball or catch it and run. Male cheerleaders, on the other hand, are tossing full-grown women high into the air and catching them. Jesse says that this argument will stop them at least temporarily. In response to wrestlers' criticisms of guy cheerleaders, Jesse responds this way: "Wrestlers get to wrestle with big ugly sweaty guys. I'm tossing a cute girl into the air and catching her. Which do you think is better?"[68]

Both responses remind the listener of the close physical relationship between men and women on coed cheerleading squads. In fact, Michael Gill, assistant cheerleading coach of Boise State University, argued that cheerleading is the only sport in which men and women are equal. He says that the trust built through grueling practices and the responsibility to each other nurtured through the dangers of stunting engender brother/sister relationships.[69]

Male and female cheerleaders may be equal, as Gill points out, but they typically have very different roles to play within the squad.[70] These roles are a way to highlight the differences between women and men on the squad, and to keep men cheerleaders from being harassed any more than they are. For example, most male cheerleaders do not dance. While the women are performing a fast-paced dance, the men typically follow the routine in the background with some simple moves, called "strong arms." This refers to arm movements that are sharply delineated, like those exhibited in a military parade. The arms jut forward or upward or to the sides and are rigid and muscle-defining. While the girls may shimmey across their shoulders and chests, the boys will not, and while the girls may use some provocative hip sways, the boys will not. Sometimes, even the strong arm movements are contested by the men. Jason Crostin confided that he and some of the other male cheerleaders at EWU would drop the strong arms and pick up megaphones to yell, just so they didn't have to be associated with the dance at all.[71]

And it's not just a division of labor during half-time entertainment that separates women and men cheerleaders. Jesse Nishikawa said that the guys on his WSU squad also act in ways to protect female cheerleaders from the catcalls and hands of inappropriate fans:

> We have a thing. It's called the Run Around. It's the Friday night before a football game. We usually go around to the fraternities and sororities and do the fight song or some kind of old chant in front of the houses. We usually go to all the bars and pubs and do it in front of them. For the most part, the guys stand back here like this with arms crossed, looking tough, but our job is to make sure nobody touches the girls.[72]

So the division of labor includes stunting as well as the traditional duty of men protecting women from other men.

For most men, stunting is what brought them into cheerleading. Man after man commented that once they tried stunting, they were hooked. University of Idaho female cheerleaders, who lost all of their male cheerleaders during the 2002–2003 season, said that the only way they could recruit men was to approach them individually and invite them to practice. Once they attend a practice, they are enamored by the athleticism of cheerleading. That has been the beginning of many of the male cheerleaders' careers with whom we talked.

Jesse Nishikawa never cheered in high school because of all of the harassment male cheerleaders received. However, during his freshmen year at WSU, he took a tumbling class, and a few of the men in this class were cheerleaders. Sometimes, other male cheerleaders would join the class, and they would practice a few stunts. Jesse thought that it looked athletic and fun. "I wanted something to keep me active. I wanted a sport. It's a lot harder than people think and it keeps you in shape." He was encouraged to try out for the squad during the spring, and made it. Meanwhile he engaged in a two-hour-a-day weight training program to build up his strength so that he could throw the stunts safely.[73]

Justin Carter, former cheerleader and choreographer for cheerleading competitions, says this about being a male cheerleader: " . . . for guys, it's an addictive sport. Girls grow up on it. But guys discover it later. We aren't burned out. I don't miss it anymore; my body is done with that. Cheerleading is unnatural to your body—jumping? Tumbling? Throwing girls? Nothing else like it. Basically, the guy is the frame. The girl's a piece of art."[74] For most male cheerleaders, just like Justin, cheerleading is about strength and power, while the girls provide the beauty, the "art" of the activity. Therefore, what men cheerleaders want to emphasize is their strength, particularly through stunting. Holding up women who are then propelled upward through the air and who plummet down to earth and are caught safely is an adrenaline high for the base cheerleaders, often male. And men take the job very seriously. As Jesse Nishikawa said, his partners would kill him if he didn't catch them.

Since strength and power are what most male cheerleaders want to emphasize in their involvement with cheerleading, it should not be surprising that muscle definition would become a component of the male role as well. Some male cheerleaders have followed the tradition of serious swimmers, power lifters, and body builders and shaved their body hair. Apparently, shaving body hair gives the toned muscles even more visibility and finer definition. One of the UCA coaches at a camp in the Northwest had shaved his body hair, and the high school girls could not get enough of looking at and caressing his bare arms. Further, some collegiate squads practice male initiation rites that involve shaving the chest as well as other areas of the body.

Because junior high and high school cheerleading has remained ensconced in femininity, the number of male cheerleaders at the secondary level is much lower than at the collegiate level. However, that is changing and many squads throughout the country now sport males, but recruiting at the high-school level can be a problem.

Liz McGivern and her fellow female cheerleaders at Bishop Guertin High School in Nashua, New Hampshire, developed a quiz for determining which boys would make good cheerleaders for a coed squad. The various scenarios that Liz provides focus on whether the guy recognizes the serious work of cheerleading. The following is one quiz question:

> On Monday morning, the principal announces that your varsity team won 1st place at a regional competition on Saturday. He turns to you and says,
> a. "Ooh, first place! Could you little girls even carry that big heavy trophy home?"
> b. "What did you get for #4 on last night's physics homework?"
> c. "That's better than you did last time—not that I'm paying attention or anything, right, guys?"
> d. "Awesome! Did you do that really cool thing where you toss Cara up in the air and catch her?"

The quiz makes no mention of whether a boy is physically capable of providing base support for stunts or tumbling to enhance the squad; rather the main concern is that potential boy cheerleaders have the right attitude. And if you hadn't figured it out, "d" is the correct answer for Liz and friends.[75]

We're certain that if Marty Beckerman, author of *Death to All Cheerleaders,* took the quiz, he would fail, because he definitely does not have the right attitude to be a cheerleader. In one essay, "My Day as a Cheerleader," Marty describes his attempt at mid-season tryouts at Anchorage's West High School and his conversation with one of the cheerleaders, Jessica:

> "Do I have to wear one of those skirt thingies?" I ask.
> "Actually, male cheerleaders wear spandex pants," Jessica explains.
> "THERE ARE REAL MALE CHEERLEADERS?!?"
> This comes as a total shock to me. I had absolutely no idea there were actually guys out there who really did cheerlead. Incredible. I am almost as excited now as I was the first time I heard the sound produced while using a hammer to smash baby raccoons![76]

The Artful Seduction of Cheerleading: Who Can be Seduced?

As Michael Gill pointed out, cheerleading is the only sport/activity in which men and women are theoretically equal. However, the sexual objectification of the female cheerleader limits the possibilities of his claim. If the man is the frame and the woman is the piece of art, what chances are there for women to be understood as athletes who exhibit self-discipline, perseverance, and physical strength? What opportunities are there for men to traverse their role of power and strength to become the piece of art? Despite the potential for male cheerleaders to challenge the cheerleader as a "disturbing erotic icon," this transformation has not taken place, as explained by Laurel Davis:

> Any feminist transformative potential that could have been enhanced when males reentered cheerleading in recent times has seemingly been lost by the construction of a sexual division of labor. The male cheerleader has become increasingly accepted because the image he has constructed and continues to construct does not challenge traditional gender notions of power relations, but rather reinforces them. Cheerleading, as a feminine preserve, remains to be seriously challenged.[77]

Men may have entered the feminine domains of cheerleading, but the sexuality of cheerleading continues to be associated with the heterosexual female. This association between cheerleading and sex is why so many feminists, parents, and young people hold such disdainful feelings about cheerleading; however, it is also one of the reasons why cheerleading continues to seduce large numbers of individuals year after year. Professional cheerleaders certainly profit from the sexual image of cheerleading. But sexuality is part of the cheerleading landscape in ways that are much more complicated than simply the Sunday afternoon routines of the Dallas Cowboys Cheerleaders. Sexuality creeps into the language of middle school coaches and high school girls; it finds its way into dances and cheer moves in every level of cheerleading; it pronounces itself in many cheerleading uniforms. It also becomes part of the selection process itself. If cheerleading represents simultaneously the ideal good girl and the sexy woman, what kind of girl or young woman is chosen to embody that cultural contradiction? In the next chapter, we explore this question by looking at the racial and ethnic representation of cheerleading squads across this country.

CHEERLEADING AS A "WHITE GIRL THING"

The Racial Politics of Cheerleading

Leader: I got it.
Crowd: What?
Leader: You need it.
Crowd: What?
Leader: It's in my eye
Crowd: Oh yeah
Leader: It's in the sky.
Crowd: Oh yeah.
Leader: It's on the roof.
Crowd: Oh yeah.
Leader: Honest truth.
Our cool team, cool![1]

Shanna, a petite seventh grade girl, was excited about trying out for the cheerleading squad at her middle school. She was popular among her peers, having been elected the secretary for the Student Government Association. She participated in a cheerleading preparation class offered at her school, and her parents seemed supportive of her desire to be a cheerleader. Shanna, a Native American girl, believed it was her responsibility to be a positive role model for younger girls in her tribal community; cheerleading, she believed, would provide this opportunity. She didn't believe that race had anything to do with who could be a cheerleader at her school, proclaiming, "cheerleading's not just the white girl's thing; it's for everybody." However, five years earlier her hometown of Wichita City[2] was a battleground over who could and should be on the local cheerleading squads. Race, ethnicity, money, privilege, and what it means to "level the playing field" became part of the community's conversation as inhabitants in this town of 26,000 struggled with the requirements for cheerleading tryouts and the composition of the squads. Wichita City is not an isolated case. Throughout the recent history of this country, the selection of cheerleading squads has been fertile ground for debates about what it means to be an inclusive, nondiscriminatory, just society. No official statistics are kept on the racial composition of cheerleaders in the United States. Yet, a visit to almost any cheerleading camp, a glance through *American Cheerleader*, cheerleading brochures promoting camps and competitions, any catalog selling cheerleading products, or a look at the nationally televised cheerleading championships reveals that cheerleading squads throughout the country are primarily white. Why have cheerleading squads, unlike some other athletic teams, remained disproportionately white? What strategies should be taken, if any, to ensure more diverse squads? What does the integration or lack of integration of cheerleading squads, both historically and today, tell us about our struggles as a nation to achieve racial equality?

Contemporary Struggles for Racial Equality

Many school districts throughout this country have found it troublesome that their cheerleading squads do not represent the diversity of their overall student body. This was certainly the problem in the Wichita school district, according to some. From 1991 to 1995, a total of 140 girls were selected to be cheerleaders at Wichita High School and Wichita Mid High. Of those 140, only 18, or 12 percent, were non-white. This number did not match the racial/ethnic composition of the school population, which was approximately 75 percent white, 14 percent American Indian, 5 percent Hispanic, 5 percent African American, and less than 1 percent Asian American. At the end of the mid-high tryouts in 1994, Alana Osborn, an African American girl, was, for the second time, not chosen for the squad. Her mother decided to present the school board with a list of concerns that focused on the amount of out-of-pocket money required for cheerleading and the criteria used for selection of the squad. Ms. Osborn pointed out that the students were asked to supply such information as the place of parental employment, favorite family vacations, their height and weight, and whether they could wear their hair in a ponytail on the tryout application. She argued that this information was used to eliminate particular groups of students.

The superintendent along with several school employees conducted an intensive investigation based on Ms. Osborn's complaint. At the same time that school officials were collecting data on the costs of school activities and sports and the numbers of students of color who participated in these, many members of the white community, particularly parents of cheerleaders, began to hold meetings on how to best respond to the obviously low numbers of minorities represented in these activities. Through newspaper announcements and a phone campaign, this group gathered a large number of supporters of the current program to speak at school board meetings and oppose any major changes in cheerleading tryout procedures.

The parent group successfully galvanized the white community. Three hundred people showed up for that next school board meeting—one of the largest crowds ever. A principal who helped conduct the investigation read the administrative report, which noted two distinct areas of discrimination, the first being the out-of-pocket expenses incurred by participants. The boys' athletic programs were funded at a much higher rate by the school district than the girls' athletic programs. Further, cheerleaders were required to purchase their uniforms and attend (at their own expense or through fundraising) a summer cheer clinic. The second distinct area of discrimination was found in the cheerleading selection process, which basically required girls to have dance and gymnastics skills in order to meet the selection criteria. Apparently, only those girls whose parents could afford gymnastics and tumbling lessons were able to make the squad. Finally, the language used in the information sheets that were given to parents and students was discussed. The belief was that the references to such items as ponytails, height, and weight requirements unfairly advantaged white students. The school administration argued that a screening process was in place that effectively eliminated many minority and low-income students. However, the audience did not see it the same way, and the principal was booed after giving his report.

The local newspaper described the meeting in this manner: "It was standing room only Monday as citizens from the community confronted the Board of Education about an issue that has been raised in regards to cheerleader selection and qualifications. . . . All speaking, with the exception of Mr. and Mrs. Osborn, were in favor of keeping the current squad as it stands. All also believe the selection process to be fair." The following excerpt from a letter sent to the local newspaper three days following the school board meeting is also representative of the pubic talk surrounding this issue:

> As adults, we understand that competition is a way of life. We compete for all of the things that we consider worthwhile, our jobs and our spouses among other things. I find it disturbing that some parents refuse to teach their children the value of that competition. It seems that in all aspects of our society today, we are teaching our children that mediocrity is okay in order to save

their self-esteem. Without competition, all things will become mediocre. . . . Success is the achievement of hard work, dedication and drive.

Dissatisfied with the outcome of the school board's narrow vote (5–4) against making changes in the selection process, Mr. and Mrs. Osborn took their complaint to the Office for Civil Rights (OCR). Within a month, the OCR filed a formal complaint against the school district. The OCR letter stated: "We have determined that the OCR has jurisdiction to process for resolution of the allegations. It appears that the complainant is alleging that the WCSS [Wichita City School System] discriminates against black and Native American students on the basis of race by deliberately excluding them from selection for participation on the cheerleader squad." Shortly thereafter, the OCR investigator, district officials, and those filing the complaint met. If a resolution could not be reached, all federal funds could be withdrawn from the district.

Recognizing the serious consequences if the discrimination complaint was not addressed, the school board attempted to resolve the issue and presented a plan at the next two school board meetings. Major facets of the plan included an after-school cheerleading clinic that would teach the seventh, eighth, and ninth grade aspiring cheerleaders the cheers and dance routines required for tryouts; the creation of a noncompetitive cheer class (called cheer preparation) that would be offered as a physical education elective for seventh, eighth, and ninth grade girls who were considering trying out for cheerleading; the recruitment of minority judges and educators; the removal of discriminatory language from literature distributed to parents and students (e.g., references to ponytails, height, and weight); and a limit to the amount of out-of-pocket expenses of $200 (grades 8–9) and $400 (grades 10–12).

Once again community groups opposed to the changes met to devise a strategy to counter these recommendations. They placed the following ad in the local newspaper, one day prior to the school board meeting.

Attention parents of students involved in athletics, band, cheerleading, choir, drill team, debate, flag corps, orchestra, Wichita City Schools traditionally have been committed to excellence for their programs. Monday night, the School Board is faced with a proposal that will start us on the road to mediocrity, beginning with cheerleading, drill team, and flag corp (and eventually other groups). Let's *support excellence* and attend the board meeting." (Paid for by Concerned Parents)

Again, the school board members were confronted by a large crowd opposed to the proposed changes. However, in a 6–3 vote, school board members approved the changes. The expected outcome of these policy changes, according to the superintendent's comments in the local newspaper, was to "create an equal footing for all students who desire to develop skills necessary to compete for the competitive programs." Obviously, another reason was to resolve the Office for Civil Rights' complaint against the district.

The Wichita City School System is not an anomaly in its struggles with race, privilege, and equality on the cheerleading squad. Throughout the country, lawsuits have been filed, policies have been implemented, and the Office for Civil Rights has intervened to address the disproportionate representation of whites on cheerleading squads. In Seminole County Public Schools in Florida, the desegregation of the cheerleading squads was one of the final steps the district had to take to comply with a suit the federal government filed against the district in 1970. The system's seven high schools had maintained mostly white squads in a district in which 14 percent of the student body is African American. A group of coaches, administrators, and parents spent two years investigating the school's cheerleading squads. What they found mimics portions of our findings at Wichita. Lack of financial resources and skills were the primary reasons that African American students did not try out for the Seminole squads. Because several of the district's cheerleading squads were nationally competitive, entrance fees to competitions along with an expanded wardrobe of warmup suits and uniforms had some cheerleaders paying $1,500 per year. Further, many African American girls did not have the opportunity to participate in tumbling and gymnastics classes. The administration formulated several strategies to address the problem: limit participation in these expensive competitions to four a year; develop a "Cheer Fest" in the county that would require a nominal fee for participation; create a countywide cheerleading camp to cut down on expenses incurred in traveling to camps sponsored on college campuses; and establish criteria for tryouts that downplay the importance of tumbling.[3]

Another case in Alabama highlights some of the same issues but provides a different approach to resolving the problem of a mostly white cheerleading squad. In 2001, 31 students tried out for the Columbiana Middle School cheerleading squad; 7 of these 31 aspiring cheerleaders were African American. The final composition of the 10-member squad consisted of only 1 African American girl. The other 9 were white. Similar to what occurred in Wichita, several African American parents confronted the school administration about the selection process. Unsatisfied with the response they received, the parents took their concerns to the Office for Civil Rights. Both the parents and the school district sought mediation in resolving the issue. A new principal conducted his own investigation of the 2001 selection process and found some discrepancies that had not been noted previously. In a move that can be found around the country, the school administration then proceeded to offer cheerleading positions to all those who initially tried out for the squad.[4] Similarly, in 1988 in Arp, Texas, two African American girls were not selected cheerleaders for their junior high team. Allegations were made that judges changed their scores and inappropriate comments had been made about the girls' weight. The Texas Education Agency stepped in and ordered Arp Independent School District to allow all 18 contestants who tried out to participate on the junior high squad or face the penalty of losing $180,000 in state funding.[5]

These four cases (Wichita, Seminole, Columbiana, Arp) were initiated due to a lack of proportional representation of a school's student body racial composition on the cheerleading squad. In these cases, race was made explicit by pointing out the unfair practice of having a racially unrepresentative cheerleading squad. However, race and ethnicity often implicitly play into discussions of who should be a cheerleader. For example, there are the unspoken or whispered assumptions and comments about differences in styles of cheerleading based on race and ethnicity, such as the lack of smiles of Native American cheerleaders, the militaristic moves of white squads, and the suggestive moves of African American cheerleaders. These simplistic characterizations speak to both national stereotypes and cultural and historical differences among racial and ethnic groups. Typically these types of conversations are not part of public discussion. However, in a recent dispute over cheerleading style in Chatham County, Georgia, direct talk about race and style did surface. In this case, the father of a Johnson High cheerleader complained that some of the squad's moves were too sexual. Hence, the squad members were told to eliminate hip movements from their routines. The parent was white, and the squad and the school is mostly African American. Although many claimed that the differences in opinions about what are considered appropriate moves for cheerleaders were generational, the two high school squads that were discussed, Beach High and Johnson High, were both predominantly African American. One former graduate of Beach High School, Lisa Wilkins, argued that the controversy was really about stylistic differences, "When we shake, as African-Americans—because we're so healthy—it's going to shake a little harder than any Caucasians. What are you going to tell me to do? Square dance?"[6]

Stylistic differences also emerge in the box-office hit *Bring It On.*[7] A subplot of the movie centers around the competition between two cheerleading squads in California, an upper-middle-class, mostly white team and a racially diverse but mostly African American squad from an inner-city school. For several years, the former captain of the white squad had stolen chants and routines from the African American squad and used them to win national championships. The stolen cheers were much more rhythmic and innovative than the traditional white cheers (for example, "I said burn. It's hot in here. There must be some Clovers in the atmosphere!" in off-beat rhythms). Without the ingenuity of the African American squad's routines, the white squad employs a choreographer to come up with a competitive routine, which turns out to be a dismal modern dance routine with bizarre hand movements. Furthermore, the choreographer had sold the same routine to other squads so the routine was useless. Once again, the lack of white cheerleaders' creativity was highlighted. The white squad eventually created its own routine; however, the African American squad won the national championship. Sophomoric in many ways, the movie does make race, social class, and stylistic differences central in a cheerleading world that tends to ignore these topics.

The histories of Southern African American cheerleading squads before desegregation also point to stylistic differences between white and African American cheerleading that are based, in large part, on the important role that popular music along with church hymns played in creating a distinctive style of African American cheering. The Easman High cheerleaders of Corinth, Mississippi, during the 1950s and 1960s are an example of that distinctive style.

Segregated Cheering at Easman High, Corinth, Mississippi

Leader: Is Tupelo going to win?
Fans: Yeah man
Leader: Is Tupelo going to win?
Fans: Yeah man
Leader: Oh you stop that lie
You know it's a sin
You know dog-gone well
Corinth is going to win.

Easman High School in Corinth, Mississippi, offers a glimpse into the culture of cheerleading at Southern African American high schools in the 1950s before desegregation. Located 80 miles southeast of Memphis, Tennessee, Corinth had a population of 11,452. Like all of the towns bordering Highway 45, Corinth was a segregated community. The African American students went to Easman High (grades 7 through 12), home of the Yellow Jackets, and the white students attended Corinth High. The schools were not integrated in Corinth, Mississippi, until the fall of 1969. Both schools had football teams that were enthusiastically supported by their segregated communities; however, the two teams never played each other. Both teams also had cheerleaders. Dr. Harold Bishop, whose father was principal of Easman High from 1930 to 1969, and who played for the Easman Yellow Jackets from 1956 to 1960 and then for Jackson State College from 1961 to 1964, remembers visiting Corinth High School with his father in the early 1950s and being fascinated with the different styles of cheering at Corinth High and at Easman. "The cheerleaders at Corinth High were sequential and militarized in the manner they cheered. They cheered by the numbers. When one arm went up, everybody's arm went up—'Go, go, go, team, go!' And everybody's head dropped the same time. It was practiced and rehearsed carefully. They were motivated, but they were militaristic."[8]

In contrast, Easman High cheerleaders were more impromptu, more emotional, less rehearsed, and more creative in their style of cheering. Bishop explains:

> A girl might yell all of a sudden "I've got it." And everyone else in tuning in would say, "Got a What?" And then she'd yell a little louder, "I got it" and the other girls would say, "Got a What?" And then they'd join the stands. She'd grab her ankles. "It's in my ankles." And they would say, "Where is it? Got a What?" "It's in my knee!" and she'd go all the way up to her brain and finally she'd come down and say, "The Easman Spirit!" And everybody would give a yell and everybody would have the Easman spirit.

Cheerleaders at Easman High were a combination of cheer and dance team. When the band broke out with a rendition of "Do the Hucklebuck," the cheerleaders would join in with unrehearsed dancing. Music was integral to cheerleading at Easman, and that music came from both the church and the blues. Heavily influenced by the music they heard on the only two African American radio stations they could pick up, WDIA (out of Memphis) and WCLA (late at night out of Nashville), the cheerleaders would often improvise on a blues tune and re-write it to fit what was transpiring on the field. The following is an improvisation of Amos Milburn's (1927–1980) "Bad, Bad Whiskey":

> I left home this morning
> I promised old Prof [the principal]
> I promised old Prof that I
> Would win this game for Easman
> Win this game or die.
> Bad, bad, Jackets, bad, bad, Jackets
> Bad, bad Jackets, gonna win this game or die.

One of the most popular Easman cheers was a take-off on Big Joe Turner's "Shake, Rattle, and Roll": "We're gonna roll, roll, football, roll. We're gonna roll, roll, football roll. Well, Booneville had a team, we rolled it over them. Hey, rolled it over them. Hey." The cheerleaders would continue the cheer by inserting the names of all the opponents they had beaten.

The cheerleaders were also heavily influenced by the Baptist church culture that permeated all facets of life in many southern African American communities. Being led by spirit, or The Spirit, the cheerleaders would often take a hymn that could be found in the standard Baptist hymnal, such as "We Shall not be Moved," and change it into something like: "We shall not, we shall not be moved. Just like the tree standing by the water, we shall not be moved. If we shall not be moved, who shall not be moved?" At that point, the cheerleaders would then interject the name of the man playing tackle or guard as the one who shall not be moved.

African American communities across the South, like that of Corinth, had high expectations of their local cheerleading squads. James Ross, former student of Second Ward High School in Charlotte, North Carolina, corroborates Dr. Bishop's emphasis on the local demand for cheerleading creativity. Ross recalled that the audience expected a good show. "There was not just rah, rah, rah. You would have to take whatever the latest song was, or the latest dance, and then come up with some cheers that incorporated your school's name and some other things and put all that stuff together. . . . And you couldn't do the same things every year. I mean, nobody wanted to hear that stuff you did last year. And so you had to come up with new cheers."[9]

Improvisation and innovative rhythms were key to successful cheers and routines in African American communities. Meanwhile, white communities were just warming up to the early versions of cheerleading camps in which cheerleading squads from surrounding white high schools were taught the same cheers. In fact, one vice president for the National Cheerleading Association commented several years ago, "I don't know where they got their cheers from before camps came along."[10] What she meant, of course, is where white cheerleaders got their routines. For Southern African American communities prior to desegregation, cheers and routines came from the minds and hearts of their cheerleaders.

Just like every other social and cultural institution in the nation during this era of segregation, cheerleading consisted of multiple worlds that existed independently from each other. After the *Brown v. Board of Education* decision was rendered by the Supreme Court in 1954, these worlds began to collide. Cheerleading became one of the important sites of these collisions.

No Blacks and Chicanos Allowed: Racial Tensions in Cheerleading During Desegregation

It's difficult today to imagine that the selection of cheerleaders would be the impetus for riots, a shooting, and school walkouts. However, when school desegregation issues came to the forefront, the selection of cheerleading squads, much more than the selection of athletes, became a highly contested issue on many high school and university campuses.[11] As African American girls found themselves having to compete with white girls for a spot on newly integrated squads, they were typically at a disadvantage because of the style of cheering that was prevalent in the African American high schools prior to integration. "The fluid improvisation of African American cheering, with its emphasis on strong rhythms, verbal eloquence, and crowd partici- pation, stood in sharp contrast to white cheerleading styles, which relied more on straight-armed, almost military precision as well as elaborate gym- nastics routines."[12] The expectation was that the African American cheer- leaders would change their style of cheering to conform to what was considered the "norm" of cheerleading, which was, in reality, the white norm. When protests about squads being disproportionately white arose, the white community typically responded that the process was fair; the African American girls simply did not have the requisite skills to be competitive for a spot on the squad.

During desegregation, it was extremely important to the African Ameri- can community that African American girls be given the same opportunity as white girls to be cheerleaders. African American citizens found it ironic that African American boys were more easily accepted on the school's ath- letic teams, yet African American girls were not allowed to cheer for them. Many in the white community fought hard to exclude African American girls from this opportunity. As Grundy notes, "the selection of cheerleading squads would, in fact, become one of the most volatile school desegregation issues around the South."[13]

When the newly integrated Walter Williams High School, in Burlington, North Carolina, held cheerleading tryouts in the spring of 1969, a small number of white students booed the African American cheerleaders who were trying out in front of the student body. The student body elected the cheerleaders and, unsurprisingly, the majority white student body elected only white girls to serve as cheerleaders. Fights erupted at school after the announcement of the squad was made. The next day African American stu- dents staged a protest on the front lawn of the school and demanded to ad- dress the issue with the superintendent. What began as a protest erupted into violence that night when buildings were burned and gunshots were fired. Leon Mebane, a fifteen-year-old, was shot to death.[14]

That same year, more than half of the 2,800 students (grades 1 through 12) in Crystal City public schools in Texas staged a 28-day walkout to protest cheerleading selection in their school district. Crystal City was 85 percent Chicano, but only one Chicano cheerleader was selected by the largely white faculty in charge of choosing cheerleaders. In addition to insisting upon more Chicano representation on the cheerleading squad, the students also demanded more Chicano teachers, the right to speak Spanish, and the right to have a curriculum that included and celebrated the contributions of Chicanos. This walkout is often cited as the birth of the Raza Unida movement.[15]

Similar protests were staged at colleges throughout the United States. In 1968, the Black Student Action committee demanded that the Purdue cheerleading squad include African American students. Certainly not taking the role of objective reporter, Pat Ryan reported the events in a 1969 article in *Sports Illustrated* in this way:

> Given their conservatism, the sorority girls and fraternity boys had to do considerable soul-searching—under administrative pressure—before agreeing to admit two Negroes arbitrarily to the squad. Neither girl, it was pointed out, had earned the right to be on the squad; they had not taken part in the regular cheerleader tryouts. The school administration, it was felt, was applying a principle of forced integration. After much discussion, the cheerleaders agreed to accept two blacks, Pam Ford and Pam King, although reluctantly. . . . [Pam King] is regarded uneasily on campus as an instigator of the Black Student Action group demonstration. Without doubt she lacks the grace and coordination to be a good cheerleader.[16]

At the University of Mississippi, John Hawkins was selected as the first African American cheerleader in the school's history. However, he refused to wave the Confederate flag. He began receiving threats, and, fearing for his safety, members of his fraternity and other supporters from the Black Student Union had to escort him around the campus. Further, his dorm room door was burned and then his room was flooded. His father's job was threatened as well. All of this during the 1982 school year—28 years after *Brown v. Board of Education* and 18 years after the passage of the 1964 Civil Rights Act.[17]

Many schools have worked diligently to resolve the issues of fair representation on their cheerleading squads. Natalie recalls that at her high school in North Louisiana, comprised of 50 percent whites and 50 percent African Americans, a policy was implemented in 1977 that called for one white and one African American cheerleader to be elected from each class (freshmen, sophomore, junior, and senior). This policy was in place for over 10 years. In North Carolina, the Charlotte-Mecklenburg Board of Education enacted a quota policy that would ensure that at least one-third of the girls elected cheerleader would be African American and one-third would be white.[18] Other schools and universities, like Wichita, have initiated policies requiring racially and ethnically diverse judges. In the 1980s, some schools, particularly at the middle and high school level, began implementing a no-cut policy, which allows everyone who wants to be a cheerleader the opportunity to participate. For example, in order to increase school involvement in general, in 1992 the Cascade Junior High in Plainsfield, Indiana, had 72 cheerleaders on their squad![19]

Certainly, discussions of numbers and proportional representation, while helpful on one level, occlude some of the more important reasons why cheerleading remains predominantly white and middle class. Stylistic differences were factors that played a role in maintaining all white squads during the era of desegregation. But what about today? Why is cheerleading still considered by many to be a "white girl thing"? We return to our study of Wichita Middle School to look at these other factors.

Wichita Middle School ... Five Years Later

When we arrived at Wichita Middle School (WMS) during the 1998–99 school year, many of the original policies aimed at "leveling the playing field" were still in place. At WMS there were two cheerleading preparation classes, which, on the surface, seemed to be serving their intended purpose: to equip all girls with the necessary skills to compete for the 20 coveted positions on the mid-high squad. Since the resolution of the OCR complaint, the composition of the judges was diverse. Discriminatory language, such as references to ponytails, height, weight, and parents' place of employment, had been removed from the literature distributed to students and parents. However, of the 64 girls enrolled in the two cheer preparation classes that we observed, only 8 were Native American, 5 African American, 2 Mexican American, and the rest were white. Two and a half months later, only 34 of the 64 competed during the formal tryouts in March, and of this 34, only 3 were girls of color, 2 Native American girls enrolled in the cheer preparation class and an African American girl who was not. Shanna, whom we introduced at the beginning of the chapter, was not one of the 3 girls of color who tried out. And, when the tryout results were tallied, the squad consisted of 19 white and 1 Native American girl. Apparently, the policies implemented five years ago had not leveled the playing field.

We wanted to know why that was the case. Why didn't Shanna and her friends try out for cheerleader? Had the African American, Native American, and poor white girls, who expressed the desire to be a cheerleader earlier, simply changed their minds? Did they no longer want to be a cheerleader? Were their grades too low? Were their parents unable to provide the support necessary for participation in an extracurricular activity? Once the threat of the OCR disappeared, did the school district become lax in enforcing the agreed upon rules and policies? There is some truth in each of these explanations. Many girls could not try out because they did not have the mandatory C average required for participation in extracurricular activities. Some did not try out because their parents were unable to provide the financial support or transportation necessary for cheerleading. And the school district had become lax in enforcing some of its policies. For example, according to the changes made in 1995, no parent was to spend more than $200 a year on eighth and ninth grade cheerleading. However, the total costs of a year of middle school cheerleading were set at $999 for the 1998–99 school year as outlined in the informational packet sent home, although the coach informed parents verbally that much of this money was not required since the squad would not attend nationals. Some of the policies simply could not "level the playing field" despite anyone's good intentions. For example, one of the goals of the new policies was to take away the privileges of middle-class students who had received private gymnastics preparation prior to the tryouts. However, tumbling could not be taught in either the semester-long cheer prep class or in the clinic, due to school liability problems. Although not required for tryouts, as it is in other schools, tumbling was one of the ways in which participants could earn more points on the judges' evaluation sheets. The girls who could afford private tumbling lessons were able to get high marks in this category. For all the above reasons, the playing field ended up not being so level after all.

But these explanations alone were not sufficient to explain why so few Native American, African American, and Mexican American girls decided not to try out, even though individually many of them said they would like to be a cheerleader. At Wichita Middle School, like so many others, cheerleading was still the highest status activity for girls. Girls talked about the cute short skirts and vests, the fact that they wanted to be the center of attention, and that they would probably get more boyfriends if they became cheerleaders. Cheerleading was also considered to be a fun activity. So why didn't these girls try out? The answer can be found, in part, in the symbolic meaning of the cheerleader. In other words, how the girls themselves understood what it meant to be a cheerleader and the kind of girl the cheerleader represented determined who did and did not try out.

Only Preps are Cheerleaders

Like most middle schools, WMS had its own hierarchy of peer groups: the Preps, the Gangsters, the Sex Mob, the Indians, the Nerds, and various other groups. The Preps were at the top of the clique pecking order; they were considered the most powerful and most influential. They were also almost all white and middle class. Other students described the Preps as the "rich kids" and the "teachers' pets," although many Preps denied such claims. But these were the kids with the good grades, the braces, the name brand shoes, the expensive backpacks, and various other markers of wealth. Ironically, the name of the elective class whose purpose was to create an equal footing for cheerleading tryouts, cheer preparation, was often abbreviated to "cheer prep" by the members of the class itself. This shortened name is significant in that cheerleading at this school was seen as an activity controlled and dominated by the Preps.

To be a Prep meant you had to talk, act, and dress in certain ways. For example, during this time period, Lucky jeans, Doc Martens, and Abercrombie & Fitch were all brand names that were worn by the Preps. Further, Prep girls often wore ribbons in their long hair, which was pulled back into a ponytail. Likewise, playing sports and being a cheerleader were also considered appropriate activities for Preps. So if you wanted to be a cheerleader, regardless of your peer affiliation, you had to start acting, dressing, and talking like a Prep or at least not act hostile to their status.

When asked about why the Preps would make the cheerleading squad, Anna, a white Prep girl who made the squad, answered in the following way: "'Cause, um, the Prep girls are usually good at almost everything. They're, they just the ones that are Preppy, the ones that are all cool and everybody, everybody wants to be like them; they're good at everything. They're, they're, they're pretty, and they're cute (slight laughter), or whatever." Members of the Prep crowd were involved in almost every facet of school-sanctioned leadership activities. Almost all of the students we interviewed responded that if teachers were asked to name the leaders of the school, they would select Preps. However, many low income and minority girls resented the power of the Preps at their school. Renee, a Mexican American girl who was considered to be one of the most athletically talented students in the school by the school's athletic director and who did not enroll in the cheer preparation class, responded this way when asked about the Preps: "Oh, God I hate them. I - I - I hate the Prep people because they act too much—they think they're too good for everything." Mandy, a Native American student who wanted to be a cheerleader and was enrolled in the cheer prep class, was so antagonistic toward the Preps that she refused to call the class by its abbreviated name; she called it "CP" so that other students supposedly would not know that she participated in the cheer prep class.

These antagonistic feelings that non-Preps felt toward Preps was a problem for the Native American and African American girls who wanted to be members of the cheerleading squad but who did not want to be criticized by their non-Prep friends. Tamara, a Native American girl, struggled with situating herself among girls' groups at WMS. During this school year, her closest friends were white, and she had begun to wear some of the markers of female Prep identity, for example, bows in her long hair. However, she was still sensitive to her Native American friends' critique of her participation in the cheer prep class. "My Indian friends think I shouldn't be, because I mean, they, I don't know. They, they just don't like me even in a Prep thing . . . They think it's like Preppy Preppy or something—and then plus, there's hardly any Indian girls in there. Like I can only think of three Indian girls that are in the whole Prep thing, in the cheer prep thing." Although she was enrolled in the cheer preparation class, she did not try out and explained that her father would not let her.

Shanna, introduced in the beginning of the chapter, explained how some Native American girls reacted to her desire to try out for cheerleading: "Some think that they're too fat or too big but last year when I told them I did, they started, they was like 'You're trying out for cheerleading?' I said 'Yeah, I think it's cool.' They was like, 'Well, you act just like a white girl,' stuff like that. I didn't care, I was saying, 'Well I don't want to be something low down.'"

Shanna's final comment corresponded to a characterization of Milea's, a Native American Prep girl who made the squad, that many Native American girls were "gangsters," an image held by many whites and others at WMS. Many Native American girls at WMS did not subscribe to the Prep's narrow dress code; there was a much wider range of clothing styles, which included baggy jeans or warm-up pants along with large Starter jackets and various T-shirts, as well as the Prep look. For members of the Prep group and others as well, baggy jeans portrayed the gangster look or the gangster wannabe look and was particularly unacceptable for cheerleading.

Furthermore, Shanna's comment that some of the Native American girls think that they are "too fat or too big" spoke to mainstream society's definition of the cheerleading body. Many of the girls who were members of the particular tribe to which Shanna was referring had developed more quickly than many of their white counterparts and appeared to be fully grown. Tamara was a good example of this: she was approximately 5'9," big boned, and appeared to be 18 instead of 12. This particular body type stood in sharp contrast to the 5'2" and 100-pound phenotype that many of the white Prep girls embodied. This petite body type was mentioned repeatedly by all the girls in their discussion of who would make the squad, and several white Prep girls who embodied this look were repeatedly used as examples. Thus, the belief that the "normal" cheerleader body was petite was infused in the girls' visions of who could become a cheerleader. In viewing the final composition of the squad, 15 of the 20 girls did indeed embody the small, petite phenotype that was discussed by most of the girls.

However, body phenotype was only one physical attribute associated with being a Prep and a cheerleader. As clearly demonstrated in the following exchange with Julie, a white Prep who made the squad, race and an appropriate display of femininity were also important characteristics of being a cheerleader. Here Julie comments on an African American girl who was trying out.

> Julie: Her toe touches are—they are really good.
> Interviewer: She's up in the air.
> Julie: Yes. But that's—I don't know that that's gonna really count very—that'll help her a lot. But I don't know if she'll make it or not, just because she's like not really the cheerleading type, at all. She's more like the sports type. She's not really out—she's outgoing, golly, she is. But she's just not—you wouldn't picture her as a cheerleader. Like the way she—she can—she can't tumble at all, but she has a really loud voice and can get up there on her toe-touches. She's got really big muscles. She's on the basketball team.

Although this African American girl has some of the requisite athletic skills, including exceptional toe touches, she does not possess the image of the "cheerleading type," or "you wouldn't picture her as a cheerleader," as Julie comments. Although in the past 20 years, cheerleading had been reconfigured to highlight the athletic skills of girls and not solely their popularity and beauty, this was not fully the case at WMS. Athleticism clearly counted, but just as important was being "the cheerleading type," which meant that one's peer group, race, and physical appearance were still central to defining what the "cheerleader type" was. Consequently, even girls who could perform most of the athletic requirements were not considered cheerleading material if they did not convey a "cheerleader look" or, in other words, the type of femininity that was necessary for cheerleading at this particular middle school. The most obvious example of this was "having a smile on your face at all times."

That Fake, Happy Look: Putting on a Cheerleading Appearance

When asked what characteristics the judges were looking for in making their selection, the girls almost universally claimed that smiling was one of the key characteristics. We found that at this school the inclination to plaster a smile on your face at a moment's notice was much easier for the white middle-class Prep girls than girls from other racial and ethnic groups. Many of the girls recognized that smiling constantly was a difficult physical and emotional ability, one that had to be practiced. Furthermore, many acknowledged that the smiles were not necessarily always genuine. When asked why she had to have a smile in cheerleading, Anna maintained, "so that everybody thinks you're having a good time," which, of course, is different than actually having a good time. In the same light, Nan, a white Prep girl who made the squad and whose affect was typically flat, noted the importance of the appearance of having fun.

Interviewer: What kind of girl do you think the judges are looking for—to be a cheerleader?

Nan: Um, someone that is real enthusiastic and has loud voice projection and someone who just acts like they're having fun.

One of the most fundamental characteristics of a cheerleader at this school, therefore, was the ability to appear to be enjoying oneself. Cheerleaders show they are enjoying themselves by smiling, even if the smile is fake. Girls who had the skills and willingness to assume this fake, "look like you're having fun" smiling face were inherently privileged over those who did not, in the quest of becoming a cheerleader. Most of the white middle-class girls, many of whom were Preps, were willing to do this, and many acknowledged the hard work of achieving it. In response to what the judges were looking for, Terry discussed what a cheerleading personality was. Furthermore, she detailed how she practiced the necessary ubiquitous cheerleading smile.

Terry: You have to be able to smile all the time and have a . . . deep cheerleading voice, you know. You have to be able to, and you have to be really cheerful, OK?

Interviewer: So some people won't make it because they don't have that, then?

Terry: Sometimes I don't smile, but now I'm getting to the habit where, whenever I'm at Louise's [the instructor for the cheerleading preparation class] house, I concentrate on one picture. And they're smiling back at me. So, I smile right at them, like, and then I just do my jumps. Even, she [Louise] goes, I don't care if it's a fake smile or not, just smile.

Lisa also acknowledged the hard work of attaining the fake smile.

Interviewer: Well, what do you think the judge, what kind of girl are the judges looking for, do you think?

Lisa: Probably one that's loud, that smiles a lot, that's really cheezy, that's pretty good at jumps and just, just looks like she's having fun, not so serious.

Interviewer: But if like, when you say the word, cheezy, now what do you mean by that?

Lisa: Like smiles a lot, like bonks her head and like makes things like turns her head like certain ways. . . .

Interviewer: But when you say cheezy, now, do you, it almost implies. Like when I use the word cheezy that it's something fake about it, I mean do you think that. . . .

Lisa: Oh yeah, fake smiles, all the time.

Interviewer: But then how do you convince the crowd that it's not fake?

Lisa: You just, like you just brighten your eyes and you look, it's, it's hard.

Both Terry and Lisa made the squad. It certainly isn't surprising that Lisa scored the most points in the cheerleading tryouts. She was named by a majority of the girls as one of the leaders of the Preps. She was petite and was known for her unwavering smile and cheerful attitude. Even though she saw smiling as hard work, Lisa had mastered the art of always *appearing* happy.

For many of the Prep girls, a permanent smile was part of their understanding of how "normal" women and girls should act. But this understanding was not shared by other girls. Chas, an African American girl in the cheer prep class, remarked that the required cheerleading smile was not natural for her. "Sometimes I have a smile on my face; sometimes I don't. Sometimes my attitude's good; sometimes it's not. You know, people get on my nerves, like the boys do." Similarly, Daneka, a Native American girl, pointed out, "Most people think that you have to be a Prep to be a cheerleader because they got that fake look about them. That fake happy look, I can't get that!" Although Shanna tried hard to emulate the smile she saw on the faces of her Prep friends, she, too, recognized the inauthenticity of their smiles: "When I watch them [the Prep girls], they're like, they have the smile, they have the jumps, everything. But sometimes, it seems like, their emotions are, like, crooked."

In the end, Shanna, Chas, Mandy, Tamara, Daneka, and the girl with the beautiful toe touches—all Native American or African American—did not even try out for the squad. With Lisa, Nan, Anna, Julie, Terry, and 14 other white girls, the cheerleading squad selected in 1999 looked the same as it did prior to the OCR's involvement and policy changes. Creating more diverse squads in Wichita was an unrealized dream.

Latin Divas and the Remaking of Cheerleading

In speaking about the girls who were cheerleaders at Easman High in the 1950s and 1960s, Harold Bishop recalls:

> When I was in high school if you would look over at the cheering squad, it would look like a rainbow. You could have a Hispanic looking young lady who was African American, or a young lady who was very light skinned with brown hair, or a lady with my skin tone. So the girls varied in physical characteristics and that was interesting. You could have a young lady that was plump next to a young lady that was totally skinny. The key word was spirit. If a young lady who was plump could move around out there and dance and could yell and bring the crowd up in their seats or cause them to laugh or smile or cheer—the young lady was out there. But things have changed since desegregation, and acculturation changes such things as that. You rarely see a plump young lady, black or white, on the sidelines even if they come from a

ninety-nine and nine-tenths black school. Now usually the standards are set by the cheerleading associations.[20]

What Bishop is speaking about is how the "cheerleader type" has changed over the years and how that change can be seen in who sets the standard for the "cheerleader look," and, more importantly, what cheerleading represents. With the feminization of cheerleading in the 1940s and 1950s, cheerleaders came to symbolize the All-American girl. Hence, the selection of cheerleaders was, in reality, the selection of what girls could best represent ideal femininity. One of the primary reasons why many whites objected so vehemently to the selection of African American girls on cheerleading squads during desegregation was based on their own notions of who could best represent ideal girlhood and womanhood. As Pamela Grundy noted, "cheerleaders were expected not simply to master routines but to project a 'look,' a combination of clothing, hairstyle, figure, and enthusiastic charm considered to embody the ideals of youthful womanhood. . . . Shutting black women out of this highly charged area could thus symbolize rejection not just of their performance but also of themselves."[21] Although Grundy is talking about the selection of cheerleaders during desegregation 40 years ago, her comments are salient for today's situation as exemplified in the above study of WMS. At WMS, cheerleaders represented a particular type of girl—one who affiliated herself with "Prep" (which meant white) and all the markers that go along with that label.

However, as we illustrate throughout this book, cheerleading is a dynamic cultural icon that changes to accommodate shifting cultural norms and beliefs. Cheerleading continues to be dominated by whites, but African Americans, Native Americans, Asian Americans, and Hispanic Americans do participate in cheerleading. In many cases, this opportunity has come about only through fierce struggles challenging racial inequalities and injustices. In other places, schools have implemented inclusive selection processes that encourage a diversity of people to participate in cheerleading. Greg Webb, senior vice president of the Universal Cheerleading Association, has noted the changing demographics of cheerleading squads over the last 10 years. At UCA camps in South Texas, half of the participants are now Mexican Americans.[22] Many of these squads have begun to challenge the assumption that cheerleading is just a "white girl thing" by insisting on a different "cheerleader look," different music, and different forms of choreography. For example, the Woodrow Wilson High School cheerleaders of Los Angeles were recently highlighted in *American Cheerleader* magazine. This mostly Hispanic squad won the 2002 NCA regional championship, even though the school for which they cheer has limited financial resources. One of their coaches, Gus Rodriguez, says that although his girls don't fit the stereotypical pattern of blond and white cheerleaders, he teaches his squad to take pride in their differences. Further, he choreographed the squad's competition routines to Latino women's music, like that of Jennifer Lopez and Thalia. He named this year's competition theme, Latin Divas.[23]

Perhaps as long as cheerleading is associated with a particular look (embodied by perkiness, fake smiles, long spiral curl ponytails with ribbons, and a certain body type), cheerleading will continue to be a "white girl thing." The question for many, such as Dr. Harold Bishop, becomes how to change that so that more racially and ethnically diverse squads can be seen in our schools and universities. Twenty years ago, one solution was to establish quotas. If the school population was 25 percent Latino, then the cheerleading squad should be 25 percent Latino. Such actions are contested today by groups who dismiss the value of quotas as a way of achieving diversity. Bishop offers another suggestion. He works with school districts in the Southeast to meet court-ordered mandates to end segregation. He notes that one of the biggest complaints from the minority community in these school districts is the lack of diverse cheerleading and dance teams. His recommendation to these school districts is to allow anyone who wants to be a cheerleader the opportunity to cheer as long as he/she meets the academic requirements. However, this response is not readily embraced in a society that lauds competition and individualism. Others have suggested a return to the more traditional aspects of cheerleading, such as leadership and school spirit, in the selection process rather than the current concern with tumbling. They argue that a return to leadership as the primary criterion for cheerleader selection would help diminish the advantage wealthier students have. Perhaps the most hopeful response lies in squads such as the Woodrow Wilson High cheerleaders, who are changing the image of cheerleading to be more congruent with their own cultural backgrounds. Highly visible as the seventh-place winner in the USA nationals, perhaps they can serve as proof that cheerleading isn't just a white girl thing; Cheerleading is for everybody.

FROM CHEER MAKING TO MONEY MAKING

The Spirit Industry

Singing in the rain
Just singing in the rain
What a glorious feeling
Pitter, patter
UCA! UCA!
Pitter, patter
UCA! UCA!

During the summer of 2002, hundreds of cheerleaders across the United States participated in the above rendition of the old classic "Singing in the Rain." They weren't cheering for a player, or a specific game, or for themselves. They were literally cheering for the largest cheerleading corporation in the United States, the Universal Cheerleading Association (UCA), and the sponsor of the cheer camp they were attending. Typically, business and cheerleading are not linked, especially in a cheer. But cheerleading is more than an activity that generates enthusiasm. It is also an activity that generates money—lots of money—to the tune of close to one billion dollars a year.[1] It is also a business that continues to prosper even in difficult economic times. As Larry Herkimer, founder of the first cheerleading association, notes: "No matter how bad times are, are you going to tell your little girl she can't have her sweater and skirt and pom-pons? Hell, you'll sell the boat before you have to tell her that."[2]

But how did cheerleading become such big business? How does the corporate, impersonal side of cheerleading mesh with a pervasive cheerleading culture that promotes intimacy, small-town patriotism, and eternal perkiness? To understand the corporate side of cheerleading, we must first turn to the stories of two cheerleading giants. It is a classic American capitalist tale— American entrepreneurship at its finest.

A Tale of Two Cheerleading Companies

Meet Lawrence (Larry) Herkimer. By all accounts he is the man responsible for institutionalizing cheerleading in American high schools and colleges. Often called "Mr. Cheerleader," he began the first cheerleading association (NCA), published the first cheerleading magazine (*The Megaphone*), wrote numerous books on cheerleading, and even created a jump that is performed by thousands of cheerleaders across the world and named after him—the herkie. Until 1974, Herkimer was the undisputed king of cheerleading.[3]

Enter Jeff Webb. If Herkimer is the "Father of Cheerleading," Webb is the ungrateful stepson. Jeff was a cheerleader at the University of Oklahoma in the late 1960s, went to work for Herkimer in 1971, and after only three years with NCA, left the company to begin a competitive company, taking several of the NCA employees with him. Acknowledged by many as the man who revolutionized cheerleading to be the sport it is today—complete with athleticism and entertainment—Webb is now the CEO and president of Varsity Spirit Company, the largest cheerleading company in the United States.[4]

Together, these two companies (Herkimer's former company, National Spirit Group and Webb's Varsity) control approximately 75 percent of the cheerleading market, both in camps and uniform sales.[5] Both have ventured overseas, both have introduced full-length glossy catalogs to sell their vast array of cheerleading products, both have begun offering cheerleading camps at resort sites throughout the United States, both have tapped into the dance market, and both recognize the importance of Herkimer's words spoken 20 years ago: "Once I have a cheerleader; she's mine for life."[6]

Larry Herkimer

Lawrence (Larry) Herkimer began his cheerleading career at North Dallas (TX) High School, where he cheered for four years and was known for his gymnastics ability. He moved on to Southern Methodist University (SMU) and cheered his freshman year there. He then took a hiatus from school and served in the Navy for two years during World War II. Upon re-entering

SMU, he once again joined the cheerleading squad and became head cheer-leader of the football team in 1946.[7] After graduating in 1948, he was hired to teach gymnastics at SMU, but he soon began receiving calls to train cheer-leading squads on the weekends. When a school offered him either a fee of $500 or a dollar per child, he opted for the latter, saying, "I'm a gambler, and I gambled. I knew the kids would come!" He was right—4,500 came, and he raked in $4,500.[8] Recognizing the potential profit of the cheerleading train-ing business, Herkimer quit his job at SMU and began working in the cheer-leading business fulltime. In 1953, with a $600 loan, he founded a for-profit cheerleading club, the National Cheerleading Association (NCA).[9]

After several years of focusing solely on training cheerleaders, Herkimer recognized another untapped market—the cheerleading uniform business. Because of the seasonal nature of cheerleading (cheerleaders are typically se-lected in late spring, attend camp in June or July, and begin cheering in Au-gust or September), cheerleading uniforms had to be custom made and delivered in a short period of time. Many apparel companies were unwilling to take on such work on a subcontract basis, so Herkimer, always the entre-preneur, began searching for alternative ways to meet this market demand. His solution: buy a knitting mill and run it himself. With $100,000 of his own money, Herkimer purchased a mill outside of Dallas and hired area women, who could work overtime in the summer, to meet the heavy sea-sonal sewing demand. He also purchased other defunct businesses to ac-commodate his growing product line. For example, he bought an old milk-carton factory and turned it into a megaphone making factory.[10] Herkimer is also credited with the invention of the pom-pom to provide more flash and pizzazz on the new color televisions. He later changed the name to "pom pon" after conducting a camp in Hawaii, where he discovered that U.S. army troops stationed in the Philippines, Japan, and Pacific Islands used "pom pom" as a slang term for sexual intercourse.[11] Over the years, Herkimer has sold over 1.5 million pom pons.[12]

But Herkimer's influence on cheerleading cannot be measured solely in dol-lars. Personally creating jumps, yells (e.g., paper bag, sputnik, and supersonic), and cheers, Herkimer was instrumental in institutionalizing a cheerleading cul-ture.[13] Indeed, Herkimer spent much of his early years actually writing many of the cheers that found their way onto high school and college campuses and are still performed today. While institutionalizing a cheerleading culture through his camps and his books (e.g., *Championship Cheers and Chants, Pep Rally Skits and Stunts, The Complete Book of Cheerleading*), he also created an in-dustry. Passionate about cheerleading and able to foster that passion in millions of others, Herkimer was extremely successful in turning passion into profit. In 1981, Herkimer could claim two-thirds of the high school cheerleading market and one-half of the college market with a pretax profit of $2 million.[14]

In 1990, Herkimer's National Spirit Group reported $45 million in annual revenues, and in 1994, 200,000 high school and college cheerleaders attended NCA camps producing (along with other parts of the business) a gross income of $60 million.[15] Although Herkimer is no longer part of the National Spirit Group, the organization, which is a private company and does not release profit figures, continues to be a "substantial company in a highly competitive niche," says Jerry Dilettuso, current CEO and president of National Spirit.[16]

However, what Herkimer didn't know 30 years ago was that by the mid-1990s his company would take a back seat to the company of his former protégé, Jeff Webb. Speaking of Webb's success, Herkimer asserted: "Jeff ought to be thrilled he ever knew me."[17]

Jeff Webb

Jeff Webb, fresh out of college, began working for Larry Herkimer in 1971. Starting out as general manager, Webb was promoted to vice president six months later. From all indications, Webb was in line to take over the daily operations of the entire company.[18] However, there was a clash of personalities and vision between the older Herkimer (who is 25 years older) and the younger Webb. Webb wanted to modernize cheerleading as he explains: "There was real resistance to bringing that organization into [modern times]. I was out there among the cheerleaders, and I knew that kids had changed and that we really weren't providing what they needed. So I decided to do it myself."[19]

In 1974, Webb left NCA and the National Spirit Group to form his own company, the Universal Cheerleading Association (UCA), with $5,000 of his own money and $80,000 borrowed from friends and relatives. The new company was headquartered in Memphis to capitalize on the connections he had in the Southeast and Midwest. When Webb left NCA, he took 12 of the instructors with him. Greg Webb, Jeff's brother, was one of them. He explains how UCA revolutionized cheerleading: "When we left NCA, all we were doing were shoulder stands. It was actually a guy who left with us, Gilmore Williams, All-American gymnast and trampolinist at Iowa, who came up with three different progressions, just like gymnastics. All these transitions these girls are doing right now, you could probably trace it back to 1975."[20] Kline Boyd was another one of the earlier UCA instructors. He explains why they left NCA:

> We thought it could be more than what it was—more athletic, more gymnastics, bring the crowd more into it. We thought we had a better way of doing it. Not that anything was wrong with the other place but they weren't

ready to be as progressive. Jeff had all this great energy—that kind of driving force and the kind of talent he brought with him, it attracted a lot of people.[21]

At the time of Webb's defection, Herkimer accused him of hiring "hot dogs" rather than "teachers."[22] However, Webb's vision for changing cheerleading to showcase athleticism and to entertain crowds paid off. After his first year of operation, Webb reported a profit of $850.[23]

In 1979, Webb and eight individuals willing to invest $25,000 each, added Varsity Spirit Fashion and Supplies, which sold uniforms, camp gear, accessories, and equipment for cheerleaders. One of the reasons for opening the apparel side of the business was that he had been asked by many of the cheerleaders at his camps for uniforms more in line with the new image of the cheerleader as an athlete and entertainer. Webb notes: "There were 2 or 3 companies that had been at the uniform business for a long time, who were basically just reprinting their catalog from year to year. Their delivery was bad and the quality of the merchandise was even worse."[24] Webb responded to these demands and introduced new styles of uniforms that were sharper, more athletic looking, and made of material that would stretch and not tear while tumbling, building, and stunting. In 1989, Webb and his original backers sold two-thirds of the company to two investors. Three years later, they took Varsity Spirit Corporation public on the NASDAQ. Original shares sold for $12.[25] At the time of this writing (May 2003), Varsity stock traded for $6.47 a share.

Credited with the transformation of cheerleading from a sideline activity to an athletic spectacle worthy of attracting its own audience, Webb began organizing national championships in 1981 and by 1983 had convinced ESPN to televise them, thus bringing cheerleading into the homes of people all over the world.[26]

Today Varsity, which continues to be run by Webb and four of the original instructors (Greg Webb as senior vice president/general manager Universal Cheerleading Association, Kline Boyd as executive vice president/general manager Varsity Spirit Fashions, Robert Tisdale as director of human resources, and Kris Shepherd as vice president of special events), claims approximately 60 percent of the cheerleading business and has posted profits every year. In 2001, the company generated revenues of $147.5 million—$82 million from the apparel side and $59.4 million from camps and special events.[27] Varsity employs 500 full-time and permanent part-time workers and more than 2,000 summer instructors and trainers. Over the years the company has dabbled in other ventures—football equipment through Riddell and soccer apparel and equipment through the acquisition of the Umbro license. Neither of those ventures proved profitable; now Varsity is back to concentrating on the bread-and-butter of their organization—cheerleading.[28]

The Selling of American Cheerleading

From Herkimer's and Webb's modest beginnings as cheerleading entrepreneurs, the spirit industry, as it is typically called, has mushroomed into a billion dollar business that includes everything from the selling of camp gear and uniforms, to pom pons and hair extensions, to how-to books and instructional videos. However, it was the selling of cheerleading training that first captured the attention of profiteers. Through cheerleading camps, young women and men are socialized into the world of cheerleading, taught the many tricks of the trade in motivating others, and inculcated with the values of leadership, ambassadorship, and cheerfulness. But, cheerleading camps serve another purpose: they are the advertisement for all the other cheerleading products and services.

Cheerleading Camps

It's a hot sultry late May afternoon. Eleven hundred junior high and high school cheerleaders and 200 dancers are gathered at the Coleman Coliseum on the University of Alabama campus for the opening ceremonies of the world's largest UCA event. The vast majority are female. All the girls look remarkably similar: they are wearing matching outfits or cheerleading uniforms; their hair is in a ponytail with a ribbon, and their bodies are physically fit. There are no waifs or Kate Moss's here. A few squads have rollers in their ponytails in preparation for the performance of their home routine tonight. The camp director, vice president of operations at UCA, Bill Seely, stands in front of the girls and says in a dynamic, motivational voice: "Hello Alabama." There are some perfunctory screams, but the response obviously doesn't please Bill. "This must be a tennis camp. Let me go and find the cheerleading camp." At this, the 1,300 campers begin screaming, pumping up the volume considerably. Bill then repeats two more times "Hello Alabama." The girls work themselves into an appropriate frenzy, so by the third time the walls are ringing with adolescent wails, shrieks, whistles, and claps.

"This year we will be working on building traditions," Bill tells the crowd just as 51 UCA staff members run into the coliseum as the Crimson Tide Fight Song is piped in. They get the crowd going by dividing the coliseum into halves—one side is ALA; the other is BAMA. ALA BAMA, ALA BAMA, ALA BAMA—again the crowd is worked into a frenzy. With loud music reverberating from the sound system, Big AL (the Alabama mascot) skateboards into the coliseum, runs onto the stage, and picks up the lid of a trashcan. On it is painted the word "Yell." He holds it up, and once again the crowd breaks into ear-splintering yells. He then pulls out a watergun from the trash can and douses the crowd with water. The girls go wild!

The campers calm down for Bill to go over the expectations of the week. He tells them they will each be assigned a Big Brother or Big Sister (one of the staff) who will work closely with them to make sure they get everything they possibly can out of camp. He talks about the awards, ribbons, and evaluations but adds that this year, they are introducing a new award, "The Traditions Award," which will be given at the end of camp to the team that best exemplifies traditional cheerleading with an emphasis on spirit raising, leadership, and athleticism. By the end of his opening comments, you can feel the energy in the building that clearly speaks to the expectations for the rest of the week: work hard but have fun. And the squads who work the hardest and have the most fun will be awarded, as Bill Sealy holds it up, the Spirit Stick. Guess what? The crowd goes wild once again.

Across the country in Moscow, Idaho, home of the University of Idaho (where the ski team has a stronger record than the football team), another UCA camp is in progress. The Northwest does not have the same reverence for cheerleading as does the South. Some attribute this to the fact that girls in this region of the country are more involved in outdoor activities such as cross-country skiing and mountain climbing, so they don't seek the physical activity that cheerleading provides. Others say that cheerleading just came late to this rugged part of the country. For example, one town in Central Idaho just formed its first cheerleading squad. Whatever the reason, the number of campers is smaller than the event in Alabama. Although small in numbers, you can hear the same kind of fierce enthusiasm in the campers' responses to their UCA instructors, Kim and Michael, in Moscow, Idaho, as you do in Tuscaloosa, Alabama.

During camp, the 100 or so girls learn a half-dozen sideline cheers, two dance routines, some basic stunting techniques and a tradition cheer that they have created themselves. But camp is not all work. On this last day of camp, they sing the boogie chant with which we began this chapter. Each time the chant is sung, the cheerleaders must sing it while they are doing something physically silly, which includes putting their thumbs out, elbows in, knees together, booty up, heads up, eyes closed and tongues out. This final rendition, if you can visualize it, with knees together, booty up, and tongues out provides quite the entertainment for those pedestrians ambling along next to the field of girls.

On the final day of camp, most of the girls are dressed in their cheerleading uniforms and have their hair in bows and glitter spray. Each squad performs the dances and cheers they have learned and debut their new tradition cheer as well. All the campers watch enthusiastically, support those who are performing, and respond to the squad's commands probably better than their home audience. Then, it's time to present the awards. No squad will leave empty handed. There are large and small trophies, red, white, and blue ribbons, and outstanding, superior, and excellent ratings. Every squad receives some kind of award, from the best dance routine to the most improved dance routine. When a team wins a trophy, the squad members scream, jump up and down, and hug each other while their captain retrieves the prize. Sometimes they hug again. This is just an emotional prelude to what is coming next: the camp goodbye scene.

Cameras are a must, and squads and individual girls take pictures with their four UCA instructors. Some of the squads present the instructors with big thank you cards, which have individual notes about how much they appreciated the help and encouragement. There are lots of "You are awesome!" written comments along with little hearts. Some senior girls are crying, since this will be their last cheerleading camp, while most of the girls give each other sisterly hugs amid calls of "See you next year."

With all the talk of tradition, Big Sister, Big Brother, teamwork, and undying affection, it's hard to imagine the corporate side of cheerleading; but cheerleading camps and training alone generate more than $100 million a year. Bill Horan was one of the first to recognize the potential profit of cheerleading training. A former World War II paratrooper and member of the University of Miami pep squad, Horan began offering cheerleading clinics in the 1940s. Described in *Life* magazine as "circuit-riding evangelist in the mystique and practice of cheerleading," [29] Horan ran his clinics like boot camps:

> You, the girl who dropped a fork at lunch, you do ten minutes extra exercise.
> And you on the end—are you chewing gum?
>   No sir.
> You're not?
>   No sir. I just swallowed it.

Mile-long runs, inspections, and strict rules were all part of this cheerleading boot camp, which cost $45 a week to attend in 1959. The purpose of these camps, as described by Horan, was to teach leadership and self-discipline to young women: "to separate the jellyfish from the real troopers. Most girls are afraid to bring out their leadership qualities. But my girls wind up running their campuses."[30]

However, it is Larry Herkimer who is given the title of the "Father of Cheerleading Clinics."[31] He offered his first cheerleading clinic when he was a senior at SMU in 1948. Fifty-two cheerleaders attended that first class.[32] In 1973 (25 years after offering his first clinic) 100,000 cheerleaders attended the 158 camps offered by NCA. The NCA camp at Illinois State in 1973 provides a glimpse into the cheerleading camps of the day. Seven hundred and thirty-five energetic, screaming girls (no boys) showed up at the five-day camp, which cost them $55. In the morning, they got up early, ate breakfast, and participated in cheer, tumbling, and pom pon workshops. After lunch in one of the university cafeterias (where the girls got to meet college boys if they were lucky), each squad received individualized instruction with some free time that was typically spent preparing for that night's evaluation (not competition). At night, each squad performed a cheer brought from home and a cheer taught that day. The NCA instructors provided written feedback and awarded either a superior, outstanding, or excellent ribbon. At night all the squads gathered again for cheering, chanting, and inspirational words such as the following, often delivered by Herkimer himself: "When you become a cheerleader, you become an 'instant.' No, not an instant cup of coffee, an instant success. You become instantly popular, instantly imitated, an instant trend-setter. What you do, what you wear, how you act, what you are—everything about you will be carefully studied—and carefully copied by all the other girls."[33] At the end of the day, the coveted red, white, and blue Spirit Stick was awarded to the squads that demonstrated the most energy and enthusiasm, the best work attitudes, and the most cooperative spirit.

During the camp, the instructors asked particular girls to be part of the annual fashion show in which they modeled the uniforms and camp gear available from NCA. Also part of the week festivities was a skit night, where different squads performed original gags, skits, songs, and dance, and a very emotional last night event in which girls often promised to be cheerleaders and best friends for life.

In 1973, Herkimer employed 230 instructors for his camps, paying them anywhere from $100 to $200 a week plus room and board. Jeff Webb was the chief instructor at the Illinois State camp in 1973.[34] Two years later he was offering his own camp under the name UCA.

Operating his new business from his apartment and his car, Jeff Webb knew he was taking a risk at the time by trying to compete with the leader of the industry, but as he describes himself, he was "opportunistic." He and the 12 former NCA instructors who came with him to start the business canvassed the greater Memphis area with announcements about the new camp. When the door opened, 4,000 showed up. He held 20 camps that first summer. Eventually surpassing NCA in the number of camps and the revenues collected, UCA in 2002 held 1,400 camps with 250,000 participants.[35]

In addition to UCA and NCA, dozens of other smaller cheerleading associations also offer camps. Cheerleaders of America (COA), The Fellowship of Christian Cheerleaders (FCC), Christian Cheerleaders of America, Americheer, Atlantic Cheer and Dance, American Cheer Power are just a few of the many organizations catering to those in search of cheerleading training. Each organization sells its camps on having something a little different to entice its customers. "Building People Before Pyramids" is the motto for the Christian Cheerleaders of America (CCA).[36] The Fellowship of Christian Cheerleaders (FCC) touts 1 instructor per 20 cheerleaders. "There's not a better instructor/camper ratio in the country!"[37] Atlantic Dance and Cheer offers cheerleading boot camps "intended to train the very toughest athletes around. We suggest only bringing cheerleaders and dancers that are brave enough to face a challenge."[38]

From boot camps to private camps to commuter camps to traditional residential camps to the most recent development, resort camps, cheerleading training comes in a variety of packages. Residential camps are the most common. Typically held on college and university campuses, cheerleaders stay in dormitories and spend several days participating in such structured activities as stunt class, pom class, cheer class, and team-building workshops. Resort camps, offered at plush resort sites such as Beaver Run, Colorado, Jeckyl Island, Georgia, and South Padre, Texas, are the newest form of cheerleading camp. Cheerleaders stay in hotels with maid service, comfortable beds, and cable television. The curriculum is less demanding, and many squads choose this kind of camp because it offers a time to bond with one another and build team camaraderie by tanning on the beach or hiking in the mountains. For those squads who don't want to attend the traditional residential camps or perhaps don't have the money to go to a resort camp, they can hire instructors for a private camp, with more personal, one-on-one instruction.[39]

Special Events

Camps are just one of the many special events in which cheerleaders can participate-events that generate money as well. At many camps, individual girls and squads receive invitations to attend regional and national championships and special invitationals. In 2001, an estimated 100,000 cheerleaders participated in some kind of championship.[40] At the 2001 UCA national championships in Orlando and California, 40,000 people participated.[41] Individual girls and squads also receive invitations to participate in such special events as the Macy's Thanksgiving Parade, the Pro Bowl, the All-Star trip to London, and the Senior trip to the French Riviera. None of these events is inexpensive, as explained by the parent of one high school cheerleader who was invited to participate in the annual Macy's Parade on Thanksgiving Day in New York. The fee: $1,600 plus airfare for the participant and $1,200 plus airfare for family members. The $1,600 covers uniform, instructional tape, jacket, bag, sweatshirt, meals, hotel accommodations for a week, one

Broadway play, one ticket to the Radio City Music Hall Christmas Spectacular, and some additional sightseeing trips.[42]

Cheerleading companies themselves seek other corporate sponsors for these events. Chick-fil-A, Nike, Claire's, AT&T, Gillette, and Thermasilk are just a few of the many companies that recognize the potential profits of cheerleading. Some merely want to put their four-ounce bottle of shampoo in the hands of 40,000 cheerleaders; others plug their products to the television audience through commercial air-time; and still others use the concentrated number of cheerleaders in one place at one time as focus groups to test their products and to market ideas.[43]

Uniforms, Camp Gear, and Accessories

Although camps, special events, and championships provide the visibility for cheerleading companies, they are not, in fact, the major revenue producer for cheerleading companies such as UCA and NCA. Rather, camps are the advertisement for the real money-maker—uniforms, camp gear, and accessories. As mentioned earlier, the cost of being a cheerleader at the junior and high school level can run as high as $1,000 a year. One uniform alone can cost as much as $250. The choices for uniforms are endless, as a quick glance at any cheerleading catalog attests. There are shell tops, bodyhuggers, bodyliners, halter tops, jumpers, jackets, midriffs, A-line flare skirts, A-line pleat skirts, A-line freestyle skirts, wrap skirts, 12-pleat freestyle skirts, 16-pleat freestyle skirts, pleated skirts, mini-pleat skirts, long pants, beltlines, sweaters, oversized sweaters, hooded pullovers, warm-up suits, vests, frat jerseys, push-down socks, crew socks, chevron socks, anklets, monogrammed socks, bodysuits, tights, Nike shoes, Adidas shoes, Kaepa shoes, gloves, two-color parade gloves, briefs, "boy cut" briefs, and, of course, pom pons (solid color, 2-color, 3-color mixed, layered, vinyl-metallic show, vinyl-metallic dazzler, mini, rooter, metallic show, and holographic). Each of these can be ordered in over 20 different colors with your choice of embroidered mascots, tackle twill lettering, chenille lettering, and monogramming.

In the last few years an interesting development in the commercial world of cheerleading has been the entrance of mainstream stores, such as Limited Too, JC Pennys, and Sears into the cheerleading market. Recognizing the growing popularity of cheerleading and the demand for camp clothing in particular, these companies have created their own line of cheerleading T-shirts, shorts, and backpacks.[44] The Limited Too retail store has even begun offering cheerleading uniforms.

And it's not just big national cheerleading associations or large specialty stores who make money from cheerleading. Numerous specialized companies have successfully targeted the cheerleading market. Take, for example, Cheer Curls Express, which specializes in customized synthetic wiglets to help create a "cheerleading look." Each member of the squad simply cuts a small clip of her hair and sends it to Cheer Curls, where the wiglet is custom made for individual color and texture. The price of the synthetic hair: $38.[45] Indeed, cheerleading has provided niche market opportunities for a vast number of small companies, from "Mom and Pop" companies who make child-size collegiate uniforms for little girls and boys, to fundraising companies offering frozen cookie dough, cheesecakes, candles, pecans, totes, stuffed bears, flower bulbs, and Boston butts (pork, that is).

These cheerleading companies and businesses now have two magazines devoted solely to their field in which they can advertise their wares. *American Cheerleader,* introduced in 1994, caters to high school and collegiate squads. Eight years later, *American Cheerleader Junior,* geared to younger cheerleaders, published its first issue. In addition to offering ample space for advertising, the magazines also feature articles on how to be a better cheerleader, how to look your best on game day, and how to master the most difficult stunts. While most companies were suffering in 2001, the conglomerate that owns *American Cheerleader* and *American Cheerleader Junior,* with 200,000 magazines in circulation and approximately 1 million readers, reported an 18 percent growth.[46]

For some readers, this discussion of cheerleading as a corporate and for profit enterprise contradicts their images of cheerleading. Indeed, image is everything in the advertising and selling of cheerleading products, services, and paraphernalia. Cheerleading sells only if people believe that cheerleading itself is worth buying. In the last 30 years, cheerleading has suffered an image problem, as many people have come to question the value and purpose of the activity itself. Thus, cheerleading has undergone a repackaging, as we have demonstrated throughout the book; with that repackaging has come a renewed commitment to sell cheerleading as not simply a fun activity for the here and now, but as excellent preparation for success in the adult world of work.

Selling the "Leader" in Cheerleader: Preparation for Corporate America

> That's all right; that's OK.
> You're gonna work for us one day![47]

Critics of cheerleading have little understanding of why so many people spend so much money on the products and services described above to support an activity that they see as having no long-term benefits. After all, how many 40-year-old cheerleaders do you see as compared to 40-year-old tennis players, swimmers, pianists, and violinists? Unlike softball, baseball, and basketball, which have adult leagues throughout the United States, very few cheerleading squads for adults exist in this country. Thus, the spirit industry must not only sell the cheerleading commodities listed above, they must also sell cheerleading as an activity that has both short-term and long-term dividends.

Advocates of cheerleading have long praised the activity for the leadership skills it teaches. Indeed, the development of leadership has been a central component of cheerleading from it very beginnings. Cheer leaders at the beginning of the twentieth century (all of whom were male) were being prepared to take their role as leaders in the competitive world of capitalism in the new industrial order of America. Like school athletes, cheer leaders were popular young men who were admired for their abilities in galvanizing others to action and struggling against adversity. "Slim" Carter, a 1924 University of Alabama cheer leader, typifies the American cheer leader of his time: "In dispensing 'Bama Spirit,' 'Slim' was an inexhaustible fountain, from which all weary, discouraged rooters drank, were filled and refreshed. So it is that the old 'Bama Spirit' raises up men to carry on as the older ones go and thus it shall ever be."[48] Even with the feminization of cheerleading, leadership ability was often one of the requisite criteria for being selected a cheerleader, as detailed by Lawrence Herkimer and Phyllis Hollander in 1975: "A cheerleader is above all a leader . . . and as such can be someone who will effectively channel and control the enormous energy of a crowd into constructive, positive behavior."[49]

Certainly, throughout this country cheerleaders continue to act as leaders for their school and community, and selling that leadership component of cheerleading is imperative for its continuation in middle schools, high schools, and colleges now and in the future. Lapwai, Idaho, home of the Lapwai High Wildcats, is located on the Nex Perce Reservation in the northern part of the state. The Lapwai High School cheerleaders are typical in many respects. They are considered leaders at their school, and a glimpse into their activities for one Homecoming weekend illuminates the responsibilities of cheerleaders and the many leadership opportunities for them. On Thursday night, they stay up late decorating the flatbed trucks that are magically turned into Homecoming floats for the Friday parade. On Friday, they ride in the parade, lead the pep rally, decorate the gym for the Homecoming Dance, practice the dance they have been saving for Homecoming, lead the fans in cheers during the game, and sponsor the Homecoming Dance after the game. Several of them are also members of the Homecoming Court, so they must excuse themselves early during the second quarter to dress for the Homecoming half-time festivities, and then return, back in their cheerleading uniforms, to the sidelines for the third quarter cheering. On Saturday morning, they bring bread, salad, spaghetti meat sauce, or noodles to the school and work a two-hour shift at the concession stand for the regional volleyball tournament. Many members of the squad are also players on the volleyball team and must sandwich their concession work between their games.

But not all squads are like the Lapwai cheerleaders. With the competitive turn in cheerleading in the last few years, many cheerleading squads skip Friday night football games to prepare for Saturday morning competitions. Hence, many administrators, fans, and parents, upset with the new priorities of these squads, have called for cheerleading to return to its roots. In fact, one of the mantras we heard at cheerleading camps held during the summer of 2002 was "Let's put the leader back in cheerleader." To encourage the leadership aspect of cheerleading, UCA introduced a new award, the Traditions Award, at its 2002 camp. Bill Seely explains:

> We've seen a trend over the last 10 years with people focusing too much on the third prong, which is the athleticism. Their stakeholders, their customers, their athletic departments, their schools and universities don't see the value of them any more. We've always preached to do the crowd stuff, but they've kind of gravitated more towards the athleticism and performance parts, so the Traditions Award is taking what has been great in the past, which created the leaders, the President Bush's, Eisenhower's, Trent Lott's, and not lose that piece and make it part of the bigger picture. That's why we brought back the traditions. Those things are important, leading the crowd is important, and getting up and doing the ambassador stuff for your school is what makes cheerleading unique and makes it different from all other activities and what draws the caliber of person to the activity.[50]

But cheerleading is not just about developing leadership for the here and now. Rather, to ensure the longevity of cheerleading in a culture that has often demeaned it as a shallow, superfluous activity, cheerleading today must be packaged and sold as excellent preparation for leadership positions in the future, particularly in the corporate and business world. Proponents of cheerleading are quick to tell you, as we have discovered throughout this book, that cheerleading is one of the best preparations for adult professional life. Debbie Purifoy, coach of the University of Alabama cheerleaders, a former cheerleader and UCA instructor, explains:

> Being a cheerleader, particularly at the college level, is like being the SGA [Student Government Association] president. You get to do things that other athletes don't do. You're a leader in your school. I tell them if you're a strong B student and you go for an interview, you'll have the interview skills and the comfort level that others won't. You'll get the job over the one with all A's. Our

cheerleaders get incredible jobs out of college because of their networking. Like the plane we're on this Saturday [to fly to the Oklahoma-Alabama game], there will be very wealthy alumni, influential people, and they'll make great friends with them. It's a high profile position.[51]

The high school cheerleaders attending camp in Ashburn Village, Virginia, would agree. These girls aspire to be engineers, lawyers, doctors, and scientists. They believe that cheerleading helps to prepare them for their future professions by teaching them to be poised, self-confident, self-disciplined, coordinated, and athletic. Stephanie Ramirez explains, "You think cheerleaders are all ditsy, but I don't think so. You're helping yourself. It helps you have confidence in yourself. I'm thinking I could be a doctor or a nurse, and this discipline is good for me."[52] According to these high school girls, cheerleading helps them build their resume, which, in turn, gives them a competitive edge in the harsh world of college admissions to top-tiered universities. Katie Boyd, 1999 *American Cheerleader* Cheerleader of the Year, 1999–2000 National Cheerleader of the Year, and World Cheerleading Association (WCA) Cheerleader of the Year, would agree. President of her university's student government association, she maintains a high grade point average majoring in economics and political science and plans to attend either law school or medical school. She was also selected first runner-up in the America's Junior Miss pageant. To what does she owe her success? "Cheerleading," she is quick to tell you, "has given me the confidence to realize I can achieve any goal I set my mind to."

Learning to speak in front of a crowd, learning how to overcome obstacles, fighting hard for what you want, leading others, and portraying a positive attitude (even when you don't feel so perky on the inside)-these are the traits often touted by cheerleading advocates as translating into good jobs in the future. Cindy Villarreal, a former Dallas Cowboys Cheerleader, contends that cheerleading is excellent preparation for success in the corporate world. This corporate recruiter would agree:

> Cheerleaders have what it takes for a challenging position in industry. They have displayed their ability to manage extremely hectic schedules; they have the high energy to succeed in the demanding job environment. They are usually capable of handling several responsibilities at one time which is central for business management. We like the balance that cheerleaders have developed in their lives.[53]

University of Kentucky's cheerleading coach, T. Lynn Williams, sees cheerleaders as a highly sought-after commodity: "I've got a note on my desk right now from a pharmaceutical company with a sales opening. I get these calls regularly. Cheerleaders know how to set goals and how to work hard to attain them. They are competitive, and they understand personality and body language."[54]

This focus on how cheerleading can prepare one to be successful in the adult world of work is exemplified in one of the regular features of *American Cheerleader*. The "Star Struck" segment highlights a famous adult who was a cheerleader when she/he was younger. Featured over the last few years have been Dixie Chicks lead singer Natalie Maines,[55] veteran actors Ann-Margaret and Jack Lemmon, Kirsten Dunst (star of *Bring it On*), *7th Heaven* actors Catherine Hicks and Beverly Mitchell, singer Christina Aguilera, and Lela Rochon, who is described this way:

> With her take-charge, spirited attitude, Lela Rochon became one of the few African-American actresses to overcome Hollywood typecasting when she landed the female lead in the John Grisham thriller *The Chamber,* winning a role originally written for a blonde. "That really let me know that my ability could stand up against anybody's," says the 34-year-old 5'9" former model who made *People Magazine's* 50 Most Beautiful list three years back. Not surprisingly, one of her performances was as a cheerleader.[56]

What is emphasized in this feature as well as throughout the magazine is that cheerleaders are not ditsy blondes who have no future goals other than dating and marrying the quarterback; rather, the cheerleader today is smart, confident, and prepared for the challenges of the adult world.

Even some of our youngest cheerleaders articulated an understanding that cheerleading puts you on a particular route that will yield dividends in the future. Here twelve-year-old Shanna talks about the future benefits of being a cheerleader: "Cheerleading helps your grades. I mean helps your diploma when you get older. So when you get older, they're going to ask you, if you want to apply at a college. If you've been a cheerleader, they'd know that they could trust you and stuff."[57]

Lynn Snowden, a writer for the magazine *Working Woman,* rather humorously agrees that trying out for cheerleader (even if you don't make it) is excellent preparation for the world of business. She explains, "For anyone who has ambitions beyond being prom queen, this [when you read the list of who made cheerleader] is the moment when you learn everything you'll ever need to know about the business world. The three most elementary maxims [are] Life Isn't Fair; Ability Doesn't Guarantee Success; and Yes, of Course Looks Count."[58] She contends, tongue-in-cheek, that former cheerleaders really do have an advantage once they get to the adult world of work: "Cheerleaders go through life with a quiet confidence, as if they never have to prove anything again, and failed cheerleaders tend to have a weird intensity, as if they have to prove everything a million times. . . . And while ex-cheerleader Meryl Streep calmly goes about her business of mastering accents and collecting Oscars, there's Jane Fonda (who tried out but lost out), compulsively molding herself into the perfect cheerleader, first aerobically, and then surgically. She even won an Oscar for her portrayal of an ex-cheerleader in *Coming Home*."[59]

We certainly haven't conducted any scientific study linking cheerleading with adult success; however, the list of former cheerleaders that are highly successful adults is impressive. If you want to go into politics, cheerleading might be excellent preparation. Franklin Roosevelt, Dwight Eisenhower, Ronald Reagan, George Bush Sr., and George W. Bush were all cheerleaders, as were Senators Trent Lott, Thad Cochran, and Kay Bailey Hutchison. If a career in journalism is what you want, consider that the highest-paid morning talk show host, Katie Couric, is a former cheerleader. And if you have aspirations to go into the entertainment industry, being a cheerleader may be better preparation than drama, band, choral classes, or participation in Little Theater. Madonna, Meryl Streep, Samuel L. Jackson, Raquel Welch, Sandra Bullock, Ashley Judd, Jack Lemmon, Steve Martin, Lela Rochon, Kathie Lee Gifford, Faith Hill, Sela Ward, Susan Lucci, Calista Flockhart, Sally Field, Paula Abdul, Kirk Douglas, Terri Hatcher, Reba McIntyre, Cybil Sheppard, and Cameron Diaz were all cheerleaders.

Cheerleading and the American Art of Making Money

As we have demonstrated throughout this book, cheerleading represents different things to many different people: leading teams to victory, motivating apathetic fans or social protestors, winning national cheerleading championships complete with money and trophies, ensuring one's place at the top of the popularity hierarchy, securing a scholarship for college. Our first chapter presented cheerleading as a uniquely American activity, one that says much about our culture. So it should be of little surprise that cheerleading is not only about all of the above, but is also a story about making money. For most people, however, the big business facet of cheerleading is a surprise. That's because, once again, cheerleading has never been taken very seriously by most adults. Ultimately, this is why Lawrence Herkimer and Jeff Webb were able to create such successful businesses that continue to thrive. They understood the passion that cheerleading elicits and gave the activity its due. They took cheerleading and cheerleaders seriously, and by doing so, opened the door for countless other entrepreneurs to sell their cheerleading products and services to an ever-expanding and loyal market. From selling camps, to curls, to cookie dough, to spirit ribbons, companies catering to cheerleaders have found what Julie Davis, president of Lifestyle Ventures, the publisher of *American Cheerleader* and *American Junior Cheerleader,* calls a "marketer's dream."[60]

In today's postindustrial order, dozens of cheerleading companies have fashioned a spirit industry that commodifies the warm feelings and nostalgia for the past role of cheerleaders as well as the athleticism and entertainment of the new role. From small-town gym owners to national corporations, cheerleading has become like many other activities and sports in the United States—a capitalist venture that has for the last 50 years sold extremely well and, from all indications, seems to have a bright future. According to Jebb Webb, CEO of UCA, his company expects an 8 percent growth in 2002, and Larry Herkimer, who is officially out of the business of selling cheerleading, still contends, even in our current economic woes: "Cheerleading is Depression-proof."[61]

CHEER EVOLUTION

The Changing Face of a Cultural Icon[1]

Chew tobacco, chew tobacco,
Chew tobacco, SPIT!
Eagle High School, we are IT![2]

hen the above cheer was yelled in 1916 at Eagle High in Nebraska, it was obviously intended to resonate with the male fans and male cheer leaders in the exclusive world of male sports. However, as we have pointed out, cheerleading today is not the cheerleading of 1916. Today 97 percent of the 3.8 million people who participate in cheerleading are females. Consequently, to take cheerleading seriously, as we have tried to do in this book, we must address the gendered meaning of cheerleading.

The history of cheerleading, with its changing practices, purposes, and roles, can be read as a story that tells us much about the dynamic nature of gender roles and expected gendered behavior in our society. From the beginning of cheerleading in the late 1800s to the late 1940s, cheerleading squads were comprised primarily of males, and males who cheered were considered manly heterosexuals. However, by the late 1950s, cheerleading had changed significantly from an activity representing ideal masculinity to one representing ideal femininity. In discussing the shift from a "naturally" masculine activity to a "naturally" feminine activity during this time period, Laurel Davis points out that cheerleaders came to symbolize "dominant ideology about how females should look and act in our society."[3] That is, females/cheerleaders were to be pretty, possess appealing figures, play a secondary role to males, and were not to be taken too seriously. Consequently, males who participated in cheerleading constantly had their masculinity and sexual identity questioned, resulting in the pervasive belief, still held by many, that "manly men" don't cheer. In the aftermath of Title IX (1972) and the second wave of feminism, ideas about the appropriate role and behavior of women in society began to shift, and cheerleading changed once again to reflect new ideals about normative femininity and ideal girlhood. In the twenty-first century, girls and women are expected to be Superwomen—slim, beautiful, and nice but also intelligent, physically fit, self-disciplined, confident, and tough.[4] The shift in cheerleading to accommodate these new ideals can be seen in the emphasis on competitive cheerleading, the demand to recognize cheerleaders as athletes, and the movement to classify cheerleading as a sport. Further, the competitive and athletic nature of cheerleading has made it easier for males to participate in the activity without having their masculinity or sexual orientation challenged.

Writing more than 50 years ago, Simone de Beauvoir, author of *The Second Sex,* recognized that the lack of physical activities for young women is one of the reasons why girls and women have not made more progress in achieving equality: "the lack of physical power leads to a more general timidity: she has no faith in a force she has not experienced in her body; she does not dare to be enterprising, to revolt, to invent; doomed to docility, to resignation, she can take in society only a place already made for her."[5] We have seen ample proof that cheerleading today offers a space to do exactly what de Beauvoir saw as essential for the progress of women—a space for some girls and young women to take pleasure in the physicality of their bodies. Through exercise, physical conditioning, mental training, and leadership-building, girls who cheer are allowed to enter a world that not too long ago was reserved only for males. Hence, many argue that cheerleading offers one opportunity, among many, for a new generation of girls to take pleasure in the physicality of their strong, fit, athletic bodies.

Cheerleading continues to be popular not simply because it allows girls and young women to be physical, athletic, and competitive. After all, participation in traditional sports fulfills those needs. Rather, cheerleading offers something else. Candance Berry, coach of one of the most successful high school cheerleading squads, Greenup County, Kentucky, believes that "cheerleading offers budding young women something that girls' basketball, track, soccer, softball can't offer: lessons in how to be a lady, how to be tough without imitating men."[6] Although we don't totally agree with Berry, we do believe that she comes closer than do many feminists to understanding why cheerleading continues to be appealing to millions of girls and women in this country. They do not have to give up their femininity (hence their sexual appeal) in order to participate. As one seventh-grade cheerleader told us, cheerleading is not like sports because it allows you to be a girly girl.

Interestingly, most of the adults with whom we talked, particularly at the middle and high school, tended to downplay the sexualized nature of cheerleading; yet, the girls themselves viewed the sexualized component of cheerleading as one of the most appealing facets, as Julie, an eighth-grade cheerleader, unabashedly told us: "I'm in for the short skirts and the guys!" Valerie Walkerdine notes that the erotic is rarely allowed to enter into schools because it is too dangerous.[7] Cheerleading, however, does allow the erotic to enter into schools, offering one of the only school-sanctioned spaces for girls to play with two different gendered identities—the all-American girl next door and the sexually provocative woman. We experienced this firsthand at a recent pep rally. The high school squad was on the field performing fairly seductive dance moves, complete with pelvic thrusts and breast juts, to a hip-hop song. Several girls in the stands stood up and began performing impromptu their own equally seductive rendition of the dance. Within seconds, a teacher reprimanded the girls in the stands and told them to sit down. The cheerleaders finished their dance and received a resounding applause. The girls in the stands were publicly shamed.

As Michelle Fine and Debra Tolman have noted, middle and high schools typically ignore female sexuality in both the formal curriculum (sex education) and informal curriculum.[8] Girls are taught that desire and being desired are something to be ashamed of—something to be hidden or dismissed. Girls get the message in a variety of ways that it is their responsibility, because they supposedly feel no such desire, to "just say no" to boys' sexual advances. Nowhere in schools is it acknowledged that girls are also sexual beings, although, outside of school, they are saturated with sexually provocative images of women and men displaying various forms of physical desire. With very few school-sanctioned places for girls to exercise sexual agency, it is no wonder, then, that the erotic appeal of cheerleading is so seductive to many girls as they are making the transition from childhood into womanhood. Cheerleading is not only approved but encouraged by the adults in the school, thus offering a safe space for girls to try on or play with a sexual identity in a public venue. Hence, cheerleading can be understood as a way for girls to try out for womanhood via a socially acceptable activity.

Further, cheerleading affords a space for girls to enjoy many of the benefits of sports and athleticism without having to face the negative repercussions that come with playing traditional sports, such as basketball and softball. When Brandi Chastain ripped off her shirt in a moment of exuberance after her soccer team had won the Women's World Cup, her actions triggered a vociferous debate about why she did what she did. What was read, by some, as an act positioning her as a sexy athlete contradicted her position as a serious athlete.[9] Female athletes all over this country are constantly barraged with questions about not only their femininity but also their sexual orientation. They are forced to take extreme measures, in some cases, to convince the public that they are heterosexual feminine women as well as accomplished athletes.[10] Cheerleaders may have to fight against stereotypical labels of "ditsy," "dumb," and "shallow," and fight for validation as serious athletes, but, unlike other female athletes, they never have their femininity questioned nor do they have to fear being stigmatized with the label lesbian and the negativity often associated with such a label. They are allowed, and some would say encouraged, to be heterosexy athletes who are tough, take risks, and sweat profusely while still maintaining a smile and exuding sex appeal.

In arguing that cheerleading offers a space for some girls to revel in the physicality of their bodies, to experiment with a sexualized identity in a safe space, to enjoy the fun and freedom of unrestrained physical activity, and to bond with other girls, we do not want to suggest that cheerleading can only be understood as a positive experience for girls and women today. The meaning of cheerleading, as we have tried to reveal, is much more complicated than that. One cannot forget that cheerleaders in many places in this country still cheer predominantly for male athletes. Or that the cheerleading companies are headed primarily by males. Or that professional cheerleaders are used as a commodity by male-dominated organizations for the purpose of selling men's sports. Or that once cheerleading became feminized it lost its status, and despite gains made in some areas, it still does not have the same status as sports, which continue to be associated with males and masculinity. It is impossible to study cheerleading in this country without facing the reality that in many places and in many ways, it is about the cultivation of a certain form of femininity and a means to socialize girls and young women into their role as supporters of men as they battle each other in the sports arena and experience all the fun, action, and excitement.[11] This really hit home with us one Friday night at a high school football game where, after a touchdown was scored, we witnessed female cheerleaders getting on their knees and bowing up and down to the male players.

This same squad that is encouraged to participate literally in male worship is, at the same time, held to the highest moral code of conduct. As leaders of their school, they are expected to be model female citizens. Indeed, despite the changes in cheerleading over the last 50 years, cheerleaders today are often expected to abide by higher moral standards than what is expected of their peers, particularly their male athletic counterparts. These standards, many would argue, are relics of a time in which women's virtue, although lauded, was used to keep women in a subservient position to men. While many football players are notorious for their immoral behavior—womanizing, drinking, using drugs, cursing, fighting—cheerleaders are expected to be beyond reproach. Admittedly, professional cheerleaders complicate the image of cheerleaders as ideal women, but it must be remembered that even though professional cheerleaders, such as the Dallas Cowboys Cheerleaders, present themselves as sexually alluring—the fantasy of every man—they, too, are held to strict moral standards. No smoking, no drinking in uniform, and no dating the football players. They can be as sexy as they want in dress and in routines on the field, but underneath they are still to exude the All-American, sweet cheerleader of the 1950s.[12]

In this way, cheerleaders are very similar to Miss America pageant contestants. Both have come to represent the contradictions of ideal American womanhood. For example, in keeping with the pure image of womanhood, no reigning Miss America is permitted to visit any establishment that serves alcohol.[13] Similarly, most high school squads must sign a code of conduct promising that they will not smoke or drink while in uniform, while most collegiate squads are not allowed to visit a bar in uniform. To win the coveted title of Miss America, contestants must engage in a variety of tricks to ensure their female perfection, from duct-taping their breasts together for greater cleavage, to applying hair spray on their buttocks so that the bottom of the swimsuit will not move during that phase of the competition.[14] Cheerleaders, even when competing in physically taxing routines, must also employ a few tricks to ensure they exude femininity—keeping rollers in their hair until seconds before their squad is called to the mat, purchasing synthetic curls to make sure their spiral ponytails are perfect, applying bright red lipstick to accentuate their mouths, and, yes, even spraying their bloomers with hairspray to keep them from moving during the competition.

Both groups of women serve as diplomats for their community, school, state, or nation and as the official hostesses for many public ceremonies such as parades and ribbon cuttings. In this public capacity, they are expected to be model girls and women. Obviously, both activities have changed in many ways to accommodate the shifting expectations for women in this society. The Miss America pageant has renamed the swimsuit phase of the competition, the "physical fitness" phase, in keeping with the same athletic trends found in cheerleading.[15] However, although Miss America contestants must be smart, beautiful, and sexy, and cheerleaders athletic and attractive, the two groups of women must continue to represent the best of ideal girlhood/womanhood, and when they don't, there is trouble. Consider the four senior cheerleaders in Hempstead, Texas, who confessed to being pregnant at the beginning of the school year and were summarily dismissed; or when Vanessa Williams lost her Miss America crown due to the publication of photos of her both nude and in various sexually provocative poses; or the more recent case with Miss North Carolina, who was stripped of her title after her ex-boyfriend shared nude pictures of her with the media.[16] Certainly, thousands of girls across this country get pregnant before they are married. Hundreds of women have allowed their boyfriends to take nude pictures of them (even Dr. Laura engaged in this behavior when she was younger), but because cheerleading and Miss America symbolically represent a form of virtuous, chaste womanhood, any individual girl or woman who violates this unwritten code of conduct must be dismissed or this icon of American womanhood itself becomes sullied or tarnished.

This regulatory function of cheerleader as the standard by which all women are judged has serious repercussions for not only high school and college girls but also for adult women as well. The late Erma Bombeck humorously alludes to this in a column she wrote in 1982: "Have you ever wondered what happens to rejected cheerleaders? Some of them, convinced there is nothing to live for, drop out of school and enter the labor market. Others put the disappointment out of their minds and go out for ice hockey. But most of us become eaten up with resentment and dwell on it for the rest of our lives."[17] When we began this research we, too, enjoyed a good laugh at the seemingly absurdity that something such as not making cheerleader would be such a life-defining moment. However, after conducting research and writing this book, we can no longer laugh in the same way we once did when we hear such stories. We certainly heard countless stories about the joys of being a cheerleader—how being a cheerleading increased one's self-confidence, offered a place for girls to revel in the pleasure of being in the limelight, provided a space to develop athletic abilities, and prepared one for positions of leadership at college and in the adult world of work. But, we have also heard the other side of the story—the stories, such as the following two, about not being selected cheerleader and the devastating after-effects of that event:

> My sister had been a cheerleader since she was in seventh grade. In her eleventh grade, she tried out for cheerleading and didn't make it. She was so devastated, as were my parents, that she moved from the town and the high school, where she had been all her life, to come live with my husband and me. My parents threatened to file a lawsuit. They even talked to an attorney. It seemed just as important to my mom as it was to my sister that she be a cheerleader. As I tried to console her tears and anguish, she told me one day, "I don't know who I am now. I'm supposed to be a cheerleader."[18]

> My daughter had been a cheerleader her sixth, seventh, eighth, ninth, and tenth grade year. She was the best tumbler on the squad, but when she tried out for the varsity squad she didn't make it, and it has ruined her life. All of her core friends left her. She withdrew from everyone and everything. She went from being the girl who did everything to the girl who was afraid to try anything. Her confidence was shot. And even now, as a college student, she is afraid to try anything, to put herself out there, for fear she will be rejected

again. I didn't realize how much her identity was wrapped up in being a cheer-leader. I don't know what to do for her and I'm afraid this is going to have se-rious repercussions when she starts looking for a job.[19]

No doubt, the cheerleader is a powerful cultural icon that symbolizes for many an ideal form of femininity, the pinnacle to which all girls and women should strive. This is why so many adult women cling to that identity long past the time that it holds any material reality. That cheerleading identity operates as proof that somehow they had, at least at one time in their life, achieved the highest status of American womanhood. They were popular, desirable, slim, and beautiful. Kim Irwin, a former cheerleader and founder of a feminist cheerleader group, realized in her mid 40's that in many ways she was still clinging to the image of the cheerleader: "I became a cheerleader in 1963 because I wanted power and love. I yearned to be popular, show off my figure and personality, and attract boyfriends. Thirty years later I still longed to be peppy, pretty, and pleasant more than anything."[20] It is no co-incidence that the traits Kim ascribes to the cheerleader are also the traits we continue to ascribe to the ideal woman in our society. By representing the ideal for which all girls and women should strive, cheerleading acts symbol-ically as a powerful agent of regulation even in the lives of women and girls who have never been a cheerleader nor have ever desired to be a cheerleader. In the following excerpt, Susan, a thirty-six-year-old woman, recounts the role cheerleaders played in her adolescent and adult identity:

> I hold cheerleaders, and what they represent, partially responsible for me being an outcast. They, the cheerleaders, set the norm, which I did not follow, so I was out. Intellectually, of course, I understand the benefits of cheerleading to some, but I also understand the damage it can do to others. At times I am envious of the confidence that cheerleading must have instilled in most cheerleaders. I have never been worshipped or looked to as a fashion and femininity (!) leader, but I imagine it must be a heady experience. I have always wondered what my life would have been like had I been petite, blonde, pretty, and bubbly.[21]

Like Susan and Kim Irwin, the identity of countless women in this coun-try is still connected in fascinating ways to their cheerleading identity or their lack thereof. For many women, it is a positive feeling that stays with them throughout their life. As one 65-year-old woman who was a cheerleader in the early 1950s told us: "Now that I'm old and overweight, I'm able to tell people that I was a cheerleader. That makes me feel good."[22] For others, not main-taining the "cheerleader look" into their adult lives causes them to have nega-tive feelings about themselves, particularly about their bodies. Repeatedly throughout our writing this book, a middle-aged woman would quietly, as though she was embarrassed, share with us that she was a cheerleader in high school. This revelation would then be followed up with some deprecating statement about how she looked now: "I'm so fat now" or "I used to be pretty" or "Can you believe I was the popular girl? You wouldn't know it now." Still other former cheerleaders have expressed that cheerleading was supposed to set you up for a particular route in life – "cheerleading, sorority, Junior League," and when one failed to achieve that route, it was proof of one's own personal failure. One 42-year-old former cheerleader told us, "unfortunately somewhere along the way you get the idea [from being a cheerleader] that you were special and if you never achieve that again, it makes you feel left out."[23] A 38-year-old woman said, "being a cheerleader in a small town gives you a sense of false importance. You realize in college and in the 'big City' that you are pretty insignificant. It's hard to go from being a somebody to a nobody."[24]

Undeniably, the cheerleader still operates as one of the most visible American cultural icons of femininity, but the norm of femininity that cheerleading represents continues to be defined very narrowly, leaving many girls and women on the margins. For all the changes in cheerleading over the years, cheerleaders do not disrupt the gendered boundaries to which this society still clings. True, they assume some of the characteristics associated with masculinity, such as intense physical training, strength, and power, but cheerleaders never step over the line. Cheerleaders merely flirt with the masculine without ever trying to actually be a man. And in our society, girls and women who do transgress gendered boundaries, who are judged by society to step too much over the accepted boundaries between men and women, continue to suffer tremendously. Women body builders know this. They understand the discomfort many men and women experience in seeing a woman who looks too much like a man, so they have to exaggerate their femininity with makeup, girlish hair, and breast implants.[25] The Women's National Basketball Association (WNBA) knows it—players are often asked to accentuate their femininity off-court through makeup, feminine hairstyles, and public affiliations with male partners.[26] The All American Girls Baseball League (the one made famous in *A League of their Own*) knew it. Recognizing the importance that female baseball players must be seen as feminine and lady-like, each player was given a Charm School Guide that they were expected to follow religiously.[27] Many would argue that all female athletes understand this all too well, and hence the push from coaches, managers, image consultants, and promoters for women athletes to present themselves as "heterosexy" athletes.[28]

Cheering for Change!

The good news is that the history of cheerleading demonstrates that it is a dynamic cultural icon that changes in response to social, cultural, historical, and economic factors. Further, individuals and groups of individuals are actively engaged in changing not only the purposes and practices of cheerleading but also the meaning of the phenomenon itself. Take, for example, a varsity squad in a Southern town in which cheerleaders have symbolically served as the vestal virgins for the male football team for years. Recently, the cheerleaders have become much more involved in the athletic and competitive nature of cheerleading and have quit performing many of the stereotypical duties of cheerleading: no more decorating the boys' lockers before the game, no more staying up late on Thursday night and getting up early on game day to secretly place goody bags in their lockers. Upset by the cheerleaders' lack of attention to their sons, the mothers of the players now have taken over the role of making goody bags. The girls have initiated new traditions: riding around late at night and "rolling" (toilet papering) the players' houses. Although some might find this new tradition juvenile and still focused on the boys, we read the girls' active attempts to remake cheerleading practices and traditions as helpful in exploring the question, What are the transformative possibilities of cheerleading for a new generation of girls and women and boys and men?

Many groups and individuals have already begun answering this question. As we have pointed out throughout this book, transgressive elements appear in all kinds of cheerleading places. Most apparent are the cheerleaders we describe in chapter 2. The Radical Cheerleaders and X-Cheerleaders take complex societal problems and transform them into provocative chants with the aim of creating a more socially just world:

> Flipping thru Vogue, What A BORE
> Ladies please Ladies, LET'S EAT MORE
> I've got booty in the back & a lot up front
> My secret is . . . I EAT LUNCH
> Now I'm in control & Ready to RIOT
> Against your demands that I need to DIET
> I'm gonna take up space & LOVE my size
> Cuz FAT & FABULOUS is on the rise
> Hey Hey FAT & FABULOUS is on the rise![29]

Gay and lesbian squads use cheerleading to bring attention to the realities of living with HIV/AIDS and to raise money to make the lives of those suffering with this deadly disease better. Cheerleading coaches throughout this country are waging a full-fledged campaign to bring attention to the athleticism involved in cheerleading so that, hopefully, outdated stereotypes will vanish, and cheerleaders will finally get the respect they deserve.

We take these transformations of cheerleading as a beginning point for rethinking what cheerleading could be. What might it mean for different kinds of people to participate in cheerleading? What might it mean for cheerleading to be practiced in a variety of venues? What might it mean if cheerleaders cheered with different purposes? What might it mean if cheerleading competitions combined intellectual and physical challenges?

What might cheerleading become if it were more multigenerational? The Wilmington Golden Pom Pom Cheerleaders certainly have taught us that cheerleading is not just for adolescents. In fact, we heard stories of the pride and pleasure that their grandchildren experienced when the squad performed at their elementary schools. What might it look like if the Wilmington Golden Cheerleaders' grandchildren had performed with them? How might grandparents, parents, and children come together for family cheer fests? Could they include riffs on their cultural heritage and family histories?

How about religious cheerleading? One Idaho Unitarian Universalist minister, Joan Montagnes, whose creative pre-offertory comments have always elicited laughs and extra change, came up with a few interesting cheers to encourage the congregation's giving. She started with:

> We've got the church
> We've got the people
> But look at our roof
> We've got no steeple

After she remembered that cheers are usually thematic and that it was water communion Sunday, her next attempt was a bit stronger:

> Drip drip drop drop
> Come on folks, put it in the pot!
> Splish splish splash splash
> Here come some baskets, put in the cash
> Crick, stream, pond, river
> Dive right in and be a big giver
> Don't be hesitant, don't be slow
> Open the flood gates and help our cash flow[30]

Although her arm movements were a bit sloppy, her cheer elicited applause and smiles from her congregation. But what could have happened if the entire congregation had joined in the cheer? What if it had been chanted a few times? Would the pockets have been deeper?

What would happen if cheerleading returned to its improvisational roots? How might that engender both athletic as well as intellectual challenges? What if cheerleading competitions provided squads with a topic and gave them a half day to create a physically challenging and clever cheer, a kind of extemporaneous cheering? What if the topics centered around local or national political and cultural events? What if cheerleading competitions started imitating the Def Jam poetry competitions in which audience members voted on the most interesting cheers? How might that play out on Friday and Saturday nights in football stadiums and basketball courts across this country? What would happen if the two opposing cheerleading squads competed as well against each other? How might improvisational cheering remake cheerleading and provide a space for different kinds of girls and boys to enter the cheerleading world? If improvisation is the heart of jazz, then could it become the heart of cheerleading? What would it mean to cheer from the heart?

What might happen if male and female cheerleaders decided to try on each others' roles? What if men became the "piece of art" and women "the frame"? Laurel Davis argues that cheerleading hasn't embraced what it could become with the re-entrance of men because it has become mired in traditional gender roles, with men supplying the brute strength and women the aesthetics.[31] What would the activity look like if men took on some of the aesthetic roles and activities that women now hold? Jesse Nishikawa, a Washington State University cheerleader, laments the fact that he isn't allowed to dance but must stand by and watch his female peers perform the cheer/dance routine that has become the mainstay of American cheerleading. His fellow male cheerleaders, intent on upholding the traditional masculine image of male cheerleaders as the solid, sturdy frame, want nothing to do with the dance part of cheerleading. But couldn't the inclusion of men in the obligatory cheer/dance open up new ways of conceptualizing it? How might the grace and beauty of male gymnastics be highlighted in cheerleading, instead of the male strength primarily? What might it look like if female strength was highlighted as we saw in a recent All-Star competition in which early adolescent girls were the bases for boy fliers? What would it look like to see women bases throwing up male flyers? That would certainly change what we see as the ideal body type of female cheerleaders. How might that image reconfigure how children, both male and female, understand what it means to be a cheerleader in this society?

What would cheerleading look like if it was not understood only as an able-bodied activity? How might those in wheelchairs, with hearing aids, and those with other physical challenges remake cheerleading in ways similar to that of several dance companies? The Axis Company in Oakland, California, and Dancing Wheels in Cleveland, Ohio, provide opportunities for "stand up" (temporarily abled) and "sit down" (disabled) dancers to participate in professionally choreographed dances that challenge the normalized view of dance.[32] The sit-down dancers are as integral to the composition as the stand-up dancers. Kathleen Farber, who participated as a temporarily abled dancer in a workshop, describes one of the dance movements: "We also did traveling movements across the floor. The sit-down dancers moved across the floor in their wheelchairs and the stand-up dancers moved across the floor using their feet and legs. Interestingly, some of the traveling movements involved turns and spins. . . . The stand-up dancers were often very envious of how the sit-down dancers could spin so readily on their wheels."[33] What would a cheerleading routine look like if it integrated the skills and strengths of both sit-down and stand-up cheerleaders? How would such a reconfiguration of cheerleading routines change the physical requirements for being a cheerleader?

What would it mean if cheerleading itself became an object of study at schools? We aren't talking about a cheerleading preparation class where students are taught tryout cheers such as that held at Wichita Middle School, but rather a class that explores critically what cheerleading is all about. "Cheering for Ourselves" does just that. Kim Irwin, creator of "The WANTED: X-Cheerleaders Project," in conjunction with the Institute for Labor and the Community (ILC), conducts workshops with New York City girls ages 9 through 12 and their teachers. In the workshop, cheerleading is the vehicle to talk about gender inequality, racism, body image, stereotypes, and sports. Kim explains why cheerleading is a powerful tool to empower all girls:

> If cheerleading's role is to inspire and motivate positive behavior, these principles must lead us to critically look at ourselves and disentangle our myths from our realities . . . The ideal cheerleader is not blonde, blue-eyed, petite, pony-tailed, White, straight, and female but intelligent, honest, confident, creative, athletic, a good performer, and a skilled leader. When I look at cheerleaders, I want to see America. I want to see all the colors, the sizes, the shapes, the moves, and the voices of America. Cheerleading that represents freedom and justice for all is really worth cheering about.

The girls conduct research about these various topics, discuss their findings, and collaboratively construct cheers, such as the following, and then share them with their peers, parents, and community members:

G-I-R-L-S
Girls, girls, we RULE!
We can play sports, we're tired of your lies
And we don't have to stay home baking cherry pies.
We can beat you any day
We're fast; we're strong
And we know how to play.

In the "Cheering for Ourselves" curriculum, cheerleading not only becomes a vehicle to explore girls' and women's status in this society, it also is a means to implode the myths and stereotypes in which females are framed.

What would happen if schools opened the activity of cheerleading to all who were interested? What would happen if there wasn't just one cheerleading squad but a myriad of squads that had different purposes and involved different strengths so that for every school competition, be it an athletic activity or a quiz bowl match, there would be cheerleaders present to motivate the team, albeit in different ways?

These reimaginings of cheerleading are helpful in addressing Nancy Fraser's questions: "What are the processes by which definitions and interpretations inimical to women's interests [here cheerleading] acquire cultural authority? What are the prospects for mobilizing counterhegemonic feminist definitions and interpretations to create oppositional groups and alliances?"[34] In other words, who has the power to define what cheerleading represents? How can that definition be re-envisioned in more positive, inclusive, and emancipatory ways? How can feminist critiques of cheerleading be used, not to abolish cheerleading, but to make cheerleading more feminist—more supportive both of individual girls, women, boys, and men and the collective good of all?

The Ambiguous Icon of Cheerleading

We must admit that we didn't begin this study with a very sympathetic leaning toward cheerleading. As feminist academics, we believed that cheerleading needed to be a quaintly remembered but extinct activity in the post - Title IX era. Like many critics of cheerleading, we thought girls should be playing between the sidelines, not cheering on the sidelines. Further, the commodification and sexual objectification of the cheerleading body and image to sell everything from men's football to pornographic films was further proof to us that cheerleading signified a particular image of women that was detrimental for all women in their continual struggle for full equality and integration into our society. However, after spending four years fully engrossed in the world of cheerleading, we have made somewhat of a turn, in that now we understand cheerleading as holding multiple meanings. Cheerleading is neither inherently good nor bad. Overzealous mothers may make the activity appear shallow and narcissistic. Shy girls who have little self-confidence can become strong, confident leaders. Radical Cheerleaders may use cheerleading to make the world a better place. Through exclusionary tryout procedures, school districts may encourage only the wealthiest to participate, or, through a more creative tryout procedure, they may make cheerleading open to everyone. Latino cheerleaders may actively rewrite what it means to be a cheerleader. Cheerleading may be the only high-status activity for girls at a school, or cheerleading may be but one of many valued activities in which girls can gain status and respect. Cheerleaders may serve as positive role models that exemplify all the traits deemed desirable in school: good grades, leadership, and responsibility; or as negative role models whose elitist attitudes create an unhealthy school environment. The point is that cheerleading can and does take on different meanings in different contexts. Some can be read as the emancipatory, transformative possibilities of cheerleading; others can be seen as solidifying a narrowly defined view of womanhood that limits the opportunities of all girls and boys—both those who cheer and those who do not. The cheerleader is an ambiguous cultural icon precisely because cheerleading is itself ambiguous.

However, we want our participants to have the final word on the significance of this American cultural icon. From the Lapwai High School cheerleaders in Idaho, to the X-Cheerleaders in New York, to the Cheer Authority All-Star Wizards in Alabama, to CHEER San Francisco, to the Wilmington (North Carolina) Golden Pom Pom Cheerleaders, all of these squads love to cheer because cheerleading brings them great pleasure and joy. In many ways we have become cheerleading converts simply because it's hard to dismiss the joy, pleasure, and fun that cheerleading brings to millions of people not only in the United States but around the world. The playfulness of cheerleading, which is so central to why cheerleaders cheer, is easily dismissed as a frivolous topic of study. Yet, when the fun is lost, the possibilities sometimes are as well. As feminist academics, we are well aware that we are often accused of having no understanding of pleasure, and, even worse, with our critical analysis, we often suck the very joy right out of any topic we study. Our hope is that this book hasn't sucked the joy out of cheerleading, but rather that we have presented cheerleading as a complex, and often contradictory, American icon that deserves, after 135 years, finally to be taken seriously.

NOTES

Introduction

1. Rick Reilly, "Sis! Boom! Bah! Humbug!" *Sports Illustrated* 91 (18 October 1999): 116.
2. John Strausbaugh, "The Anti-Cheerleader," *New York Press* 30, 4–10 October 2000, <http://www.nypress.com/13/40/news&columns/publishing.cfm> (20 January 2003).
3. This is the number of cheerleaders according to the American Sports Data, a firm that tracks participation in sports, as cited in Marilyn Elias, "Cheerleading Leaps into the Dangerous-Sport Camp," *USA Today,* 22 October 2002, <http://web5epnet.com/citation.asp?tb=1 . . .   98024+sm+KS+so+b+ss +SO+84BA&fn=31&rn=37> (22 January 2003).
4. Kathy O'Malley, "The Reluctant First Lady: Jesse's Girl: Terry Ventura Wrestles with Her New Role," *McCall's* 126 (July 1999): 58–60.
5. During the early years, cheer leader was written as two separate words. By the 1920s, a hyphen had been added. Later, the hyphen was omitted, and the spelling became one word, cheerleader.
6. "Organized Cheering," *The Nation* 92 (1911): 5–6.
7. "November Yells that Win Games," *Literary Digest* 83 (8 November 1924): 36.
8. Mary Ellen Hanson, *Go! Fight! Win!: Cheerleading in American Culture* (Bowling Green, OH: Bowling Green University Press, 1995), 2.
9. Pamela Grundy, *Learning to Win: Sports, Education, and Social Change in Twentieth-Century North Carolina* (Chapel Hill: The University of North Carolina Press, 2001), 7.
10. Greg Webb, senior vice president/general manager, Universal Cheerleading Association; interview by author, tape recording, Memphis, Tennessee, 24 June 2002.
11. For an excellent description of the role of football in small towns and communities, see H. G. Bissinger *Friday Night Lights* (New York: Harper Perennial, 1990); Dianne Divoky and Peter Schrag, "Football and Cheers," *Saturday Review* (11 November 1972): 58–65; Douglas Foley, "The Great American Football Ritual: Reproducing Race, Class, and Gender Inequality," *Sociology of Sport Journal* 7 (1990): 111–135.

12. Arturo Gonzales, "The First College Cheer," *American Mercury* 83 (1956): 100–104.

13. Hanson, *Go! Fight! Win!;* Gonzales, "The First College Cheer."

14. For an excellent discussion of how norms of femininity are changing around the world, see Sherrie Inness, ed., *Millennium Girls: Today's Girls around the World* (Lanham, MD: Rowman & Littlefield, 1998).

15. For a thorough discussion of status groups and the activity of cheerleading in elementary, middle, and secondary school, see Patricia Adler and Peter Adler, "Dynamics of Inclusion and Exclusion in Preadolescent Cliques," *Social Psychology Quarterly* 58 (1995): 145–162; Penelope Eckert, *Jocks and Burnouts: Social Categories and Identity in the High School* (New York: Teachers College Press, 1989); Donna Eder and Stephen Parker, "The Cultural Production and Reproduction of Gender: The Effects of Extracurricular Activities on Peer Group Culture," *Sociology of Education* 60 (1987): 200–213; Don Merten, "Burnout as Cheerleader: The Cultural Basis for Prestige and Privilege in Junior High School," *Anthropology and Education* 27 (1996): 51–70; Don Merten, "The Meaning of Meanness: Popularity, Competition, and Conflict among Junior High School Girls," *Sociology of Education* 70 (1997): 175–191.

16. Title IX was enacted in 1972 and prohibits any program receiving federal aid to discriminate based on sex. Its implementation has been highly contentious in college and high school athletics.

17. Christa Grizzle, interview by author, tape recording, Tuscaloosa, Alabama, 1 October 2002.

18. Milea [pseud], interview by author, tape recording, Wichita [pseud], 2 March 1999. This interview was part of an ethnographic study we conducted in 1998–99 in which all participants were promised anonymity.

19. Grundy, *Learning to Win.*

20. Dr. Harold Bishop, professor, interview by author, tape recording, Tuscaloosa, Alabama, 27 September 2002.

21. For a discussion of the integration of high school and college athletics, see Derrick Gragg, "Race in Athletics: Integration or Isolation?" in *Sports in School: The Future of an Institution,* ed. John Gerdy (New York: Teachers College Press, 2000), pp. 79–90; Grundy, *Learning to Win;* C. Richard King and Charles F. Springwood, *Beyond the Cheers: Race as Spectacle in College Sport* (Albany: State University of New York Press, 2001); Gary Sailes, ed., *African Americans in Sport* (New Brunswick, NJ: Transaction Publications, 1998); John Watterson, *College Football: History, Spectacle, Controversy* (Baltimore: The Johns Hopkins University Press, 2000).

22. Grundy, *Learning to Win,* 285.

23. Teresa Gutierrez, "Tamsey Muniz, La Raza Unida Party and the Chicano," 26 May 1997, <http://burn.ucsd.edu/archives/raza/1997.05/msg0001.html > (19 September 2002).

24. When Larry Herkimer led a camp in Hawaii, he discovered that "pom pom" was a slang term used by military men to denote "sexual intercourse."

Hence, Herkimer changed the name to "pom pon," although the general public still continues to refer to these cheer accessories using the original term. See Harold Wentworth and Stuart Flexner, ed., *Dictionary of American Slang* (New York: Thomas Y. Crowell Co., 1975).

25. Ann Bagamery, "Go! Fight! Win!" *Forbes* 130 (27 September 1982): 136–140; Sonja Steptoe, "The Pom-Pom Chronicles," *Sports Illustrated* 75 (30 December 1991–6 January 1992): 38–44, 46.

26. Ken Woodmansee, "Cheers: Jeff Webb's Multicolored World Wide Spirit Machine," *Memphis Business* 3 (Third Quarter 1993): 14–19.

27. Erik Brady, "Cheerleading in the USA: A Sport and an Industry," *USA Today* (26–28 April 2002): 1A.

28. Marlene Cota, vice president-marketing, Universal Cheerleading Association, interview with author, tape recording, Memphis, Tennessee, 25 June 2002.

29. Data for this book was derived from a variety of sources. We conducted a large ethnographic study about girls and leadership at a middle school in the Midwest in 1998–99 in which we conducted 93 interviews with 61 middle school girls. In 1999, we surveyed 31 former cheerleaders from the 1940s to 1990s. We interviewed 12 people employed by the Universal Cheerleading Association in June 2002. We conducted formal interviews with seven coaches at the middle, high school, and collegiate level in 2002. We also conducted field observations of two UCA camps in the summer of 2002, 12 high school football games, 4 collegiate practices, 4 high school practices, 20 All-Star practices, and a regional cheerleading competition. However, much of the data presented in this book was derived from informal interviews, conversations, and communications that occurred as we made contacts through a variety of people from all over the United States as well as overseas. From conversations with strangers in photography shops, to acquaintances at social gatherings, to colleagues at academic conferences, to contacts made through our connection to the Universal Cheerleading Association, to e-mail conversations with perfect strangers who have now become our friends, we have literally communicated with hundreds of cheerleaders, former cheerleaders, and cheerleader pundits during the last four years. Their insights have greatly informed this book.

Chapter 1

1. Marcie Frazee, "Patriotic Cheers," 3 September 2002, <cheerleader@imagi-comm.com> (5 September 2002).

2. Shelia Angalet, "Patriotic Cheers," 2 September 2002, <cheerleader@imagi-comm.com> (5 September 2002).

3. Eddie Adams, "Our American Spirit," *Parade Magazine* (8 September 2002): 4–5.

4. Leigh Stope, "Workers Blame Corporate Cheerleading for Huge Retirement Losses with BC-Enron Investigation," *AP Worldstream,* 8 February 2002,

<wysiwyg://211/http://web1.epnet.com/cit . . .
04187+sm+KS+so+b+ss+SO+6C48&fn=41&m=43> (23 August 2002).

5. John Strausbaugh, "The Anti-Cheerleader," *The New York Press* 30, 4–10
October 2000, <www.nypress.com/13/40/news&columns/publishing.cfm>
(20 January 2003).

6. Ronald Smith, *Sports and Freedom: The Rise of Big-Time College Athletics*
(New York: Oxford University Press, 1988), 70.

7. For an excellent discussion of this first intercollegiate football game, see
Richard Mandell, *Sport: A Cultural History* (New York: Columbia University
Press, 1984); Smith, *Sports and Freedom;* and John Watterson, *College Foot-
ball* (Baltimore: The Johns Hopkins University Press, 2000).

8. Arturo Gonzales, "The First College Cheer," *American Mercury* 83 (1956):
100–104; "Tiger," *The New Yorker* 23 (12 July 1947): 18–19.

9. Gonzales, "The First College Cheer."

10. "Tiger," 19.

11. See Michael Hurd, *Black College Football: 1892–1992* (Virginia Beach, VA:
The Donning Company, 1993).

12. Robert Park, "Sport, Gender and Society in a Transatlantic Victorian Per-
spective," in *From 'Fair Sex' to Feminism: Sport and the Socialization of
Women in the Industrial and Post-Industrial Eras,* ed. J. A. Mangan & Roberta
Park (Totowa, NJ: Frank Cass, 1987), 58–93.

13. Mandell, *Sport,* 188.

14. George Sage, *Power and Ideology in American Sport* (Champaign, IL: Human
Kinetics Books, 1990), 172.

15. Sage, *Power and Ideology in American Sport,* 98–99; Park, "Sport, Gender
and Society in a Transatlantic Victorian Perspective," 74.

16. Mary-Ellen Hanson, *Go! Fight! Win: Cheerleading in American Culture*
(Bowling Green, OH: Bowling Green State University Press, 1995).

17. Craig Lambert, "Cheerleaders Take Flight," *Harvard Magazine*
<http:www.harvard-magazine.com/archive/00so/so00.jhj.sports.html> (22
August 2002).

18. Kathleen Thames, "A Look Back at 100 Years," *La Louisiane* 11 (Fall 2000): 13.

19. "Organized Cheering," *The Nation* 92 (1911): 6.

20. Ibid., 5.

21. Ibid.

22. Hanson, *Go! Fight! Win!*

23. Ibid., 17.

24. Gonzales, "The First College Cheer"; Charles Morton, "Accent on Living,"
Atlantic Monthly 189 (January 1952): 92–93.

25. The two "T's" are intentional for the rhythm of the chant.

26. All quotes cited in this section were derived through personal correspondence between the authors and the former cheerleaders, July-December
1999.

27. For a more detailed discussion of the role of extracurricular activities in the
early high schools, see Joel Spring, *The American School 1642–1990* (New

York: Longman, 1990) and Charles Foster, *Extra-curricular Activities in the High School* (Richmond, VA: Johnson Publishing Company, 1925).

28. Universal Cheerleading Association, *UCA Advisor/Coach Manual 2002* (Memphis, TN: Universal Cheerleading Association, 2000), 7.

29. Jim Lord, executive director, American Association of Cheerleading Coaches and Advisors (AACCA), interview with author, tape recording, Memphis, Tennessee, 25 June 2002.

30. Kline Boyd, executive vice president/general manager, Varsity Spirit Fashions, interview with author, tape recording, Memphis, Tennessee, 25 June 2002.

31. Shelia Angalet "Spread Good Cheer," 30 August 2002 <cheerleader@imagi-comm.com> (5 September 2002).

32. Laurie Wager, "Spread Good Cheer," 30 August 2002 <cheerleader@imagi-comm.com> (5 September 2002).

33. Boyd, interview.

34. Ginger Hopkins, "That Unchampionship Season," *Seventeen* 38 (January 1979): 115.

35. "President Leads Cheers at Summit," *The Tuscaloosa News* (14 August 2002), 6A.

36. We discuss Radical Cheerleaders in more detail in chapter 2.

37. Radical Cheerleaders, "About Us," <www.geocities.com/radicalcheerleaders/index.html> (12 September 2002).

38. *Bring it On,* Universal Studios, Los Angeles, 2000.

39. "Let's Hear it For Pep Squad Beauty," *Teen* 27 (September 1983): 94.

40. Strausbaugh, "The Anti-Cheerleader."

41. "Jokes About $C Cheerleaders," <http://www.bol.ucla.edu/~ddacumos/cheer.html1> (22 August 2002).

42. For more details on this sensational story, see Anne McDonald Mayer, *Mother Love, Deadly Love* (Secaucus, NJ: Birchlane Press Book, 1992).

43. Gabrielle Cosgriff, "Verna Heath Puts a Murder Plot Behind Her," *People Weekly,* 15–22 March 1999, <http://proquest.umi.com/pqdweb? TS=931895&Fmt=3&Sid=1&Idx=33&Deku=1&ROT=309&Dtp=1> (13 July 1999).

44. Mayer, *Mother Love, Deadly Love,* 154.

45. Sandy Banks, "Inspiring Tears as Well as Cheer," *Los Angeles Times,* 15 January 2002, <wysiwg://bodyframe.13/http://ehostvgw2 . . . =34%boolean-Term=cheerleading&fuzzyTerm=> (22 May 2002).

46. "Pompomgate is Not Worth Cheering About," *Los Angeles Times,* 13 January 2002, <wysiwyg://bodyframe.13/http://ehostvgw2 . . . =35boolean-Term=cheerleading&fuzzyTerm=> (22 May 2002).

47. Ibid.

48. Scott Ostler, "Dump the Cheerleaders," *Sport* 85 (August 1994): 20.

49. "Let's Hear it for Pep Squad Beauty," 95.

50. "Leader of the Pack," *American Cheerleader Junior* 3 (Winter 2003): 54.

51. Cheer Curls, 29 October 2002, <www.expage.com/cheercurlz> (16 September 2002).

52. Celso, "New Guy From Brazil!—This is the Tird [sic] Time I Try to Send it,"
    31 August 2002, <cheerleader@imagicomm.com> (16 September 2002).

Chapter 2

1. Radical Cheerleaders, "Radical Cheers," <www.geocities.com/radicalcheer-
   leaders/about.htm> (4 September 2002).
2. Lianne Stewart, "Cheerleading Takes on a Radical New Form," *Toronto Observer,* 17 April 2001, <http://observer.thecentre.centennialcollege.ca/fea-
   tures/lianne_radical_041702.htm> (12 September 2002).
3. See Mary Ellen Hanson, *Go! Fight! Win!: Cheerleading in American Culture*
   (Bowling Green, OH: Bowling Green State University Popular Press, 1995)
   and Laurel Davis, "Male Cheerleaders and the Naturalization of Gender," in
   Sport, Men, and the Gender Order, ed. Michael Messner and Donald Sabo
   (Champaign, IL: Human Kinetics Books, 1990), 153–161.
4. Lawrence Brings, *School Yells: Suggestions for Cheerleaders* (Minneapolis: Northwestern Press, 1944), 9, quoted in Mary-Ellen Hanson, *Go! Fight! Win!,* 23.
5. John Gach, "The Case For and Against Girl Cheerleaders," *School Activities*
   9 (February 1938): 301–302.
6. Ibid., 302.
7. See Sarah Banet-Weiser, *The Most Beautiful Girl in the World: Beauty
   Pageants and National Identity* (Berkeley: University of California Press,
   1999); Hanson, *Go! Fight! Win!;* Christopher Lucas, *American Higher Education* (New York: St. Martin's Press, 1994); Kate Mulvey and Melissa
   Richards, *Decades of Beauty: The Changing Image of Women 1890s–1990s*
   (New York: Reed Consumer Books, 1998); Edward Wagenknecht, *Stars of
   the Silence* (Metuchen, NJ: Scarecrow Press, 1987).
8. Hanson, *Go! Fight! Win!*
9. "High School Cheerleaders: Agile Trio at Whiting, Ind. Specialize in
   Rhythm-nastics," *Life* 11 (10 November 1941): 58.
10. Hanson, *Go! Fight! Win!*
11. Arturo Gonzales, "The First College Cheer," *The American Mercury* 83 (No-
    vember 1956): 101–104.
12. Craig Lambert, "Cheerleaders Take Flight," *Harvard Magazine* <http:har-
    vard-magazine.com/archive/00so/so00.jhj.sports.html> (22 August 2002).
13. Kris Axtman, "Texas School Where Pompoms Aren't Welcome," *Christian
    Science Monitor* 94 (6 December 2001): 3.
14. Dana Curry, "Fears Over Cheers," *Chronicle of Higher Education* 48 (7 De-
    cember 2001): A6.
15. Axtman, 3.
16. David Nakamura, "Jeers, Boos for Female Cadets on VMI's Cheerleading
    Squad," *The Washington Post,* 24 November 1998, <http:proquest.umi.com/
    pqdweb?TS=931896 . . .&Fmt=3&Sid=1&Idx=81&Deli=1&RQT=309&
    Dtp=1> (13 July 1999).

17. Dana Van Iquity, "Cheer San Francisco Celebrates 20 Years," *San Francisco Bay Times* (22 June 2000): 22; CHEER San Francisco, "Team History," <http://www.cheersf.org > (12 August 2002).

18. Steve Burke, personal correspondence, 24 December 2002.

19. LoAnn Halden, "Pride's Cheering Section: Tops and Bottoms," *The Weekly News* (South Florida's Gay Community Newspaper), 3 February 1999.

20. CHEER San Francisco, "Our Mission," <http://www.cheersf.org > (12 August 2002); CHEER New York, "Our Mission," <http://www.cheerny.org > (12 September 2002).

21. Steve Burke, "Cheer SF Picture," 27 August 2002, personal e-mail (29 August 2002).

22. Van Iquity, "Cheer San Francisco Celebrates 20 Years," 22.

23. *WANTED: X-Cheerleaders: A Performance Art Event,* 1997, a video by Andrea DeGette. For a copy of the video, contact producer and director Kim Irwin at <http://www.mindspring.com/x-cheerleaders/ourstory/history.html> (5 September 2002).

24. Linda Haac, "No Bull," *Independent Weekly,* 30 October–5 November 1996, <http://www.mindspring.com/~x-cheerleaders/gigs/clips/indy1.html > (5 September 2002).

25. X-Cheerleaders, "WANTED: X-Cheerleaders," <http://www.mindspring.com/x-cheerleaders/ourstory/history.html> (22 August 2002).

26. Linda Belans, "X-Cheerleaders Know the Real Score," *The News and Observer,* 24 October 1996, <http://www.mindspring.com/~x-cheerleaders/gigs/clips/nando.html > (5 September 2002).

27. Erin Ward, "Behind the Pom-Poms: Halifax's Radical Cheerleaders," *NovaNewsNet,* 1 February 2002, <http://novanewsnet.ukings.ns.ca/stories/01–02/020131/wardhalirads.htm> (12 September 2002).

28. See Mary Jessica Hammes, "Radical Road Trip," *Online Athens,* 18 July 2001, <http://www.onlineathens.com/stories/071901/ent_0719010009.shtml> (12 September 2002); Krystalline Kraus, "Rah-Rah Revolution," <wysiwyg://501/http://rabble.ca/news_ful . . . tm=f40219cc4a5cflafa28b182 flabcbb08&r=1> (12 September 2002); Radical Cheerleaders, "About Us," <http://www.geocities.com/radicalcheerleaders/about.htm > (4 September 2002).

29. Pat Ryan, "Once it was Only Sis-Boom-Bah!" *Sports Illustrated* 30 (6 January 1969): 45–55.

30. Carol Matzkin, "Peacenik in the Center Ring," *Mademoiselle* 67 (May 1968): 56, 62.

31. Ibid.

32. Ryan, 54.

33. NYC Radical Cheerleaders, "What is Radical Cheerleading All About?" <wysiwyg://433/http://www.geocities.com/nycradicalcheerleaders/about.html> (12 September 2002).

34. Radical Cheerleaders, "About Us," <http://www.geocities.com/radicalcheerleaders/about.htm> (4 September 2002).

35. Abbie Jarman, "The Jenning Sisters: Aimee, 28, Cara, 25, and Coleen, 23," *Utne Reader* (September-October 2002): 55.
36. Stewart, "Cheerleading Takes on a Radical New Form."
37. Kraus, "Rah-Rah Revolution."
38. Zines and posters can be purchased from Cara and Aimee Jennings, P.O. Box 961, Lakeworth, Florida 33460.
39. Womyn Centre, "Radical Conference," <http://www.carleton.ca/womyn-centre/events/marchconference.htm> (12 September 2002).
40. Graig Uhlin, "The Act of Activism . . . Las Sinfronteras Exemplifies the Intersection," *Arizona Daily Wildcat*, 7 May 2002, <wildcat.arizona.edu/papers/95/115/04 1.html> (12 October 2002).
41. Mary Xmas, personal communication, 21 February 2003.
42. Aimee Jennings, personal communication, 20 February 2003.
43. Katie Mears, "2,4,6,8! Our Forests are Dying at a Terrible Rate," *The Scarlet & Black* 118, 16 November 2000, <http://web.grinnell.edu/sandb/archives/volume118/111601/features/cheerleaders.html> (12 September 2002).
44. Kraus, "Rah-Rah Revolution."
45. Phil Leckman, "Give me a F-E-M-I-N-I-S-M," *Arizona Daily Wildcat*, 23 October 2000, <http://wildcat.arizona.edu/papers/94/45/04_2_m.html> (12 September 2002).
46. See Amy Argetsinger, "When the Cheerleaders are the Main Event: For Private Teams, Victory is Their Own," *The Washington Post*, 10 July 1999, <http://proquest.umi.com/pqdweb?TS=931894 . . . 1&Fmt=3&Sid=1&Idx=1&Deli=1&RQT=309&Dtp=1> (13 July 1999); Elsa Brenner, "Cheerleading Changes as Boys Join Sidelines," *New York Times*, 2 May 1999, <http:proquest.umi.com/pqdweb?TS=931895 . . . &Fmt=3&Sid=1&Idx=22&Deli=1&RQT=309&Dtp=1> (13 July 1999); James T. McElroy, *We've Got Spirit!: The Life and Times of America's Greatest Cheerleading Team* (New York: Simon & Schuster, 1999).
47. Cheer Ltd., "CANAM 2003 is Hotter than Ever," <http://cheerltd.com/canam.html> (12 November 2002).
48. Liz Benston, "Central California Firms Foresee Profit in Cheerleading Training Programs," *The Record*, 4 March 2002, <wysiwyg://bodyframe.13//http://ehostvgw2 . . . =19&booleanTerm=cheerleadingandfuzzyTerm=> (22 May 2002); Erik Brady, "Cheerleading in the USA," *USA Today* (26–28 April 2002); Jennifer Walsh, "Houston-Area Gym Facilities Thrive when Offering Cheerleading," *Houston Chronicle*, 8 July 1999, <wysiwyg://247/http://web1.epnet.com/cit . . . 187+sm+KS+so+b+ss+SO=6C48&fn=131&rn=138> (23 August 2002).
49. Julia Deardorff, "Cheerleaders Want R-E-S-P-E-C-T," *Chicago Tribune* (30 May 1999): 1–3.
50. Michael Alpert, "As Cheering Gains Respect, Georgia Keeps Producing Champions," *The Atlanta Journal-Constitution* (21 January 1999), JG11, <http://proquest.umi.com/pqdweb?TS=931896 . . . &Fmt=3&Sid=1&Idx=63&Deli=1&RQT=309&Dtp=1> (13 July 1999).

51. Arian Campo-Flores, "Cheerleading Gets Tough," *Newsweek* 137, 21 May 2001, <wysiwyg://bodyframe.13/http://ehostvgw2 . . . 103&boolean-Term=cheerleading&fuzzyTerm=> (22 May 2002).

52. Ibid.

53. Argetsinger, "When the Cheerleaders are the Main Event."

54. Liz Benston, "Central California Firms Foresee Profit in Cheerleading Training Program."

55. Alyssa Roenigk, "It's A Cheer World After All," *American Cheerleader,* February 2002, <wysiwyg://76/http://www.americancheerleader.com/backissues/feb02/cheerworld.html> (14 October 2002).

56. Katarina Ericsson, "Need your Help About Cheerleading," 5 October 2002, personal e-mail (7 October 2002).

57. Bob Kiralfy, "Cheerleading Book," 12 September 2002, personal e-mail (12 September 2002); Alyssa Roenigk, "It's a Cheer World After All," *American Cheerleader* (February 2002). <wysiwyg://76/http://www.americancheerleader.com/backissues/feb02/cheerworld.html> (14 October 2002); World Cheerleading Association, "Special Events," <http://www.cheerwca.com/Special%20Events.htm> (23 August 2002).

58. Greg Webb, interview with author, tape recording, Memphis, Tennessee, 24 June 2002.

59. Mike Fultz, interview with author, tape recording, Memphis, Tennessee, 25 June 2002.

60. Bob Kiralfy, "Cheerleading Book," 13 September 2002, personal e-mail (13 September 2002).

61. Jean Eve, "Cheerleading Book," 24 September 2002, personal e-mail (25 September 2002).

62. Cheerparadise, "Cheerleading in Japan," 4 October 2002, personal e-mail (4 October 2002).

63. British Cheerleading Association, "History of Cheerleading in Britain," <http://www.cheerleading.org.uk/handbook/history/htm> (24 September 2002).

64. Katarina Ericsson, "Need Your Help about Cheerleading in Sweden," 5 October 2002, personal e-mail (7 October 2002).

65. Bob Kiralfy, "Cheerleading Book," 13 September 2002, personal e-mail (16 September 2002).

66. Bob Kiralfy, "Anyone Seen This Yet," (10 December 2002, <cheerleader@imagicomm.com> (12 December 2002).

67. Alyssa Roenigk, "It's A Cheer World After All."

68. Mary Jones, personal communication, 13 January 2003.

69. According to the coach Mary Jones, cheerleading is not included in the National Senior Games; however, officials for that event are considering adding cheerleading if the numbers nationally warrant such a move.

70. Sylvia Auten, written correspondence, November 2002.

71. Jones, personal communication.

Chapter 3

1. Parts of this chapter were previously published in *Gender and Society*. Reprinted with permission from Sage Publications.

2. Varsity Spirit, *Varsity Catalog* (Memphis, Tennessee: Varsity, 1999), 1.

3. Marlien Rentmeester, "The Bomb Squad," *Seventeen* (November 1997): 84–86; Carey Walker, "The Bod Squad," *Muscle & Fitness* 60 (April 1999): 170–174.

4. For a detailed explanation of the impact of Title IX, see National Coalition for Women and Girls in Education, "Title IX at 30: Report Card on Gender Equity," June 2002, <http://www.newge.org/title9at30–6–11.pdf> (14 July 2002); "Title IX: Gender Equity in College Sports: 6 Views," *The Chronicle Review* (6 December 2002): Section 2, pp. B7-B10. For a counterargument of the impact of Title IX, see Jodi Schneider, "The Fairness Factor," *U.S. News & World Report* 132 (18 March 2002): 63–65.

5. Amy Argetsinger, "When Cheerleaders are the Main Event: For Private Teams, Victory is Their Own," *Washington Post*, 10 July 1999, <http://proquest.umi.com/pqdweb?TS=931894 . . . 1&Fmt=3&Sid=1&Idx=1&Deli=1&RQT=309&Dtp=1>, (13 July 1999).

6. Nancy Lesko, "We're Leading America: The Changing Organization and Form of High School Cheerleading," *Theory and Research in Social Education* 16 (Fall 1988): 263–278; James McElroy, *We've Got Spirit! The Life and Times of America's Greatest Cheerleading Team* (New York: Simon & Schuster, 1999).

7. Mary Ellen Hanson, *Go! Fight! Win: Cheerleading in American Culture* (Bowling Green, OH: Bowling Green State University Popular Press, 1995).

8. Erik Brady, "Cheerleading in the USA: A Sport and an Industry," *USA Today* (26–28 April 2002): 2A.

9. "Outside the Lines. Cheerleading: Controversy and Competition," televised program, ESPN, 5 November 2002.

10. Middle Tennessee State University, "Cheerleading Teams," <http://www.mtsu.edu/~mtcheer/bstryouts.htm> (13 September 2002).

11. Alyssa Roenigk, "Cheer Safety: Setting the Record Straight," *American Cheerleader* 8 (August 2002): 46–48.

12. Arian Campo-Flores, "Cheerleading Gets Tough," *Newsweek*, 21 May 2001, <wysiwyg://bodyframe.13/http://ehostvgw2 . . . 103&booleanTerm=cheerleading&fuzzyTerm=> (22 May 2002); Debbie Purifoy, cheerleading coach, interview with author, tape recording, Tuscaloosa, Alabama, 30 September 2002.

13. Elsa Brenner, "Cheerleading Changes as Boys Join Sidelines: Stereotypes Slip Away, Attitudes Shift and a Sport Calls for More Acrobatics," *The New York Times*, 2 May 1999, <http:proquest.umi.com/pqdweb?TS=931895 . . . &Fmt=3&Sid=1&Idx=22&Deli=1&RQT=309&Dtp=1> (13 July 1999).

14. Chris Darby, interview with author, tape recording, Memphis, Tennessee, 25 June 2002.

15. Barby Ingle, cheerleading coach, interview with author, Pullman, Washington, 9 August 2002.

16. "Outside the Lines: Cheerleading: Controversy and Competition," televised program.

17. Frederick Mueller and Robert Cantu, 2001, *National Center for Catastrophic Sport Injury Research Report: Eighteenth Annual Report,* <http://www.unc.edu/depts/nccsi/SportList.htm> (19 June 2002).

18. Mark Hutchinson, "Cheerleading Injuries," *The Physician and Sportsmedicine* 25, September 1997, <http://proquest.umi.com/pqdweb?TS=945715 . . . &Fmt=3&Sid=4&Idx=64&Deli=1&RQT=309&Dtp=1> (20 December 1999).

19. Gerald George, ed., *AACCA Cheerleading Safety Manual* (Memphis, TN: The UCA Publications Department, March 1997).

20. Jim Lord, interview with author, tape recording, Memphis, Tennessee, 25 June 2002.

21. Varsity, "Varsity Brands, Inc., National Federation of State High School Associations Form Strategic Alliance on Cheerleading," <www.varsity.com /index.asp?category=1&article=856> (7 October 2002).

22. "New Coaches Safety Council Formed," *American Cheerleader* 9 (June 2003): 15.

23. "NU, Former Cheer Squad Member Reach Agreement," UNL News Release, 13 April 2001, <www.unl.edu/pr/2001/0401/041301bnews.html> (23 August 2002).

24. Laurie Schreier, "Byrne Bans Cheerleaders' Stunts," *Daily Nebraskan,* 12 March 2002, <www.dailynebraskan . . . T2002/03/12/3c8da10e10d14?in_archive=1> (23 August 2002).

25. Allison Roenigk, "Ground (Bound) Breaking," *American Cheerleader* 8 (August 2002): 159.

26. In February 2003, UNL's new athletic director, Steve Pederson, eased the ground-bound restrictions somewhat by allowing the UNL Husker Spirit Squad to perform partner stunts beginning in the 2003 football season. However, they still cannot perform basket tosses or pyramids. They also cannot tumble.

27. Mueller and Cantu, "*National Center for Catastrophic Sport Injury Research Report*"; "Cheerleaders Unhappy with Temporary Ban on Stunts," <www.sportserver.com/newsroo . . . /feat/archiv/022698/acc68005.html > (11 June 1999).

28. See Jay Mariotti, "The Tragic Cost of Pride," *The Sporting News* 225 (13 August 2001): 6; Herman Masin, "Putting on the Heat (Stroke)," *Scholastic Coach & Athletic Director* 71 (October 2001): 11; David Noonan, "How Safe are Our Youngest Athletes?" *Newsweek* 140 (16 September 2002); 50; "Sidelines," *Chronicle of Higher Education* 48 (9 August 2002): A39; "Study Reveals 23 Football Players Died During 2001 Season," *Black Issues in Higher Education* 19 (15 August 2002): 12.

29. Roenigk, "Cheer Safety."

30. Schreier, "Byrne Bans Cheerleader Stunts."
31. "Cheerleaders Unhappy with Temporary Ban on Stunts," 1998.
32. "Outside the Lines," televised program.
33. "It Pays to Cheer!" *American Cheerleader* 9 (February 2003): 89–100.
34. Ingle, interview.
35. "It Pays to Cheer," 95, 98,100.
36. Purifoy, interview.
37. Deirdre Wulf, personal communication, 18 October 2002.
38. Purifoy, interview. According to Purifoy, in the event that the men's basketball team advances to the second round of the NCAA tournament, they surpass the cheerleaders in revenues produced for the university.
39. Brady, "Cheerleading in the USA," 1A.
40. Erik Brady, "Sport v. Activity," *USA Today* (26–28 April 2002): 2A.
41. Women's Sports Foundation, "Cheerleading, Drill Team, Danceline and Band as Varsity Sports: The Foundation Position," (20 July 2000) <www.womenssportsfoundation.org/cgi-bin/iowa/issues/rights/article.html?record=95> (19 June 2002).
42. Rick Reilly, "Sis! Boom! Bah! Humbug!" *Sports Illustrated* 91 (18 October 1999): 116.
43. The quotes cited in this section are derived from an ethnographic study we conducted in 1998–99. All participants as well as the location of the school were promised anonymity.
44. "NBC Dateline: Personal Best," televised program, June 2002.
45. For an excellent history of the role sports have played in inculcating a certain form of American masculinity, see Susan Cahn, *Coming on Strong: Gender and Sexuality in Twentieth-Century Women's Sport* (Cambridge, MA: Harvard University Press, 1994); Richard Mandell, *Sport: A Cultural History* (New York: Columbia University Press); George Sage, *Power and Ideology in American Sport: A Critical Perspective* (Champgain, IL: Kinetics Books).
46. For a more thorough discussion of this role, see Cahn, *Coming on Strong* and Pamela Grundy, *Learning to Win: Sports, Education, and Social Change in Twentieth-Century North Carolina* (Chapel Hill: The University of North Carolina Press, 2000).
47. Ibid.
48. John Watterson, *College Football* (Baltimore: The Johns Hopkins University, 2000).
49. Cahn, *Coming on Strong*.
50. Louise Weisiger, "The Status of Interscholastic Athletics in Secondary School for Girls," *School Activities* 22 (February 1951): 184–187.
51. See Cahn, *Coming on Strong*.
52. Susan Cahn, "From the 'Muscle Moll' to the 'Butch' Ballplayer: Mannishness, Lesbianism, and Homophobia in U.S. Women's Sport," *Feminist Studies* 19 (1993): 343–370.
53. Shirley Castelnuovo and Sharon Guthrie, eds., *Feminism and the Female Body: Liberating the Amazon Within* (Boulder, CO: Lynne Rienner Publishers, 1998).

54. B. Palzkill, "Between Gymshoes and High-Heels: The Development of a Lesbian Identity and Existence in Top Class Sport," *International Review for the Sociology of Sport* 25 (1990): 226.
55. Mark Hyman, "The 'Babe Factor' in Women's Soccer," *Business Week* (1999): 118; Griffen, "Changing the Game."
56. Vikki Krane, "We Can be Athletic and Feminine, but Do We Want to?: Challenging Hegemonic Femininity in Women's Sports," *Quest* 53 (2001): 122.
57. Helen Lenskyji, "Sexuality and Femininity in Sport Contexts: Issues and Alternatives," *Journal of Sport & Social Issues* 18 (1994): 356–377.
58. Marnie Ko, "How to Play the Game," *Newsmagazine* 26 (2000): 38–39.
59. For a detailed discussion of how the threat of being labeled a "lesbian" regulates both lesbian and heterosexual female athletes, see Cahn, "From the 'Muscle Moll' to the 'Butch' Ballplayer"; Griffin, "Changing the Game"; Palzkill, "Between Gymshoes and High-Heels"; and Maria Veri, "Homophobic Discourse Surrounding the Female Athlete," *Quest* 51 (1999): 355–368.
60. Veri, "Homophobic Discourse Surrounding the Female Athlete."
61. Dan Hansen, "Apple Cup: Cougars' No. 3 Ranking Attracts Long-Distance Fans," *Spokesman-Review,* 24 November 2002: A1, A8-A9.

Chapter 4

1. Pat Ryan, "Once it was Only Sis Boom Bah," *Sports Illustrated* 30 (6 January 1969): 45.
2. Ibid., p. 53.
3. Bruce Newman, "Gimme an S," *Sports Illustrated* 48 (22 May 1978): 18.
4. Aaron Schatz, "The XFL Looks Ready to Rumble," *The Lycos 50 Daily Report,* 10 November 2000, <wysiwyg://7/http://50.lycos.com/111000.html> (17 January 2003).
5. McKenna & Marconi Law Offices, "Former Eagles Cheerleaders Expand Lawsuit Against NFL Teams," <http://www.digitmedia.com/mckenna/release.html > (7 November 2002); "More Cheerleaders to Sue Eagles Over Alleged Peephole," *CBS SportsLine* <http://footballlive.sportsline.com/u/wire/stories/0,1169,5073864_59,00.html > (7 November 2002).
6. Kostya K
    ennedy and Richard Deitsch, "Sports Beat," *Sports Illustrated* 7 (26 August 2002): 30.
7. Kelley King, "Cheesecake Sport: Overrated Cheerleading," *Sports Illustrated* 97 (4 November 2002): 73.
8. Jason Zinoman, "Debbie's Doing New York, But Rate Her PG," *The New York Times,* 27 October 2002, <http://proquest.umi.com/pqdweb?Did=0000 . . . &Fmt=3&Deli=1&Mtd=1&Idx=7&Sid=8&RQT=309 > (5 November 2002).

9. Joe Flower, "Survival of the Fittest," *Sport* 75 (October 1984): 94.
10. George Kurman, "What Does Girls' Cheerleading Communicate?" *Journal of Popular Culture* 20 (Fall 1986): 58.
11. *Flesh Gordan Meets Cosmic Cheerleaders,* Home Video, New Concorde, 1993.
12. Kurman, "What does Girls' Cheerleading Communicate?" 58.
13. F. B. Kutz, "Cheerleading Rules, Desirable Traits, and Qualifications," *School Activities* 26 (May 1955): 310.
14. Ruth Doan MacDougall, *The Cheerleader* (Centersandwich, NH: Frigate Books, 1998), 36.
15. Maxine Paetro, "Cheerleader Envy," *New Woman* 26 (March 1996): 93.
16. *Debbie Does Dallas,* New York, Pussycat Cinema, 1978.
17. Shannon T. Nutt, "More Cheerleaders!" *Adult DVD Empire, 28 August 2001, <http://www.pornopopdvd.com/exec/news/article.asp?media_id=114 >* (9 January 2003).
18. Robert Shaw, "Cowgirls," *Esquire* 88 (October 1977): 80.
19. Suzette, Stephanie and Sherry Scholz, *Deep in the Heart of Texas: Reflections of Former Dallas Cowboy Cheerleaders.* (New York: St. Martins Press, 1991), 146.
20. Gary Fine and Bruce Johnson, "The Promiscuous Cheerleader: An Adolescent Male Belief Legend," in *Manufacturing Tales: Sex and Money in Contemporary Legends,* ed. Gary Fine (Knoxville: The University of Tennessee Press, 1992), 59–68.
21. Ibid., 65.
22. This cheer is attributed to Georgia Tech. See "SI Rankings," *Sports Illustrated* 97 (7 October 2002): 74.
23. "The Broadening Curriculum," *New York Times,* 25 January 1924: 16, quoted in Mary Ellen Hanson, *Go! Fight! Win!: Cheerleading in American Culture* (Bowling Green, OH: Bowling Green State University Popular Press, 1995), 2.
24. Arturo Gonzales, "The First College Cheer," *American Mercury* 83 (November 1956): 104.
25. Anne Dingus, "The Dallas Cowboy Cheerleaders," *Texas Monthly* 26, January 1998, <http://ehostvgw1.epnet.com/fulltext.asp?resultsSetId=R00000011&hit-Num=3&booleanTer . . . > (16 April 2002); Kristen Morse, "Where are They Now?: Dallas Cowboy Cheerleaders," *Sports Illustrated* 95 (2 July 2001), 87–89; Joe Nick Patoski, "Dallas Cowboy Cheerleaders," *Texas Monthly* 29 (September 2001): 124, 157–158.
26. Hanson, *Go! Fight! Win!,* 70.
27. Dingus, "The Dallas Cowboy Cheerleaders."
28. Patoski, "Dallas Cowboy Cheerleaders."
29. Morse, "Where are They Now?" 88.
30. Patoski, "Dallas Cowboy Cheerleaders," 124.
31. For a discussion of the role of pinups in World War II, see John Costello, *Love, Sex and War: Changing Values 1939–1945* (London: Collins, 1985); Philomena Goodman, *Women, Sexuality and War* (New York: Palgrave,

2002); Charles Martignette and Louis Meisel, *The Great American Pin-Up* (New York: Taschen, 1996).

32. Dallas Cowboy Cheerleaders, "History," <http://www.dallascowboys.com/cgi-bin/Cowboys/cheerleaders/history.jjsp?BV_SessionID= . . . > (15 July 2002).

33. Edward Wagenknecht, *Stars of the Silence* (Metuchen, NJ: Scarecrow Press, 1987).

34. Scholz, *Deep in the Heart of Texas,* 143.

35. Ibid., 140.

36. Morse, "Where are They Now?"

37. Diane Shah, Stephen Gayle, and Mary Lord, "Sis-Boom-Bah!" *Newsweek* 90 (7 November 1977): 87–89; Joanne Schneller, "The Sis Boom Babes," *Mademoiselle* 97, (February 1991): 134–137.

38. Shah, Gayle, and Lord, "Sis-Boom-Bah!" 87.

39. Newman, "Gimme an S," 19.

40. Zondra Hughes, "African-American NFL Cheerleaders," *Ebony* 58 (November 2002): 162–164,166; Gail Shister, "The Pro Football Cheerleaders," *Glamour* 79 (February 1981): 166–167; Judith Timson, "Bounce for Glory," *Maclean's* 91 (21 August 1978): 29–32.

41. Scott Ostler, "Dump the Cheerleaders," *Sport* 85 (August 1994): 20.

42. Hanson, *Go! Fight! Win!*

43. *Dallas Cowboy Cheerleaders, Inc. v. Pussycat Cinema, Ltd. 604 F 2d 200* (2d Cir 1979).

44. "Microsoft Sued by Cheerleading Site Over Porn Ads," Computergram International <http://www.findarticles.com/csf_0/m0CGN/ . . . 1e.jhtml?term=cheerleading+and+lawsuits > (22 August 2002).45. Linda Haugsted, "See Nude Pics of Superbowl Winner! (XFL)," *Multichannel News,* 19 February 2001. <http://www.findarticles.com/cf_0/m3535/ . . . 808/p1/article.jhtml?term=cheerleading+ > (22 August 2002).

46. Ibid.

47. Ibid.

48. *Bring it On,* Universal Studios, Los Angeles, 2000.

49. Chris Darby, interview with author, tape recording, Memphis, Tennessee, 25 June 2002.

50. Debbie Purifoy, interview with author, tape recording, Tusacaloosa, Alabama, 30 September 2002.

51. Allison Glock, "Made You Look," *Gentlemen's Quarterly* 68 (1 June 1998): 236–243, 280.

52. For a more detailed discussion of how "slut" is used to regulate the behavior of teenage girls, see Joyce Canaan, "Why a 'Slut' is a 'Slut': Cautionary Tales of Middle-Class Teenage Girls' Morality," in *Symbolizing America,* ed. Herve Varenne (Lincoln: University of Nebraska Press, 1986), 184–208; Karin Martin, *Puberty, Sexuality, and the Self: Girls and Boys at Adolescence* (New York: Routledge, 1996); Emily White, *Fastgirls: Teenage Tribes and the Myth of the Slut* (New York: Scribner, 2002).

53. Kurman, "What Does Girls' Cheerleading Communicate?"

54. Peter Annin, "The Day the Cheering Stopped," *Newsweek* 122 (October 18, 1993). http://ehostvgw1.epnet.com/fulltext.asp?resultsSetId=R00000001 &hitNum=1&booleanTer . . . > (16 April 2002): Jack Chambers, "Not Much to Cheer About," *National Review* 45 (November 29, 1993): 22, 24.

55. "On the Art of Cheerleading," *Saturday Review* (20 October 1962): 73.

56. Gretchen Norton, "Cheerleading Doesn't Deserve a Bad Image," *Seventeen* 36 (June 1977): 64.

57. These were the regulations governing tryouts at Wichita Middle School.

58. Bill Seely, interview with author, tape recording, Memphis, Tennessee, 25 June 2002.

59. Don Merten, "Burnout as Cheerleader: The Cultural Basis for Prestige and Privilege in Junior High School," *Anthropology & Education Quarterly* 27 (1996): 51–70.

60. All quotes in this section were derived from a study conducted in 1998–1999 in which participants were promised anonymity.

61. Michelle Fine, "Sexuality, Schooling and Adolescent Females: The Missing Discourse of Desire," *Harvard Educational Review* 58 (1988): 29–53; Deborah Tolman, "Doing Desire: Adolescent Girls' Struggles for/with Sexuality," *Gender & Society* 8 (September 1994): 324–342.

62. Joel Spring, *American Education* (New York: McGraw Hill, 1996).

63. Jim Lord, interview with author, tape recording, Memphis, Tennessee, 25 June 2002.

64. Purifoy, interview.

65. Laurel Davis, "Male Cheerleaders and the Naturalization of Gender," in *Sport, Men, and the Gender Order,* ed. Michael Messner and Donald Sabo (Champaign, IL: Human Kinetics Books, 1990), 153–161.

66. Jason Crostin, former Eastern Washington University cheerleader, interview with author, Moscow, Idaho, 30 August 2002.

67. Elsa Brenner, "Stereotypes Slip Away, Attitudes Shift and a Sport Calls for More Acrobatics," *New York Times,* 2 May 1999, <http://proquest.umi.com/pqdweb?TS=931895 . . .&Fmt=3&Sid=1&Idx=22&Deli=1&RQT=309& Dtp=1 > (13 July 1999).

68. Jesse Nishikawa, Washington State University varsity cheerleader, interview with author, tape recording, Pullman, Washington, 10 October 2002.

69. Michael Gill, assistant cheerleading coach, Boise State University/UCA instructor, and Kim Budvarson, captain of Boise State University Cheerleading Squad/UCA instructor, interview with author, Moscow, Idaho, 18 June 2002.

70. Davis, "Male Cheerleaders and the Naturalization of Gender."

71. Crostin, interview.

72. Nishikawa, interview.

73. Ibid.

74. "What They Were Thinking," *New York Times Sunday Magazine* (May 26, 2002): 20.

75. Liz McGivern, "Is He 'Cheerleading' Material?" <wysiwyg://14/http://www. varsity.com/index.asp?article=117> (7 October 2002).
76. Marty Beckerman, *Death to all Cheerleaders* (Flat Rock, NC: Infected Press, 2000): 42–43.
77. Davis, "Male Cheerleaders and the Naturalization of Gender."

Chapter 5

1. Pat Ryan, "Once it Was Only Sis Boom Bah," *Sports Illustrated* 30 (6 January 1969): 45.
2. Wichita City is a fictitious name as are all the names of the people at Wichita Middle School, whom we interviewed as part of a study we conducted in 1998–1999. For more details about that study, see Pamela Bettis and Natalie Adams, "The Power of the Preps and a Cheerleading Equity Policy," *Sociology of Education* 76 (April 2003): 128–142.
3. Michele Popke, "Diverse Spirit: A Florida School District Hopes to Attract More African-American Cheerleaders," *Athletic Business* 2 (October 2001): 34.
4. Nancy Wilstach, "Officials: All Who Tried Out Can Cheer," *Birmingham News* (AL), 31 July 2002, < http://n19.newsbank.com/nl-search/ we/Archives?p_action=doc&p_docid=0F5461C76D7C . . . > (23 August 2002).
5. Jeannie Ralson, "Rah! Power," *Texas Monthly* 22 (October 1994): 150+ <http://ehostvgw1.epnet.com/fulltext.asp?resultSetId=R00000004&hit-Num=1&booleanTer . . . > (16 April 2002).
6. Russ Bynum, "GA Seeks Sexy Cheerleading Crackdown," *Associated Press Online,* 21 November 2001, <wysiwyg://bodyframe.13/http://ehostvgw2 . . . =60&booleanTerm=cheer-leading&fuzzyTerm=> (22 May 2002).
7. *Bring It On,* Universal Studios, Los Angeles, 2000.
8. Dr. Harold Bishop, Professor, interview with author, tape recording, Tuscaloosa, Alabama, 27 September 2002.
9. Pamela Grundy, *Learning to Win: Sports, Education and Social Change in 20th Century North Carolina* (Chapel Hill: The University of North Carolina Press, 2001), 174.
10. Sonja Steptoe, "The Pom-Pom Chronicles," *Sports Illustrated* 75 (30 December 1991–6 January 1992): 44.
11. Grundy, *Learning to Win,* 285.
12. Ibid., 286.
13. Ibid., 285.
14. Ibid., 267.
15. Teresa Guterierrez, "Tamsey Muniz, La Raza Unida Party and the Chicano," 26 May 1997, <http://ehostvgw1.epnet.com/fulltext.asp?resultSetId= R00000010&hitNum=1&booleanTer . . . > (16 April 2002); Hanson, *Go! Fight! Win!,* 35.

16. Ryan, 47.
17. Jenny Dodson, "Rebel Flag Made Debut at UM in 1948, Prof Says," *The Daily Mississippian,* 21 October 1997, <http://dm.olemiss.edu/archives/97/9710/971021/971021N4flag.HTML> (21 November 2002); Keith Wright, "Summit on Race at Ole Miss," *Z Magazine,* <http://www.zmag.org/ZMag/articles/dec1999wright.htm> (21 November 2002).
18. Grundy, *Learning to Win,* 289.
19. C. Guyon, "Cheering Unlimited," *People Weekly* 37 (10 February 1992):72.
20. Dr. Harold Bishop, interview.
21. Grundy, *Learning to Win,* 287.
22. Greg Webb, senior vice president/general manager, Universal Cheerleading Association, interview with author, tape recording, Memphis, Tennessee, 24 June 2002.
23. Beth Whiffan, "Latin Divas," *American Cheerleader* 8 (December 2002): 71–72.

Chapter 6

1. Erik Brady, "From Megaphones to Mega-Profits," *USA Today* (26–28 April 2002): 3C.
2. Ann Bagamery, "Go! Fight! Win!" *Forbes* 130 (27 September 1982): 140.
3. See Bagamery, "Go! Fight! Win!"139; Rex Lardner, "Herkimer Tells How to Make 'Em Holler," *Sports Illustrated* 15 (27 November 1961): 41–46; Sonja Steptoe, "The Pom-Pom Chronicles," *Sports Illustrated* 75 (30 December 1991–6 January 1992): 38–44, 46; Marisa Walker, "10 Questions with Herkie," *American Cheerleader* 8 (October 2002): 45–46.
4. Cheryl Rodgers, "Spirit! Let's Hear It!" *Nation's Business* 82 (June 1994): 16; R. Lee Sullivan, "School for Cheerleaders," *Forbes* (25 October 1993): 118–119.
5. Erik Brady, "From Megaphones to Mega-Profits," *USA Today* (26–28 April 2002): 3C.
6. Bagamery, "Go! Fight! Win!" 136.
7. Bagamery, "Go! Fight! Win!" 139; Jim Sirmans, "Cram Course for Cheerleaders," *Seventeen* 32 (September 1973): 114–115, 17; Walker, "10 Questions with Herkie," 45–46.
8. Sirmans, "Cram Course for Cheerleaders," 171.
9. Steptoe, "The Pom-Pom Chronicles," 44.
10. Bagamery, "Go! Fight! Win!" 140.
11. Walker, "10 Questions with Herkie," 46. For the slang definition of "pom pom," see Harold Wentworth and Stuart Berg Flexner, ed., *Dictionary of American Slang* (New York: Thomas Y. Crowell Co., 1975).
12. Steptoe, "The Pom-Pom Chronicles," 44.
13. Lardner, "Herkimer Tells How to Make 'Em Holler," 42.
14. Bagamery, "Go! Fight! Win!" 139.

15. Steptoe, "The Pom-Pom Chronicles," 43.
16. Erik Brady, "From Megaphones to Mega-Profits," 3C.
17. Sullivan, "School for Cheerleaders," 119.
18. Ken Woodmansee, "Cheers: Jebb Webb's Multicolored World Wide Spirit Machine," *Memphis Business* 3 (Third Quarter 1993): 14–19.
19. Steptoe, "The Pom-Pom Chronicles," 46.
20. Greg Webb, senior vice president/general manager, UCA, interview with author, tape recording, Memphis, Tennessee, 24 June 2002.
21. Kline Boyd, executive vice president/general manager, Varsity Spirit Fashions, interview with author, tape recording, Memphis, Tennessee, 25 June 2002.
22. Steptoe, "The Pom-Pom Chronicles," 44.
23. Erik Brady, "From Megaphones to Mega-Profits," 3C.
24. Woodmansee, "Cheers," 17.
25. Rodgers, "Spirit! Let's Hear It!" 16; Sullivan, "School for Cheerleaders," 119; Ray Arnold, corporate controller—Apparel Division, Varsity Brand, Inc., interview with author, tape recording, Memphis, Tennessee, 26 June 2002.
26. Steptoe, "The Pom-Pom Chronicles," 46; Woodmansee, "Cheers," 18.
27. Securities and Exchange Commission, *Quarterly Report Pursuit to Section 13 or 15 (d) of the Securities Exchange Act of 1934, Varsity Brands, Inc.* (Washington, D.C: 0–19298, 2002), 1-S-2.
28. Kavin Finley, controller-Apparel Division, Varsity Brands, Inc., interview with author, tape recording, Memphis, Tennessee, 25 June 2002.
29. "Go, You Jelly Fish, Go!" *Life* 59 (17 September 1965): 72.
30. Ibid.
31. Sirmans, "Cram Course for Cheerleaders," 114–115, 171.
32. "Mr. Cheerleader," *American Magazine* 161 (March 1956): 47.
33. Sirmans, "Cram Course for Cheerleaders," 171.
34. Ibid.
35. Flaum, "Memphis, Tenn.-Based Varsity Brands Gets National Development Deal."
36. Christian Cheerleaders of America, "Camps," <http://www.chcercca.com/camps.html> (13 January 2003).
37. Fellowship of Christian Cheerleaders, "Summer Camps," <http://www.cheerfcc.org/pages/newsumcamp.html > (12 November 2002).
38. Atlantic Cheer & Dance, "Boot Camps," <http://atlantic-cheer-n-dance.com/camps/ (12 November 2002).
39. Mike Fultz, program director of camp administration/international special events coordinator, interview with author, tape recording, Memphis, Tennessee, 25 June 2002; Sean Ellis, financial analyst, UCA/UDA, interview with author, tape recording, Memphis, Tennessee, 25 June 2002.
40. "Outside the Lines: Cheerleading: Controversy and Competition," televised program, ESPN, 5 November 2002.
41. Securities and Exchange Commission, *Quarterly Report.*
42. Pam Crawford, personal communication, 6 November 2002.

43. Marlene Cota, vice president, marketing (UCA), interview with author, tape recording, Memphis, Tennessee, 25 June 2002.

44. Finley, interview.

45. Cheer Curls, 29 October 2002, <wysiwyg://2/http://www.expage.com/page/cheercurlz> (16 September 2002).

46. Erik Brady, "Cheerleading in the USA: A Sport and an Industry," *USA Today* (26–28 April 2002): 1A.

47. A classic American cheer chanted by students of elite high schools and universities when their team is losing.

48. *The Corrolla,* 1924, p. 401. Found in the Special Collections Library, University of Alabama, Tuscaloosa, Alabama.

49. Lawrence Herkimer and Phyllis Hollander, *The Complete Book of Cheerleading* (New York: Doubleday & Company, 1975), 11.

50. Bill Seely, vice president of operations and development, UCA, interview with author, tape recording, Memphis, Tennessee, 25 June 2002.

51. Debbie Purifoy, cheerleading coach, interview with author, tape recording, Tuscaloosa, Alabama, 30 September 2002.

52. Jennifer Lenhart, "Camp Gives Cheerleaders An Extra Lift: At Ashburn Program, Girls Dispel 'Airhead' Stereotype," *The Washington Post,* 8 July 1999, <http://proquest.umi.com/pqdweb?TS=981894 . . .   1&Fmt=3&Sid=1&1dx=3&Deli=1&RQT=309&Dtp=1>
(13 July 1999).

53. Cindy Villarreal, *The Cheerleader's Guide to Life* (New York: Harper Perennial, 1994), 183.

54. Erik Brady, "Cheerleading in the USA," 2A.

55. Interestingly, the two other members of the Dixie Chicks, sisters Martie Seidel and Emily Robison, were discouraged by their father from being cheerleaders. He wanted his daughters to be the ones cheered for rather than the ones doing the cheering.

56. "Lela Rochon: Breaking Boundaries," *American Cheerleader* 5 (June 1999): 19.

57. Shanna, [pseud], personal interview with author, tape recording, Wichita [pseud], 9 December 1998.

58. Lynn Snowden, "The Roots of Rejection," *Working Woman* 17 (September 1992): 74.

59. Ibid.

60. Erik Brady, "From Megaphones to Mega-Profits," 3C.

61. "Outside the Lines," ESPN televised program.

Chapter 7

1. Portions of this chapter appear in *Gender & Society.* Used with permission by Sage Publications.

2. Charles Kuralt, "Those Good Old Cheers Gone By," *Reader's Digest* 117 (September 1980): 54–55.

3. Laurel Davis, "Male Cheerleaders and the Naturalization of Gender," in *Sport, Men and the Gender Order,* ed., Michael Messner and Donald Sabo (Champaign, IL: Human Kinetics Books, 1990), 153–161.

4. Susan Bordo, *Unbearable Weight: Feminism, Western Culture and the Body* (Berkeley: University of California Press, 1993); Susan Douglas, "Girls 'n' Spice: All things Nice?" *Nation* 265, 25 August 1997, <wysiwygillbodyframe.5/http://ehostgw13 . . . =39&booleanTerm=Girl%20Power& fuzzyTerm=> (16 October 2000).

5. Simone de Beauvoir, *The Second Sex* (New York: Vintage Books, 1952), 331.

6. James McElroy, *We've Got Spirit: The Life and Times of America's Greatest Cheerleading Team* (New York: Simon & Schuster, 1999), 119.

7. Valerie Walkerdine, "Girlhood Through the Looking Glass," in *Girls, Girlhood, and Girls' Studies in Transition,* ed. Marion de Ras and Mieke Lunenberg (Amsterdam: Het Spinhuis, 1993).

8. Michele Fine, "Sexuality, Schooling, and Adolescent Females: The Missing Discourse of Desire," *Harvard Educational Review* 58 (February 1988): 29–53; Deborah Tolman, "Doing Desire: Adolescent Girls' Struggles for/with Sexuality," *Gender & Society* 8 (September 1994): 324–342.

9. See Elise Ackerman, "She Kicks. She Scores. She Sells," *U.S. News & World Report* 127 (26 July 1999): 42; Tim Crothers, "Spectacular Takeoff," *Sports Illustrated* 93, 3 July 2000, <http://web22.epnet.com/citation.asp?tb= . . . 46693+sm+KS+so+b+ss+SO+53B6&fn=61&rn=68 >(16 January 2003); Tanya Davies, "Brandi's Brazen Celebration," *Maclean's* 112 (26 July 1999): 10; Mark Hyman, "The 'Babe Factor' in Women's Soccer," *Business Week* (26 July 1999): 118; Robert Sullivan, "Goodbye to Heroin Chic: Now It's Sexy to be Strong," *Time* 154, 19 July 1999, <http://web22.epnet.com/citation.asp?tb= . . . 6693+sm+KS+so+b+ss+SO+53B6&fn=91&rn=100> (16 January 2003).

10. Pat Griffen, "Changing the Game: Homophobia, Sexism, and Lesbians in Sport," *Quest* 44 (1992): 251–265; Vikki Krane, "We Can be Athletic and Feminine, but Do We Want To?: Challenging Hegemonic Femininity in Women's Sports," *Quest* 53 (2001): 115–133; B. Palzkill, "Between Gymshoes and High-Heels: The Development of a Lesbian Identity and Existence in Top Class Sport," *International Review for the Sociology of Sport* 25 (1990): 221–234.

11. Lois Weis, "Gender and the Reports: The Case of the Missing Piece," in *Feminist Critical Policy Analysis: A Perspective from Primary and Secondary Schooling,* ed. Catherine Marshall (London: The Falmer Press, 1997).

12. Anne Dingus, "The Dallas Cowboy Cheerleaders," *Texas Monthly* 26, January 1998, <http://ehostgv1.epnet.com/fulltext.asp?resultSetId=R00000011 &hitNum=3&booleanTer . . . > (16 April 2002); Kristin Morse, "Dallas Cowboy Cheerleaders: Where are They Now?" *Sports Illustrated* 95 (2–9 July 2002): 87–89; Joe Nick Patoski, "Dallas Cowboy Cheerleaders," *Texas Monthly* 29 (September 2001): 124, 157–158.

13. Sarh Banet-Weiser, *The Most Beautiful Girl in the World: Beauty Pageants and National Identity* (Berkeley: University of California Press, 1999).

14. Ibid.
15. Ibid.
16. For a discussion of these scandals, see Peter Annin, "The Day the Cheering Stopped," *Newsweek* 122, 18 October 1993, <http://ehostgw1.epnet.com/fulltext.asp?resultSetId=R00000001&hitNum=1&booleanTer . . . > (16 April 2002); Jack Chambers, "Not Much to Cheer About," *National Review* 45 (November 29, 1993): 22, 24; Sarah Banet-Weiser, *The Most Beautiful Girl in the World* (Berkeley: University of California Press, 1999); Jeffrey Gettleman, "In North Carolina, The 2-Tiara State, A Beauty of a Fight," *New York Times* 151 (6 September 2002): A1; Michele Orecklin, "She Couldn't Even Win the Lawsuit Competition," *Time* 160 (23 September 2002): 89.
17. Erma Bombeck, "Desire to be a Cheerleader Never Fades," *News-Star World* (14 March 1982): 8D.
18. Susie Smith [pseud], personal communication, September 2002.
19. Janice Knowles [pseud], personal communication, September 2002.
20. Kim Irwin, personal correspondence, January 2003.
21. Susan Lucas, written correspondence, May 2003.
22. Lisa Largent [pseud], personal communication, July 1999.
23. Julie Junkin [pseud], personal communication, July 1999.
24. Gabby Hebert [pseud], personal communication, July 1999.
25. Maria Lowe, *Women of Steel: Female Bodybuilders and the Struggle for Self-Definition* (New York: New York University Press, 1998).
26. Krane, "We Can be Athletic and Feminine, But Do We Want To?"
27. National Baseball Hall of Fame—Women in Baseball, "A Guide for All-American Girls," <http:www.assumption.edu/HTML/Academic/history/Hil13net/AAGPBL%20Charm%20> (2 December 2002).
28. Griffen, "Changing the Game," 255; Krane, "We Can be Athletic and Feminine, but Do We Want To?" 116–118; Palzkill, "Between Gymshoes and High-Heels," 221–234.
29. A. Jax, "Fat and Fabulous," *Radical Cheerleader Handbook #3*, p. 30. Copy available by writing Cara and Aimee Jennings, P.O. Box 961, Lakeworth, Florida 33460.
30. Joan Montagnes, personal communication, October 2002.
31. Davis, "Male Cheerleaders and the Naturalization of Gender."
32. For more information, visit their websites at http://www.axisdance.org and http://www.gggreg.com/dancingwheels.htm.
33. Kathleen Farber, "When Bodies Matter: Teaching Adolescents about Community, Critical Consciousness, and Identity through Movement," in *Educating Young Adolescent Girls*, ed. Patricia O'Reilly, Elizabeth Penn, and Kathleen deMarrais (Mahwah, NJ: Lawrence Erlbaum Associates, 2001), 103–121.
34. Nancy Fraser, "The Uses and Abuses of French Discourse Theories/or Feminist Politics," in *Revaluing French Feminism: Critical Essays on Difference, Agency, and Culture*, ed. Nancy Fraser and Susan Bartkey (Bloomington: Indiana University Press, 1992), 180.

REFERENCES

Ackerman, Elise. 1999. "She Kicks. She Scores. She Sells." *U.S. News & World Report*, 26 July, 42.

Adams, Eddie. 2002. "Our American Spirit." *Parade Magazine*, 8 September, 4–5.

Adams, Natalie and Pamela Bettis. 2003. "Commanding the Room in Short Skirts: Cheering as the Embodiment of Ideal Girlhood." *Gender & Society* 17: 73–91.

Adler, Patricia and Adler, Peter. 1995. "Dynamics of Inclusion and Exclusion in Preadolescent Cliques." *Social Psychology Quarterly* 58:145–162.

Alpert, Michael. 1999. "As Cheering Gains Respect, Georgia Keeps Producing Champions." *The Atlanta Journal-Constitution*, 21 January, <http://proquest.umi.com/pqdweb?TS=931896 . . . &Fmt=3&Sid=1&Idx=63&Deli=1&RQT=309&Dtp=1> (13 July 1999).

Annin, Peter. 1993. "The Day the Cheering Stopped." *Newsweek*, 18 October, <http://ehostvgw1.epnet.com/fulltext.asp?resultsSetId=R00000001&hitNum=1&booleanTer . . . > (16 April 2002).

Argetsinger, Amy. 1999. "When the Cheerleaders are the Main Event: For Private Teams, Victory Is Their Own." *The Washington Post*, 10 July, <http://proquest.umi.com/pqdweb?TS=931894 . . . 1&Fmt=3&Sid=1&Idx=1&Deli=1&RQT=309&Dtp=1> (13 July 1999).

Atlantic Cheer & Dance. "Boot Camps." <http://atlantic-cheer-n-dance.com/camps/ >(12 November 2002).

Axis Dance Company. "About Axis Dance Company." <*http://www.axisdance.org/about/about.html*> (27 January 2003).

Axtman, Kris. "Texas School Where Pompoms Aren't Welcome." *Christian Science Monitor*, 6 December, 3.

Bagamery, Ann. 1982. "Go! Fight! Win!" *Forbes*, 27 September, 136–140.

Banet-Weiser, Sarah. 1999. *The Most Beautiful Girl in the World: Beauty Pageants and National Identity*. Berkeley: University of California Press.

Banks, Sandy. 2002. "Inspiring Tears as Well as Cheer." *Los Angeles Times*, 15 January, <wysiwg://bodyframe.13/http://ehostvgw2 . . . =34%booleanTerm=cheerleading&fuzzyTerm=> (22 May 2002).

Beckerman, Marty. 2000. *Death to All Cheerleaders*. Flat Rock, NC: Infected Press.

Belans, Lind. 1996. "X-Cheerleaders Know the Real Score." *The News and Observer*, 24 October, <http://www.mindspring.com/~x-cheerleaders/gigs/clips/nando.html > (5 September 2002).

Benston, Liz. 2002. "Central California Firms Foresee Profit in Cheerleading Training Programs." *The Record,* 4 March, <wysiwyg://bodyframe.13//http:// ehostvgw2 . . . =19&booleanTerm=cheerleadingandfuzzyTerm=> (22 May 2002).

Bissinger, H.G. 1990. *Friday Night Lights.* New York: Harper Perennial.

Bombeck, Erma. 1982. "Desire to be a Cheerleader Never Fades." *News-Star World,* 14 March, 8D.

Bordo, Susan. 1993. *Unbearable Weight: Feminism, Western Culture and the Body.* Berkeley: University of California Press.

Brady, Erik. 2002. "Cheerleading in the USA: A Sport and an Industry." *USA Today,* 26–28 April, 1A.

———2002. "Sport v. Activity." *USA Today,* 26–28 April, 2A.

———2002. "From Megaphones to Mega-profits." *USA Today,* 26–28 April, 3C.

Brenner, Elsa. 1999. "Cheerleading Changes as Boys Join Sidelines." *New York Times,* 2 May, <http:proquest.umi.com/pqdweb?TS=931895 . . . &Fmt=3&Sid= 1&Idx=22&Deli=1&RQT=309&Dtp=1> (13 July 1999).

Bring It On. 2000. Los Angeles: Universal Studios.

Brings, Lawrence. 1944. *School Yells: Suggestions for Cheerleaders.* Minneapolis: Northwestern Press. Quoted in Mary-Ellen Hanson, *Go! Fight! Win! Cheerleaders in American Culture,* (Bowling Green, OH: Bowling Green State University Popular Press), 23.

British Cheerleading Association. "History of Cheerleading in Britain," <http://www.cheerleading.org.uk/handbook/history/htm> (24 September 2002).

"The Broadening Curriculum." 1924. *New York Times,* 25 January, 16. Quoted in Mary Ellen Hanson, *Go! Fight! Win! Cheerleading in American Culture* (Bowling Green, Ohio: Bowling Green Statue University Popular Press), 2.

Bynum, Russ. 2001. "GA Seeks Sexy Cheerleading Crackdown." *Associated Press Online,* 21 November, <wysiwyg://bodyframe.13/http://ehostvgw2 . . . =60& booleanTerm=cheerleading&fuzzyTerm=> (22 May 2002).

Cahn, Susan. 1993. "From the 'muscle moll' to the 'butch' ballplayer: Mannishness, lesbianism, and homophobia in U.S. women's sport." *Feminist Studies* 19: 343–370.

———1994. *Coming on Strong: Gender and Sexuality in Twentieth-century Women's Sport.* Cambridge, MA: Harvard University Press.

Campo-Flores, Arian. 2001. "Cheerleading Gets Tough." *Newsweek,* 21 May, <wysiwyg://bodyframe.13/http://ehostvgw2 . . . 103&booleanTerm=cheerleading &fuzzyTerm=> (22 May 2002).

Canaan, Joyce. 1986. "Why a 'Slut' is a 'Slut': Cautionary Tales of Middle-class Teenage Girls' Morality." In *Symbolizing America,* edited by Herve Varenne. Lincoln: University of Nebraska Press.

Castelnuovo, Shirley and Sharon Guthrie, ed. 1998. *Feminism and the Female Body: Liberating the Amazon Within.* Boulder, CO: Lynne Rienner Publishers.

Chambers, Jack. 1993. "Not Much to Cheer About." *National Review,* 29, November, 22, 24.

Cheer Curls. <wysiwyg://2/http://www.expage.com/page/cheercurlz > (16 September 2002).

Cheer Ltd. "CANAM 2003 is Hotter than Ever." <http://cheerltd.com/canam.html> (12 November 2002).

CHEER New York. "Our Mission." <http://www.cheerny.org > (12 September 2002).CHEER San Francisco. "Our Mission." <http://www.cheersf.org > (12 August 2002).

————"Team History." <http://www.cheersf.org > (12 August 2002)."Cheerleaders Unhappy with Temporary Ban on Stunts." <http://www.sportserver.com/newsroo . . . /feat/archive/022698/acc68005.html>(11 June 1999).

Christian Cheerleaders of America. "Camps." <http://www.cheercca.com/camps.html >(13 January 2003).

The Corrolla, 1924, p. 401.

Cosgriff, Gabrielle. 1999. "Verna Heath Puts a Murder Plot Behind Her." *People Weekly,* 15–22 March, http://proquest.umi.com/pqdweb?TS=931895& Fmt=3&Sid=1&Idx=33&Deku=1&ROT=309&Dtp=1> (13 July 1999).

Costello, John. 1985. *Love, Sex and War: Changing Values 1939–1945.* London: Collins.

Crothers, Tim. 2000. "Spectacular Takeoff." *Sports Illustrated,* 3 July, <http://web22 .epnet.com/citation.asp?tb= . . . 46693+sm+KS+so+b+ss+SO+53B6&fn=61&rn=68 > (16 January 2003).

Curry, Dana. 2001. "Fears over Cheers." *Chronicle of Higher Education* 48: A6.

Dallas Cowboys Cheerleaders. "History." <http://www.dallascowboys.com/cgi-bin/Cowboys/cheerleaders/history.jjsp?BV_SessionID= . . . > (15 July 2002).

Dallas Cowboy Cheerleaders, Inc. v. Pussycat Cinema, Ltd. 604 F 2d 200 (2d Cir 1979).

Dancing Wheels. <http://www.gggreg.com/dancingwheels.htm> (27 January 2003).Davies, Tanya. 1999. "Brandi's Brazen Celebration." *Maclean's,* 26 July, 10.

Davis, Laurel. 1990. "Male Cheerleaders and the Naturalization of Gender." In *Sport, Men, and the Gender Order,* edited by Michael Messner and Donald Sabo. Champaign, IL: Human Kinetics Books.

de Beauvoir, Simone.1952. *The Second Sex.* New York: Vintage Books.

Deardorff, Julia. 1999. "Cheerleaders Want R-E-S-P-E-C-T." *Chicago Tribune,* 30 May, 1, 3.

Debbie Does Dallas. 1978. New York: Pussycat Cinema.

Dingus, Anne. 1998. "The Dallas Cowboy Cheerleaders." *Texas Monthly,* January, <http://ehostvgw1.epnet.com/fulltext.asp?resultsSetId=R00000011&hit-Num=3&booleanTer . . . > (16 April 2002).

Divoky, Dianne and Peter Schrag. 1972. "Football and Cheers." *Saturday Review,* 11 November, 58–65.

Dodson, Jenny. 1997. "Rebel Flag Made Debut at UM in 1948, Prof Says." *The Daily Mississippian,* 21 October, <http://dm.olemiss.edu/archives/97/9710/971021/ 971021N4flag.HTML> (21 November 2002).

Douglas, Susan. 1997. "Girls 'N' Spice: All Things Nice?" *Nation,* 25 August, <wysi-wygillbodyframe.5/http://ehostgw13 . . . =39&booleanTerm=Girl%20Power &fuzzyTerm=> (16 October 2000).

Eckert, Penelope. 1989. *Jocks and Burnouts: Social Categories and Identity in the High School.* New York: Teachers College Press.

Eder, Donna and Stephen Parker. 1987. "The Cultural Production and Reproduction of Gender: The Effects of Extracurricular Activities on Peer Group Culture." *Sociology of Education* 60: 200–213.

Elias, Marilyn. 2002. "Cheerleading Leaps into the Dangerous-Sport Camp." *USA Today,* 22 October, <http://web5.epnet.com/citation.asp?tb=1 . . . 98024+sm+KS+so+b+ss+SO+84BA&fn=31&rn=37> (22 January 2003).

Farber, Kathleen. 2001. "When Bodies Matter: Teaching Adolescents about Community, Critical Consciousness, and Identity through Movement." In *Educating Young Adolescent Girls,* edited by Patricia O'Reilly, Elizabeth M. Penn, and Kathleen deMarrais. Mahwah, NJ: Lawrence Erlbaum Associates.

Fellowship of Christian Cheerleaders. "Summer Camps." <http://www.cheerfcc.org/pages/newsumcamp.html > (12 November 2002).

Fine, Gary and Bruce Johnson. 1992. "The Promiscuous Cheerleader: An Adolescent Male Belief Legend." In *Manufacturing Tales: Sex and Money in Contemporary Legends,* edited by Gary Fine. Knoxville: The University of Tennessee Press.

Fine, Michelle. 1988. "Sexuality, Schooling and Adolescent Females: The Missing Discourse of Desire." *Harvard Educational Review* 58: 29–53.

Flaum, David. 2002. "Memphis, Tenn.-Based Varsity Brands Gets National Development Deal." *The Commercial Appeal,* 3 October, <http://web12.epnet.com/citation.asp?tb= . . . 0004169+sm+KS+so+b+ss+SO+BE46&fn=1&rn=2> (9 October 2002).

Flesh Gordon 2: Flesh Gordon Meets the Cosmic Cheerleaders. 1993. Los Angeles: New Concorde Home Entertainment.

Flower, Joe. 1984. "Survival of the Fittest." *Sport,* October, 94.

Foley, Douglas. 1990. "The Great American Football Ritual: Reproducing Race, Class, and Gender Inequality." *Sociology of Sport Journal* 7: 111–135.

Foster, Charles. 1925. *Extra-curricular Activities in the High School.* Richmond, VA: Johnson Publishing Company.

Fraser, Nancy. 1992. "The Uses and Abuses of French Discourse Theories/or Feminist Politics." In *Revaluing French Feminism: Critical Essays on Difference, Agency, and Culture,* edited by Nancy Fraser and Susan Bartkey. Bloomington: Indiana University Press.

Gach, John. 1938. "The Case for and against Girl Cheerleaders." *School Activities* 9: 301–302.

George, Gerald, ed. 1997. *AACCA Cheerleading Safety Manual.* Memphis, TN: The UCA Publications Department.

Gettleman, Jeffrey. 2002. "In North Carolina, the 2-tiara State, a Beauty of a Fight." *New York Times,* 6 September, A1.

Glock, Allison. 1998. "Made You Look." *Gentlemen's Quarterly,* 1 June, 236–243, 280.

"Go, You Jelly Fish, Go!" 1965. *Life,* 17 September, 71–72.

Gonzales, Arturo. 1956. "The First College Cheer." *American Mercury* 83: 101–104.

Goodman, Philomena. 2002. *Women, Sexuality and War.* New York: Palgrave.

Gragg, Derrick. 2000. "Race in Athletics: Integration or Isolation?" In *Sports in School: The Future of an Institution,* edited by John Gerdy. New York: Teachers College Press.

Griffin, Pat. 1992. "Changing the Game: Homophobia, Sexism, and Lesbians in Sport." *Quest* 44: 251–265.

Grundy, Pamela. 2001. *Learning to Win: Sports, Education, and Social Change in Twentieth-century North Carolina.* Chapel Hill: The University of North Carolina Press.

Gutierrez, Teresa. "Tamsey Muniz, La Raza Unida Party and the Chicano." 26 May 1997, <http://burn.ucsd.edu/archives/raza/1997.05/msg0001.html > (19 September 2002).

Guyon, C. 1992. "Cheering Unlimited." *People Weekly,* 10 February, 72.

Haac, Linda. 1996. "No Bull." *Independent Weekly,* 30 October–5 November, <http://www.mindspring.com/~x-cheerleaders/gigs/clips/indy1.html > (5 September 2002).

Hammes, Mary Jessica. 2001. "Radical Road Trip." *Online Athens,* 18 July, <http://www.onlineathens.com/stories/071901/ent_0719010009.shtml> (12 September 2002).

Hansen, Dan. 2002. "Apple Cup: Cougars' no. 3 Ranking Attracts Long-distance Fans." *Spokesman-Review,* 24 November, A1, A8-A9.

Hanson, Mary Ellen. 1995. *Go! Fight! Win! Cheerleading in American Culture.* Bowling Green, OH: Bowling Green University Press.

Haugsted, Linda. 2001. "See Nude Pics of Superbowl Winner! (XFL)." *Multichannel News,* 19 February, <http://www.findarticles.com/cf_0/m3535/ . . . 808/p1/article.jhtml?term=cheerleading+ > (22 August 2002).

Herkimer, Lawrence and Phyllis Hollander. 1975. *The Complete Book of Cheerleading.* New York: Doubleday & Company.

"High School Cheerleaders: Agile Trio at Whiting, Ind. Specialize in Rhythmnastics." 1941. *Life,* 10 November, 58–60.

Hopkins, Ginger. 1979. "That Unchampionship Season." *Seventeen,* January, 115.

Hughes, Zonda. 2002. "African-American NFL Cheerleaders." *Ebony,* November, 162–164,166.

Hurd, Michael. 1993. *Black College Football: 1892–1992.* Virginia Beach, VA: The Donning Company.

Hutchinson, Mark. 1997. "Cheerleading Injuries." *The Physician and Sportsmedicine* 25, September, <http://proquest.umi.com/pqdweb?TS=945715 . . . &Fmt=3&Sid=4& Idx=64&Deli=1&RQT=309&Dtp=1> (20 December 1999).

Hyman, Mark. 1999. "The 'Babe Factor' in Women's Soccer." *Business Week,* 26 July, 118.

Inness, Sherrie. ed. 1998. *Millennium Girls: Today's Girls around the World.* Lanham, MD: Rowman & Littlefield.

Irwin, Kim. "WANTED: X-Cheerleaders," <http://www.mindspring.com/x-cheerleaders/ourstory/history.html> (22 August 2002).

"It Pays to Cheer!" 2003. *American Cheerleader,* February, 89–100.

Jarman, Abbie. 2002. "The Jenning Sisters: Aimee, 28, Cara, 25, and Coleen, 23." *Utne Reader,* September-October, 55.

Jax, A. "Fat and Fabulous." *Radical Cheerleader Handbook #3,* 30.

"Jokes About $C Cheerleaders." <http://www.bol.ucla.edu/~ddacumos/cheer.html1> (22 August 2002).

Kennedy, Kostya and Richard Deitsch. 2002. "Sports Beat." *Sports Illustrated,* 26 August, 30.

King, C. Richard and Charles F. Springwood. 2001. *Beyond the Cheers: Race as Spectacle in College Sport.* Albany: State University of New York Press.

King, Kelley. 2002. "Cheesecake Sport: Overrated Cheerleading." *Sports Illustrated,* 4 November, 73.

Ko, Marnie. 2000. "How to Play the Game." *Newsmagazine* 26: 38–39.

Krane, Vikki. 2001. "We Can be Athletic and Feminine, but do We Want to?: Challenging Hegemonic Femininity in Women's Sports." *Quest* 53: 115–133.

Kraus, Krystalline. "Rah-Rah Revolution." <wysiwyg://501/http://rabble.ca /news_ful . . . tm=f40219cc4a5cflafa28b182flabcbb08&r=1> (12 September 2002).

Kuralt, Charles. 1980. "Those Good Old Cheers Gone By." *Reader's Digest,* September, 54–55.

Kurman, George. 1986. "What Does Girls' Cheerleading Communicate?" *Journal of Popular Culture* 20: 57–64.

Kutz, F. B. 1955. "Cheerleading Rules, Desirable Traits, and Qualifications." *School Activities,* May, 310.

Lambert, Craig. "Cheerleaders Take Flight." *Harvard Magazine,* <http:www.harvard-magazine.com/archive/00so/so00.jhj.sports.html> (22 August 2002).

Lardner, Rex. 1961. "Herkimer Tells How to Make 'em Holler." *Sports Illustrated,* 27 November, 41–46.

"Leader of the Pack." 2003. *American Cheerleader Junior,* Winter, 54.

Leckman, Phil. 2000. "Give Me a F-E-M-I-N-I-S-M." *Arizona Daily Wildcat,* 23 October, <http://wildcat.arizona.edu/papers/94/45/04_2_m.html> (12 September 2002).

"Lela Rochon: Breaking Boundaries." 1999. *American Cheerleader,* June 19.

Lenhart, Jennifer. 1999. "Camp Gives Cheerleaders an Extra Lift: At Ashburn Program, Girls Dispel 'Airhead' Stereotype." *The Washington Post,* 8 July, <http://proquest.umi.com/pqdweb?TS=981894 . . . 1&Fmt=3&Sid=1&1dx=3&Deli= 1&RQT=309&Dtp=1>(13 July 1999).

Lenskyji, Helen. 1994. "Sexuality and Femininity in Sport Contexts: Issues and Alternatives." *Journal of Sport & Social Issues* 18: 356–377.

Lesko, Nancy. 1988. "We're Leading America: The Changing Organization and Form of High School Cheerleading." *Theory and Research in Social Education* 16: 263–278.

"Let's Hear it for Pep Squad Beauty." 1983. *Teen,* September, 94–95.

Lowe, Maria. 1998. *Women of Steel: Female Bodybuilders and the Struggle for Self-definition.* New York: New York University Press.

Lucas, Christopher. 1994. *American Higher Edicuation.* New York, NY: St. Martin's Press.

Mayer, Ann McDonald. 1992. *Mother Love, Deadly Love.* Secaucus, NJ: Birchlane Press Book.

MacDougall, Ruth Doan. 1998. *The Cheerleader.* Center Sandwich, NH: Frigate Books.

MacKenna & Marconi Law Offices. 2002. "Former Eagles Cheerleaders Expand Lawsuit Against NFL Teams." <http://www.digitmedia.com/mckenna/release.html>(7 November 2002).

Mandell, Richard. 1984. *Sport: A Cultural History.* New York: Columbia University Press.

Mariotti, Jay. 2001. "The Tragic Cost of Pride." *The Sporting News,* 13 August, 6.

Martignette, Charles and Louis Meisel. 1996. *The Great American Pin-up.* New York: Taschen.

Martin, Karin. 1996. *Puberty, Sexuality, and the Self: Girls and Boys at Adolescence.* New York: Routledge.

Masin, Mark. 2001. "Putting on the Heat(stroke)." *Scholastic Coach & Athletic Director,* October, 11.

Matzkin, Carol. 1968. "Peacenik in the Center Ring." *Mademoiselle,* May, 56, 62.

McElroy, James T. 1999. *We've Got Spirit!: The Life and Times of America's Greatest Cheerleading Team.* New York: Simon & Schuster.

McGivern, Liz. "Is He 'Cheerleading' Material?" <wysiwyg://14/http://www.varsity.com/index.asp?article=117> (7 October 2002).

Mears, Katie. 2000. "2,4,6,8! Our Forests Are Dying at a Terrible Rate." *The Scarlet & Black,* 16 November, <http://web.grinnell.edu/sandb/archives/volume118/111601/features/cheerleaders.html> (12 September 2002).

Merten, Don. 1996. "Burnout as Cheerleader: The Cultural Basis for Prestige and Privilege in Junior High School." *Anthropology and Education* 27: 51–70.

———1997. "The Meaning of Meanness: Popularity, Competition, and Conflict among Junior High School Girls." *Sociology of Education* 70: 175–191.

"Microsoft Sued by Cheerleading Site over Porn Ads." *Computergram International,* <http://www.findarticles.com/csf_0/m0CGN/ . . . 1e.jhtml?term=cheerleading+and+lawsuits > (22 August 2002).

Middle Tennessee State University. "Cheerleading Teams." <http://www.mtsu.edu/~mtcheer/bstryouts.htm> (13 September 2002).

"More Cheerleaders to Sue Eagles over Alleged Peephole." *CBS SportsLine* <http://footballlive.sportsline.com/u/wire/stories/0,1169,5073864_59,00.html > (7 November 2002).

Morse, Kristen. 2001. "Where are they Now?: Dallas Cowboys Cheerleaders." *Sports Illustrated,* 2 July, 87–89.

Morton, Charles. 1952. "Accent on Living." *Atlantic Monthly,* January, 92–93.

"Mr. Cheerleader." 1956. *American Magazine,* March, 47.

Mueller, Frederick and Robert Cantu. 2001. "National Center for Catastrophic Sport Injury Research Report: Eighteenth Annual Report." <http://www.unc.edu/depts/nccsi/SportList.htm> (19 June 2002).

Mulvey, Kate and Melissa Richards. 1998. *Decades of Beauty: The Changing Image of Women: 1890s–1990s.* New York: Reed Consumer Books.

Nakamura, David. 1998. "Jeers, Boos for Female Cadets on VMI's Cheerleading Squad." *The Washington Post.* 24 November, <http:proquest.umi.com/pqdweb?TS=931896 . . . &Fmt=3&Sid=1&Idx=81&Deli=1&RQT=309&Dtp=1> (13 July 1999).

National Baseball Hall of Fame—Women in Baseball. "A Guide for All-American Girls." <http:www.assumption.edu/HTML/Academic/history/Hi113net/AAGPBL%20Ch arm%20> (2 December 2002).

National Coalition for Women and Girls in Education. 2002. "Title IX at 30: Report Card on Gender Equity." <> (14 July 2002).

NBC Dateline Personal Best. 2002. Televised program, June.

"New Coaches Safety Council Formed." 2003. *American Cheerleader,* June 15.

Newman, Bruce. 1978. "Gimme an S." *Sports Illustrated,* 22 May, 18–19.

Noonan, David. 2002. "How Safe are our Youngest Athletes?" *Newsweek* 16 September, 50.

Norton, Gretchen. 1977. "Cheerleading Doesn't Deserve a Bad Image." *Seventeen,* June, 64.

"November Yells that Win Games." 1924. *Literary Digest,* 8 November, 34–40.

"NU, Former Cheer Squad Member Reach Agreement." 2001. *UNL News Release,* 13 April, <www.unl.edu/pr/2001/0401/041301bnews.html> (23 August 2002).

Nutt, Shannon T. 2001. "More Cheerleaders!" *Adult DVD Empire.* 28 August, <http://www.pornopopdvd.com/exec/news/article.asp?media_id=114 > (9 January 2003).

NYC Radical Cheerleaders. "What is Radical Cheerleading All About?" <wysiwyg://433/http://www.geocities.com/nycradicalcheerleaders/about.html> (12 September 2002).

O'Malley, Kathy. 1999. "The Reluctant First Lady: Jesse's Girl: Terry Ventura Wrestles with her New Role." *McCall's,* July, 58–60.

"On the Art of Cheerleading." 1962. *Saturday Review,* 20 October, 73.

Orecklin, Michele. 2002. "She Couldn't Even Win the Lawsuit Competition." *Time,* 23 September, 89.

"Organized Cheering." 1911. *The Nation,* 5 January, 5–6.

Ostler, Scott. 1994. "Dump the Cheerleaders." *Sports,* August, 20.

"Our Mission." Cheer San Francisco website, <http://www.cheersf.org> (12 August 2002); "Our Mission." Cheer New York homepage, <http://www.cheerny.org> (12 August 2002).

Outside the Lines. Cheerleading: Controversy and Competition. Televised program, ESPN, 5 November 2002.

Paetro, Maxine. 1996. "Cheerleader Envy." *New Woman,* March, 91–93, 142.

Palzkill, B. 1990. "Between Gymshoes and High-heels: The Development of a Lesbian Identity and Existence in Top Class Sport." *International Review for the Sociology of Sport* 25: 221–234.

Park, Robert. 1987. "Sport, Gender and Society in a Transatlantic Victorian Perspective." In *From 'Fair Sex' to Feminism: Sport and the Socialization of Women in the Industrial and Post-industrial Eras,* edited by J. A. Mangan and Roberta Park. Totowa, NJ: Frank Cass.

Patoski, Joe Nick. 2001. "Dallas Cowboys Cheerleaders." *Texas Monthly,* September, 124, 157–158.

"Pompomgate Is Not Worth Cheering About." 2002. *Los Angeles Times,* 13 January, <wysiwyg://bodyframe.13/http://ehostvgw2 . . . =35booleanTerm=cheerleading&fuzzyTerm=> (22 May 2002).

Popke, Michele. 2001. "Diverse Spirit: A Florida School District Hopes to Attract More African-American Cheerleaders." *Athletic Business,* October, 34.

"President Leads Cheers at Summit." 2002. *The Tuscaloosa News,* 14 August, 6A.

Radical Cheerleaders. "About Us." <www.geocities.com/radicalcheerleaders/index.html> (12 September 2002).

Radical Cheerleaders. "Radical Cheers," <www.geocities.com/radicalcheerleaders/about.htm> (4 September 2002).

Ralson, Jeannie. 1994. "Rah! Power." *Texas Monthly,* October, 150+, <http://ehostvgw1.epnet.com/fulltext.asp?resultSetId=R00000004&hitNum=1&boolea nTer . . . >(16 April 2002).

Reilly, Rick. 1999. "Sis! Boom! Bah! Humbug!" *Sports Illustrated,* 18 October, 116.

Rentmeester, Marlien. 1997. "The Bomb Squad." *Seventeen,* November, 84–86.

Rodgers, Cheryl. 1994. "Spirit! Let's Hear It!" *Nation's Business,* June, 16.

Roenigk, Allyssa. 2002. "Ground (bound) Breaking." *American Cheerleader,* August, 159.

Roenigk, Allyssa. 2002. "It's a Cheer World After All." *American Cheerleader,* February, <wysiwyg://76/http://www.americancheerleader.com/backissues/feb02/cheerworld.html> (14 October 2002).

———2002. "Cheer Safety: Setting the Record Straight," *American Cheerleader,* August, 46–48.

Ryan, Pat. 1969. "Once it Was Only Sis-boom-bah!" *Sports Illustrated,* 6 January, 45–55.

Sage, George. 1990. *Power and Ideology in American Sport.* Champaign, IL: Human Kinetics Books.

Sailes, Gary. 1998. *African Americans in Sport.* New Brunswick, NJ: Transaction Publications.

Saint Louis, Catherine. 2002. "What They Were Thinking." *New York Times Sunday Magazine,* 26 May, 20.

Schatz, Aaron. 2000. "The XFL Looks Ready to Rumble." *The Lycos 50 Daily Report* 10, November, <wysiwyg://7/http://50.lycos.com/111000.html> (17 January 2003).

Schneider, Jodi. 2002. "The Fairness Factor." *U.S. News & World Report,* 18 March, 63–65.

Schneller, Johanne. 1991. "The Sis Boom Babes." *Mademoiselle,* February, 134–137.

Scholz, Suzette, Stephanie and Sherry. 1991. *Deep in the Heart of Texas: Reflections of Former Dallas Cowboys Cheerleaders.* New York: St. Martins Press.

Schreier, Laurie. "Byrne Bans Cheerleaders' Stunts." *Daily Nebraskan,* 12 March, <T2002/03/12/3c8da10e10d14?in_archive=1 > (23 August 2002).

Securities and Exchange Commission. 2002. *Quarterly report pursuit to section 13 or 15 (d)of the Securities Exchange Act of 1934, Varsity Brands, Inc.* Washington, D.C: GPO.

Shah, Diane, Gayle Stephen and Mary Lord. 1977. "Sis-Boom-Bah!" *Newsweek,* 7 November, 87–89.

Shaw, Robert. 1977. "Cowgirls." *Esquire,* October, 80–83.

Shister, Gail. 1981. "The Pro Football Cheerleaders." *Glamour,* February, 166–167.

"SI Rankings." 2002. *Sports Illustrated,* 7 October, 74.

"Sidelines." 2002. *Chronicle of Higher Education*, 9 August: A39.

Sirmans, Jim. 1972. "Cram Course for Cheerleaders." *Seventeen*, September, 114–115, 171.

Smith, Ronald. 1988. *Sports and Freedom: The Rise of Big-time College Athletics*. New York: Oxford University Press.

Snowden, Lynn. 1992. "The Roots of Rejection." *Working Woman*, September, 72–74, 100.

Spring, Joel. 1996. *American Education*. New York: McGraw Hill.

———1990. *The American School: 1642–1990*. New York: Longman.

Steptoe, Sonja. 1991–92. "The Pom-pom Chronicles." *Sports Illustrated*, 30 December–6 January, 38–44, 46.

Stewart, Lianne. 2001. "Cheerleading Takes on a Radical New Form." *Toronto Observer*, 17 April, <http://observer.thecentre.centennialcollege.ca/features/lianne_radical_041702.htm> (12 September 2002).

Stope, Leigh. 2002. "Workers Blame Corporate Cheerleading for Huge Retirement Losses with BC-Enron Investigation." *AP Worldstream*, 8 February, <wysiwyg://211/http://web1.epnet.com/cit . . .   04187+sm+KS+so+b+ss+SO+6C48&fn=41&m=43> (23 August 2002).

Strausbaugh, John. 2000. "The Anti-Cheerleader." *New York Press*, 4–10 October, <http://www.nypress.com/13/40/news&columns/publishing.cfm> (20 January 2003).

"Study Reveals 23 Football Players Died During 2001 Season." 2002. *Black Issues in Higher Education* 19, 15 August: 12.

Sullivan, R. Lee. 1993. "School for Cheerleaders." *Forbes*, 25 October, 118–119.

Sullivan, Robert. 1999. "Goodbye to Heroin Chic: Now It's Sexy to be Strong." *Time*, 19 July, 62.

"Team History." Cheer San Francisco website, <http://www.cheersf.org> (12 August 2002).

Thames, Kathleen. 2000. "A Look Back at 100 Years." *La Louisiane*, Fall, 8–29.

"Tiger." 1947. *The New Yorker*, 12 July, 18–19.

Timson, Judith. 1978. "Bounce for Glory." *Maclean's*, 21 August, 29–32.

"Title IX: Gender Equity in College Sports: 6 Views." 2002. *The Chronicle Review*, 6 December: B7–B10.

Tolman, Deborah. 1994. "Doing Desire: Adolescent Girls' Struggles for/with Sexuality." *Gender & Society* 8: 324–342.

Uhlin, Graig. 2002. "The Act of Activism . . . Las Sinfronteras Exemplifies the Intersection." *Arizona Daily Wildcat*, 7 May, <http://wildcat.arizona.edu/papers/95/115/04_1.html> (12 October 2002).

Universal Cheerleading Association. 2002. *UCA Advisor/coach Manual 2002*. Memphis, TN: Universal Cheerleading Association.

Van Iquity, Dana. 2000. "Cheer San Francisco Celebrates 20 Years." *San Francisco Bay Times*, 22 June, 22.

Varsity Brands, Inc. 2002. "National Federation of State High School Associations Form Strategic Alliance on Cheerleading." <www.varsity.com/index.asp?category=1&article=856> (7 October 2002).

Varsity Spirit. 1999. *Varsity Catalog.* Memphis, TN: Varsity.

Veri, Maria. 1999. "Homophobic Discourse Surrounding the Female Athlete." *Quest* 51: 355–368.

Villarreal, Cindy. 1994. *The Cheerleader's Guide to Life.* New York: Harper Perennial. Wagenknecht, Edward. 1987. *Stars of the Silents.* Metuchen, NJ: Scarecrow Press.

Walker, Carey. 1999. "The Bod Squad." *Muscle & Fitness,* April, 170–174.

Walker, Marisa. 2002. "10 Questions with Herkie." *American Cheerleader,* October, 45–46.

Walkerdine, Valerie. 1993. "Girlhood Through the Looking Glass." In *Girls, Girlhood, and Girls' Studies in Transition,* edited by Marion de Ras and Mieke Lunenberg. Amsterdam: Het Spinhuis.

Walsh, Jennifer. 1999. "Houston-Area Gym Facilities Thrive When Offering Cheerleading." *Houston Chronicle,* 8 July, <wysiwyg://247/http://web1.epnet.com/cit . . . 187+sm+KS+so+b+ss+SO=6C48&fn=131&rn=138> (23 August 2002).

WANTED: X-Cheerleaders. "History of the Project." <http://www.mindspring.com/x-cheerleaders/ourstory/history.html> (22 August 2002).

Ward, Erin. 2002. "Behind the Pom-Poms: Halifax's Radical Cheerleaders." *NovaNewsNet, February, <http://novanewsnet.ukings.ns.ca/stories/01–02/020131/wardhalirads.htm>* (12 September 2002).

Watterson, John. 2000. *College Football: History, Spectacle, Controversy.* Baltimore: The Johns Hopkins University Press.

Weis, Lois. 1997. "Gender and the Reports: The Case of the Missing Piece." In *Feminist Critical Policy Analysis: A Perspective from Primary and Secondary Schooling,* edited by Catherine Marshall. London: The Falmer Press.

Weisiger, Louise. 1951. "The Status of Interscholastic Athletics in Secondary School for Girls." *School Activities,* February, 184–187.

Wentworth, Harold and Stuart Flexner, ed. 1975. *Dictionary of American Slang.* New York: Thomas Y. Crowell Co.

Whiffan, Beth. 2002. "Latin Divas." *American Cheerleader,* December, 71–72.

White, Emily. 2002. *Fastgirls: Teenage Tribes and the Myth of the Slut.* New York: Scribner.

Wilstach, Nancy. 2002. "Officials: All Who Tried Out Can Cheer." *Birmingham News,* 31 July, <http://n19.newsbank.com/nsearch/we/Archives?p_action=doc&p_docid= 0F5461C76D7C . . . > (23 August 2002).

Women's Sports Foundation. 2000. "Cheerleading, Drill Team, Danceline and Band as Varsity Sports: The Foundation Position." 20 July, <www.womens sportsfoundation.org/cgi-bin/iowa/issues/rights/article.html?record=95> (19 June 2002).

Woodmanse, Ken. 1993. "Cheers: Jeff Webb's Multicolored World Wide Spirit Machine." *Memphis Business,* Third Quarter, 14–19.

World Cheerleading Association. "Special Events," <http://www.cheerwca.com/Special%20Events.htm> (23 August 2002).

Womyn's Centre. "Radical Conference," <http://www.carleton.ca/womyncentre/events/marchconference.htm> (12 September 2002).

Wright, Keith. n.d. "Summit on Race at Ole Miss." *Z Magazine*, <http://www.zmag.org/ZMag/articles/dec1999wright.htm> (21 November 2002).

Zinoman, Jason. 2002. "Debbie's Doing New York, But Rate her PG." *The New York Times*, 27 October, <http://proquest.umi.com/pqdweb?Did=0000 . . . &Fmt= 3&Deli=1&Mtd=1&Idx=7&Sid=8&RQT=309 > (5 November 2002).

INDEX